sybil leek's astrological guide to successful everyday living

sybil leek's astrological guide to successful everyday living

by sybil leek

BELL PUBLISHING COMPANY
New York

This 1988 edition is published by
Bell Publishing Company, distributed by
Crown Publishers, Inc., 225 Park Avenue South,
New York, New York 10003, by arrangement
with Prentice Hall Press, a division of
Simon & Schuster, Inc.

Printed and Bound in the United States of America

Library of Congress Cataloging-in-Publication Data

Leek, Sybil.
    [Astrological guide to successful everyday
living]
    Sybil Leek's astrological guide to successful
everyday living / by Sybil Leek.
        p.   cm.
    Reprint. Originally published: Englewood Cliffs,
N.J. : Prentice-Hall, 1970.
    ISBN 0-517-67664-8
    1. Astrology.   I. Title.   II. Title: Astrological
guide to successful everyday living.
BF1701.L37   1988   88-29352
133.5—dc19   CIP

                    h g f e d c b a

DEDICATED TO
ROZ CARLTON COLE
with affection
and gratitude for her
Sagittarian-Capricorn friendship.

CONTENTS

sybil leek's astrological guide to successful everyday living

INTRODUCTION

Since the beginning of time, as civilizations have succeeded each other, many sciences and sub-sciences have appeared. From history we can learn *how* a man lived and what he did, but rarely are we told *why* he acted or reacted in a specific manner. The six-thousand-year-old science of astrology is one of the means available for understanding everything that has taken place, or is taking place in the gigantic jigsaw of life.

Like other systems of thought, astrology has suffered from wild speculations and has often been confused with unimaginable superstitions. The greatest disadvantage for astrology has been its downgrading into something between occultism and fortune-telling. In the last few hundred years, unfortunately, astrologers themselves have deliberately fostered the myths of mystic forces, thus leaving themselves vulnerable to criticism. Despite this, astrology has survived the test of time.

1

Astrology was cradled in its infancy in the early civilization of the Euphrates Valley, and integrated in the religion of Egypt. The Golden Age of Greece saw it keeping pace with philosophies and the pantheon of their gods when it was raised to maturity under the guidance of Greek mathematicians. It flourished in Imperial Rome, especially during the reign of Tiberius. Through the evolution of the Judaic and Christian religions it survived, but as it became divorced from its involvement with religion to become more and more viewed as a science, so did its enemies grow in proportion. The first major attacks on astrology came from the religious, who fought it simply because it *was* regarded as a science. Today there is a swing of the pendulum: its enemies declare it is *not* a science but the remnant of a superstitious age. The arguments will probably go on forever, each age producing some remarkably viru-lent discussions about it.

Yet in the twentieth century, astrology is becoming a stronger force every day. Many condemn it on the grounds that it is a mixture of myth and superstition. But many superstitions, once you dust away the cobwebs, are founded on ancient and basic truths. The word "supersti-tion" comes from the Latin *supersto,* meaning "to stand over." A dic-tionary definition gives it as "originally a standing still at, in fear or amazement." All fears have their roots in a lack of understanding.

There are those who condemn astrology without any investigation whatsoever—these are the same people who, had they lived in another age, would be condemning surgery, vaccination, the steam engine or any innovation beyond their comprehension.

Many fine astrologers today have to subsidize their interest in astrology by doing other work, just as Galileo and Kepler did, but as the world goes from the Piscean into the Aquarian Age, life will become much easier for astrologers. We are beginning to understand that the natural laws of the universe based simply on action and reaction, also apply to men. We already have a solid foundation for the validity of astrology as a science necessary to man—what concerns us now is to con-tinue to build on the foundation. It is a highly cerebral pursuit, not a way-out hobby, as any reasonably intelligent person can see if they take the trouble to look at a well-prepared astrological chart. We still use a special kind of shorthand in setting up a chart, but then a doctor's pre-scription for medicine is not the clearest thing for a layman to read! Yet it generally gets results.

The horoscope is really a personal map of an individual's life, but it can be set up for other things as well—such as predicting the weather and the influence of the celestial bodies on all natural things. Despite the evolution of a highly sophisticated society such as we find ourselves in today, men still retain a link with the ancients who lived in the Euphrates Valley six thousand years ago. Men still have a desire to know what tomorrow will bring, and must always live with hope. This looking forward into the future is not the exclusive prerogative of prophets, some of whom had the rare quality of extrasensory perception to a high degree. Side by side with the prophets, there has always been a group who has studied celestial maps, charted routes for trading, and indeed paved the way for the first man to descend on the moon. Like the prophets, they are men of vision, but attribute their vision not to some mysterious intangible force but to a practical application of wisdom. Occasionally there are rare beings who have the gift of prophecy together with the capability of scientifically studying the influence of the planets on all living things. On these people rests a double burden: they have to be true to their visions, but also have to bear the brunt of an interested public "standing still in fear and amazement." Again we arrive at a point where a lack of public understanding deliberately tries to make the astrologer-prophet-scientist wear a cloak of mysticism.

On looking at a horoscope for the first time, an uninformed person invariably asks "But what are all those mysterious signs?" Actually they are no more mysterious than the shorthand done by an efficient stenographer. Astrologers stick to their own brand of shorthand simply because they have to condense a great deal of information into the limited space of the 360-degree circle which becomes the horoscope. The horoscope's final interpretation into everyday language can take up many pages of typewritten script. This is done in order to communicate with the client, but it is not necessary for an astrologer to have anything more than his own one-to-three page chart to see the précis of an entire lifetime.

Astrological shorthand is not intended to impress or confuse. Several times I have tried avoiding its use. The result was that my chart began to look cumbersome, and it was not as easy to draw in the lines of the trines, squares, quincunxes and the other geometrical patterns which show the linking of the planetary influences.

The correct interpretation of a horoscope involves a complete understanding of the position of the planets and their patterns. The astrologer finds the position of the Sun, Moon, and the sign rising on the eastern horizon at the time of birth which is called the *ascendant*. The position is then plotted on to the chart. From an ephemeris (whose name is derived from the Greek word meaning "diary") the astrologer finds the placement of all other planets, and these in turn are plotted onto the chart. The ephemeris is a publication showing the placement of the heavenly bodies throughout the year, an astronomical almanac that takes much of the pain out of the initial stages of preparing the horoscope.

The *aspects* are then worked out by drawing a line from the center of the earth to one planet and another line to another planet. The angle between the two is then measured. Continuing to take each planet in turn, the planetary patterns begin to emerge.

One of the most common complaints about astrology stems from the fact that everyone has a secret desire to be unique. Thus when a group horoscope in a newspaper or magazine is read, it causes many people to say, "But I have a friend who is an Aries, and she isn't a *bit* like me." She probably isn't, although I should be surprised if the two friends did not find some characteristics in common.

Every one is, indeed, an individual. No two charts can ever be alike, since the value of a horoscope is that it relates only to you and cannot be for anyone else. Yet you belong to a group with which you share many or a few basic characteristics—it's the other traits which make you into a single, distinctive unit. You have a specific birthday, but thousands of other people share this birthday with you. You all are placed within the one of the twelve divisions of zodiacal signs, just as the actual day of your birth is placed within a specific month. At the time of your birth, every planet is in a certain position in relationship to the sun—and therefore to your birthday. Each sign has its own ruling planet, although Pisces is jointly ruled by Jupiter and Neptune, whilst Scorpio is jointly ruled by Pluto and Mars. The planet ruling your sun sign is dominant at birth, but can be weakened or strengthened by the position of the other planets.

Nothing in the celestial map of the planets is static. The planets are moving in a constant orderly procession, the ones nearest the sun such as Mercury and Venus move more quickly than Uranus and Pluto, which are farther away from the sun. Mars rules both Aries and Scorpio, and if this planet is found in either the sign of Aries or Scorpio at birth (presuming that your birthday falls within the area of Aries) then you will feel the influence of your ruling sign to a greater degree than if Mars was, say, in a house farther away from your birth sign. Even though you are officially recognized as an Aries, because Mars also rules Scorpio, some of the Scorpian characteristics, either negative or positive will have spilled over into your character. You may be not a typical Aries, but much nearer to being a typical Mars type.

Other factors enhance a planet's power. If a planet is found at any of the four highly sensitive points in the heavens such as the ascendant, its opposite, the descendant; the midheaven, or the nadir—the opposite to the midheaven—it will have something extra to say to you. This is strikingly emphasized if your ruling planet is rising on the eastern side of the horizon at the time of your birth and so becomes the ascendant or rising sign. If you are born under Taurus, celebrating your birthday between April 21 and May 21, Venus is your ruling planet. If you have Venus rising—that is, the Ascendant—at the time of your birth, it will have a double impact on your life.

There are dozens of permutations which an astrologer goes through in order to find out whether you are typical of your sign. It is a mistake to think that because you are born on April 25th, you are a typical Taurean. As the astrologer progresses, your actual birthday—although used as a means of starting her calculations—becomes less important than studying the planetary patterns at the time of birth. She sees it only as the time when the sun was transiting through your sign.

Although my own birthdate places me under the sign of Pisces, because of the ascendant position on the day I was born, it would be wrong for me to consider myself "typically Piscean." Certainly I have many Piscean characteristics—such as an interest in occultism, poetry, and music—but I have Scorpio rising, and this dominates any of the dreaming, retiring, mysterious, rather nebulous basic characteristics of the true Piscean. Another complication is that may birthdate falls on the cusp of Aquarius and Pisces with only 2 degrees in Pisces—just enough to get me into the sign but definitely not enough to produce many totally Piscean characteristics about me. Add my moon's position of being in Aquarius, and many of the emotions felt by typical Pisceans is replaced by a much more serene nature, more calculated and unemotional and with a distinct leaning toward the sciences and inventions. The sun in Pisces enables me to write and includes a certain musical ability. The Scorpio rising makes me see and feel much more dramatically than any Piscean ever could, encouraging me to probe into research projects and urging me to live quite recklessly sometimes.

On the whole if I read a general astrological column in a newspaper, Scorpio always applies to me more than Pisces. If I was only the creature of my sun sign, there have been many times in my life when I would have retired hurt, full of tears, needing a shoulder to cry on and frightened of life. But the Scorpio rising rears up with its attendant ruling planet of Mars. So instead of retiring, I am apt to slash back, become aggressive, and fight. Fortunately the moon in Aquarius comes to my aid, enabling reason to help cool down what would be a dynamic Mars-orientated temper.

Always consider the three parts of yourself: body, mind, and spirit —which the astrologer will see as your sun sign, rising sign, and moon sign.

I am frequently asked what type of people go to an astrologer to have a chart prepared. It is rather like asking how long is a piece of string! People from all walks of life, all points of the world are increasingly interested in astrology. In my personal practice lately, I have probably done more horoscopes for people who were first sceptical than for outright believers.

One newspaperman has called me a "society astrologer," but I am not sure what he meant by this. Certainly I move around the world meeting many interesting and famous people and have done a great deal of astrological work for royalty and politicians. But I have also done the horoscopes of many ordinary people who needed the help which a well prepared horoscope can give. Mainly my clientele is drawn from people who have been recommended to me by others. This, I think, is how many of the best known astrologers work.

One of my great annoyances is to have someone come with a prepared chart and ask me to interpret it. It is either one they have had made up very cheaply or the result of their own work. In some cases, the chart has been done well, but the accompanying interpretation has left the client completely bewildered by its archaic language. To tell a client that "your Uranus is squaring the sun" needs to be translated. It is best to explain that Uranus is the planet of unexpected happenings who nevertheless telegraphs its action, and a square indicates that the unexpectedness of Uranus' action is not for anything good. Always remember that the major characteristics of any planet is strengthened or weakened by the patterns the other planets make with it. The understanding of this linking system of the planets is perhaps the most difficult thing for an amateur astrologer to learn. The fundamentals of astrology are not beyond the grasp of anyone with reasonable intelligence, arithmetic, and the willingness to spend quite a lot of time in practice. The snag is that many students can learn to draw the plan of a building, but may not be able to build one that will stand up.

The first principle to remember is that the horoscope is a *geocentric* map of the solar system at a given moment of time. On this map the positions of the Sun, Moon and eight planets are calculated in relation to the signs of the zodiac. Secondly, the zodiac is an imaginary band of sky representing the sun's yearly path through the fixed stars. The sun's apparent movement along this path is actually produced by the earth's annual movement around the sun. The astrologer needs plenty of paper including scratch pads to makes notes and calculations, and a protractor to plot the positions, besides an ephemeris and the date, place, and time of birth of his subject. Chart sheets can be purchased singly or in bulk from many bookshops.

Most astrologers use sidereal time, which is measured by the stars and not like ordinary clock time, measured by the sun. In a sidereal day, the stars appear to make one complete circuit of the sky, while the sun has not quite completed its apparent circuit. So the sidereal day is shorter than the ordinary sun day by four minutes. In order to use the tables, the astrologer must translate his basic information of birth time and place into sidereal time, since most ephemeris use Greenwich Mean Time as a standard.

Imagine that you have a subject who was born on July 5, 1960 at 7:20 p.m. On that date, the sidereal time at noon was 6 hours 53 minutes, 56 seconds. Because the subject was born 7 hours and 20 minutes after high noon, this is added to the sidereal noontime. Add to this ten seconds for each hour to find:

	hr.	min.	sec.
Sidereal Time	6	53	56
Hour of Birth	7	20	00
Acceleration		1.	13.
	14 —	15 —	09

Complications arise when the astrologer begins to study world time zones. Eastern Standard Time in the United States is five hours slow; Central European Time one hour fast by comparison to Greenwich Mean Time. For all people born elsewhere than on the Greenwich meridan, the longitude of the place of birth must be found in degrees and minutes and must be translated into minutes and seconds of time. Longitude is transformed into time by multiplying by four. When this is done, the minutes and seconds are added to the sidereal time of Greenwich for all places east of Greenwich or subtracted for all points west. Obviously a good map showing the earth divided into the twenty-four time zones is useful. It is possible to obtain a map in which each zone shows the corresponding time to noon in Greenwich Mean Time.

Latitude is the measurement north or south of the equator. In the table of houses, the now-calculated sidereal time is found at the given latitude of birth. At this point a planet is rising at a certain degree on the eastern horizon, and this is the ascendant. It is impossible to guess latitude; it must always be looked up on the map. Within a twenty-four hour period, there are 360 possible ascendants, and a different degree of the zodiac rises above the horizon every four minutes. When twins are born in the same place—perhaps even within five minutes of each other—they will have a different degree of the zodiac for their ascendants. If one twin has an ascendant of 30 degrees in Pisces, the second twin born five minutes later will have 1 degree in Aries. The difference in the twins' personalities would be specially remarkable because this particular cusp is extremely unlike any other and the contrast in personalities likely to be more noticeable.

The calculated ascendant is marked on the blank circle of the horoscope chart. A line is drawn connecting the ascendant with a point exactly opposite on the other side of the chart—like drawing the diameter of a circle. The ascendant-descendant line is then bisected from the center top of the chart—the midheaven—to the center bottom of the chart—the *imum coeli*—so that the chart now has four angles in it. The houses are then filled in, commencing at the ascendant which is the beginning of the first house—and all other sectors are filled in, making twelve in all.

The position of all the planets is filled in, starting with the faster-moving ones such as Venus, again using the tables. (Raphael's Ephemeris is excellent to use although many people in America use the Waite Ephemeris. It becomes a matter of personal taste—the ephemeris you are first introduced to generally becomes the one you will continue to use.) All planetary positions in the ephemeris are given for noon on the day of birth, and adjustments have to be calculated according to the time of birth. Only practice can add to the efficiency of looking up the logarithms and calculating the adjustments.

Astrology is not something that can be learned in a day. The best way to learn is from a teacher giving verbal instruction. A student should take the opportunity to watch a qualified astrologer build up a chart, and the good teacher will explain every point as he is doing it. The student should make her own notes, although in time she will see that she has really learned what seems to be a new language. This language can be transformed into the special shorthand helpful to the astrologer, but causes complete confusion to anyone looking at a chart for the first time. It is a good idea to have the individual steps in the horoscope made into a chart which you can refer to quickly until you are able to remember them automatically.

1. Obtain the date, exact time and place of birth.

2. Find the longitude and latitude of place of birth.

3. Use the ephemeris to find the sidereal time at noon, Greenwich Mean Time for the given day of birth.

4. By addition or subtraction find the equivalent sidereal time for the moment of birth as expressed in Greenwich Mean Time.

5. Convert the longitude of the place of birth into hours, minutes and seconds by multiplying it by four.

6. Find the local sidereal time for the place of birth by adding or subtracting the longitude to or from the Greenwich sidereal time, remembering that places *east* of Greenwich are added to the Greenwich sidereal time and all points *west* subtracted.

7. Look up the local sidereal time in the table for houses to find the ascendant and midheaven positions.

8. Fill in the ascendant, descendant, midheaven and *imum coeli* on the chart.

9. According to the tables, fill in the positions of the houses.

10. Fill in the positions of the planets according to the tables, always converting Greenwich sidereal time into local sidereal time.

11. Begin to interpret the horoscope from the squares, trines, and conjunctions made by the planets.

It will take you a long time to reach number 11, for interpretation can be the stumbling block of the academic, technically good horoscope maker. Sometimes I have employed students who have reached a point of efficiency in making charts, but I have never let them do any interpretation except as a means of teaching. All my clients get my personal interpretation, and I still find this one of the most difficult things to teach. The beginner needs the help of as many books as possible so that he can grasp the nature of each planet, sign, house and aspect, and then apply the related knowledge to any chart. The dedicated student will probe into books ranging from archaic to modern, and will ask questions from his teacher that can go on for years. But the unexplainable "something" which makes a good interpretation of a horoscope is rather like the mysterious thing which divides one author from another. Astrologers have to use part of themselves to express what they have been taught. Yet the good astrologer cannot be emotional or use the author's poetic license. At the same time, a well interpreted horoscope can carry the hallmark of the astrologer and be completely understood by the subject. It is by interpretation that an astrologer will be remembered.

If you want to be an astrologer, practice and read, practice and read for the rest of the days of your life and the more you know will lead you into a constant thirst to discover more. It can become your personal treadmill but never a vicious circle; as you understand people through their horoscopes, so you will understand them when you meet them in the flesh, and understanding can make the astrologer more tolerant of the whims and foibles of his fellowmen. He is traditionally and ethically bound to reveal his findings truthfully.

Unfortunately, this does not always please the subject of the horoscope, since many people deliberately present a facade to the world which is totally different from their real self. There are valid reasons for this. Sometimes the facade is a defensive or protective maneuver, whereby it may be necessary to present a stern face lest the bearer be thought weak. In other cases, social conditions, the demands of society, and educational conditioning can force a man to adopt a different character than one he was destined to fulfill and to parade through life as something which he is not. Life becomes much more complex for these people and there is always an element of fear that the mask may slip and some weakness be revealed.

Today the astrologer is receiving more and more clients who are not concerned with "having their fortunes told" so much as finding out who and what they are. Despite increased education, the knowledge of philosophy and religion, and an increase in the material things of the world, man still knows his unhappy moments. He begins to ask why, with so much around him, he still is not at peace within himself. In the midst of plenty it becomes vital to know why he should feel as if he has nothing. In fact, unless he understands himself, his place in the universe, and is in harmony with his environment, he has virtually nothing.

Astrology has become one route of knowing yourself. And the average person is not alone in his journey to the door of the nearest astrologer. It is very rare for any day to pass without a doctor or psychologist calling to consult me about a difficult case. Naturally, this is done with the utmost discretion. No names are mentioned, and all I have to work on is the date of birth. My diagnoses are almost always correct.

The majority of astrologers are a long way from having such opportunities. It is sad, also, that an element of secrecy has to shroud a major part of such activities. For instance, I receive the grateful thanks of professional men, and I know they are sincere in this—but it is they who collect the fee and the praise from their patients, not me. I have no objection, but some time in the near future, provision has to be made for astrologers such as myself to work openly with professional men with both parties dedicated to the good of the patient or client. Fortunately, I keep very accurate records of every case I have dealt with (especially the medical ones) and one day these may be useful for others. The time cannot be too far ahead when astrologers receive the same dignified respect afforded to other professionals. But before this happens, we have to be prepared to strip away all the mysticism which has been built into astrology's image, and to understand that astrology is not fortune-telling.

In my monthly column written for the *Ladies Home Journal*, I present group astrology in a readable form that has proved to be most successful. Instead of giving diffuse group characteristics each month, I have taken every known *aspect* of life, to which I have applied a complete astrological analysis. The result is that we have covered such unusual subjects as interior decorating, dieting, how to be a hostess, investments, and the care of children, among many other things. This book should stand as evidence that modern astrology, based though it is on traditional astrology, can serve as a guide to everyday living.

Sybil Leek

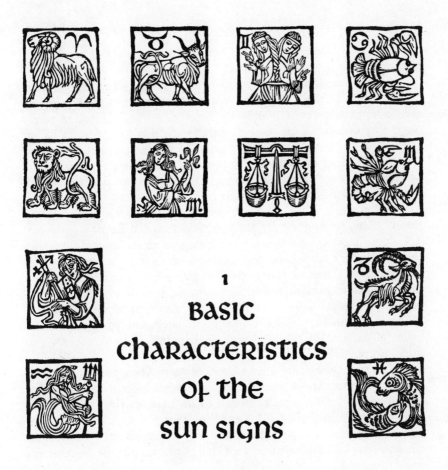

1
BASIC characteristics of the sun signs

ARIES ♈ MARCH 21ST-APRIL 20TH

You are the first of the fire signs of the zodiac. Something of the fieriness shows itself in your temperament and in flashes of temper. Fortunately, though you have your say in no uncertain terms, you're always willing to bury the hatchet.

Your major attributes—energy, self-reliance, and impulsiveness—lead you into exciting areas of life with the spirit of a pioneer. Very often, even though you can't sustain the effort of completing plans, you hold a unique place in the zodiac as an innovator of ideas.

In youth, you often have a compulsion to get involved with dangerous pursuits. You don't always choose your companions with discrimination but this is part of your need to experiment with living. Maturity doesn't always bring wisdom, and being cautious in any sphere of life is always difficult for you.

Sometimes you seem inconsiderate of others—especially to your family—and you don't like to be reproved unless it's done with utmost tact. You like to feel all ideas emanate from you and you're rarely coerced or threatened into doing anything you don't want to do. What you lack in emotional restraint, calmness of thought, and consideration to others, is offset by boundless energy and enthusiasm. You can show courage in times of emergency, but this usually happens when your back is to the wall and nothing but your own resources and quick thinking can extricate you. Then you're at your best with your dynamic ruling planet, Mars, coming to your aid in his most martial form.

Your most positive sign, when living up to its highest form, can channel all your best characteristics into a successful personal and professional life. Those of you who are negative find yourselves involved in a series of emotional, and often traumatic, conditions which can develop into mental anguish and alter the whole pattern of your life. When this happens, small hurts are accentuated, and you go from one resentful moment to another, rarely taking time to think of how you might improve the situation.

Despite the seeming waywardness of most Aries, you show a great response to affection. Approval or encouragement seem to propel you to your best. While you can't respond to any hard, driving, whip-in-the-hand tactics from others, you have enough energy to be a tireless worker without any sense of martyrdom. You may resent efforts to drive you, but once you've decided to do something, you supply the impetus for success.

You can be led to water, but you can't be forced to drink. Coerce or attempt to bully you, and you're quite likely to leave home, throw up your job in a sudden fit of temper, or sometimes even seek revenge for what you consider a personal slight.

You thrive on constant change, whether in environment, interests, friendships or love affairs. Because you hate restrictions—even if some of them may be only imaginary—you also want to be in the front of any public movement for freedom. Your agile mind is constantly saturated with new ideas. But you can rarely visualize the end product and frequently leave your inspirations for others to carry out. This isn't entirely due to losing interest, but more because you feel others move more slowly than you do and while waiting for them to get at it, other ideas start collecting in your head.

So many of you find yourselves spreading your ideas and energies too thinly that there's always a danger of being diverted from the area in which you could find success. You can be an important catalyst to other people if you're patient and realize that some people can't move as quickly as you.

Conversation is one of your greatest pleasures, and there's nothing you like better than holding forth with your latest ideas. Sometimes you're more inclined to rhetoric than to conversation, but you're rarely boring to people even if the speed at which you talk may leave them a little breathless. Conversation can bring you into the limelight—which you enjoy—and there's a tendency to deliberately upstage other people by allowing your imagination (and often exaggeration) to run riot.

If you use the positive attribute of your sign—the great driving power of Mars—by channelling it into decisive action and sustaining this action until your ideas bear fruit, you can be successful as a reformer and pioneer in just about any sphere of life. If other planets weaken the drive of Mars, you're reduced to a negative approach to life. In this case, aggressiveness comes out just for the sake of being awkward and disruptive and you become touchy, showing a complete lack of consideration for others. Ultimately, you suffer the most, because friends drift away and the last thing *you* like is to be alone or to feel unwanted.

You can be one of the easiest or most difficult people to get along with, and friends have to try to keep up with you. You might help sometimes by pausing for breath and waiting for others to catch up. While this is just about the hardest thing for you to do, it can be done if you direct some of your remarkable energy into the realms of thinking as well as into physical drive.

Your symbolic zodiac animal is the Ram.

TAURUS ♉ APRIL 21ST-MAY 20TH

You are the first of the earth signs of the zodiac.

This shows itself in the major attributes of your character—practical, reserved, very determined and set in your purposes. Sometimes you're slow-moving, but you have many attractive qualities of mind and body.

Your strength of will and determination come out in marked degree when you decide to use them to mould others to your way of thinking. Your preceding sign, Aries, creates an idea. But you have the ability to see someone else's idea, evaluate its potential, and then execute it.

You aren't adaptable to changes of environment, work, or people, preferring to be with those you've probably known from youth. Strange faces find you stiff and ill at ease and you're not likely to show your best qualities. Once you know a person, no one will be a more faithful friend, especially in times of need. You give help and advice, but rarely lend money, except in a strictly businesslike manner. It takes a great deal to make you angry, but once roused, you can be a veritable display of fireworks with no inclination to forgive and forget.

Your associates should be careful not to get on your wrong side since your qualities of generosity and faithfulness can turn to ruthlessness—and you never forget a wrong or a slight. Often, you have a tendency to provoke quarrels within your own family circle, almost as if you enjoy making amends afterward. Perhaps this is a catalystic method of finding out what your associates think and feel. You need constant assurance of affection, although not in a sentimental manner—but rather with someone always being available when you need them or remembering that you like special attention.

If you're unable to live up to the most positive quality of your sign—stability—you'll indulge in gambling, over-indulge in eating and drinking, and concentrate on satisfying your more sensual parts. There'll also be many degrees of personal conceit in order to impress others. As a positive Taurean, you can be one of the most charming individuals of the zodiac. Females, especially, can combine grace of manner with great talents in the kitchen and homemaking. Your best attributes are in concentration, indomitable perseverance, and combining practicality with objectivity of purpose. Once you love a person, you can be generous to a fault. But you need to have both yourself and your gifts fully appreciated.

There's a tendency, particularly in the last twenty-five years, for you to make regrettable marriages—if you marry young. It's much better for you to sow any of your wild oats before considering marriage. As you mature, marriage is another form of stability and security which you need to help produce your best work and the better side of yourself. Often, you're condemned as a born sceptic. But this is because you aren't willing to make changes. Once the pattern of your life is set, you will form definite views and will be outspoken about them. This can lead to some of you being very dogmatic parents with not too much understanding of your children when they are adolescents. Your parents' religion is likely to remain with you all your life, as you have a tendency to adhere to the orthodox, being impressed with ritual and ceremony of all kinds.

You like to impress people with your stability and show what you've achieved in your working life; and you also like to mix with people who show similar stable trends and who are also impressive.

You'll be faithful to your friends, but always with the proviso that they return the same amount of fidelity. Your practical nature exerts itself even in romantic affairs, although you enjoy a gracious and unhurried courtship. Once married, you're more inclined to be dutifully attentive than just romantic. You expect marriage to be a partnership in every way with each party understanding his role. There's sometimes a danger in this. You may expect your wife to be an excellent housekeeper, and if she's a Taurean, she may expect her husband to be the breadwinner. When this happens, some of the more exciting parts of the relationship fall apart. It's a point you should guard against, but this depends as much on your marital partner as it does on you.

Your symbolic animal of the zodiac is the Bull, standing firmly on the earth, showing strength, and a little arrogance, as if to defy the world—which is what you're literally capable of doing. Not, however, as a pioneer like your preceding sign. You demonstrate defiance by showing the world how stable you are and how well you hold on to what you've attained by hard work and determination.

Venus is your ruling planet, influencing you to love many forms of beauty.

Gemini Ⅱ May 21st-June 20th

You are the first air sign of the zodiac, which also brings the first signs of sensitivity into it.

You can be as restless as the air itself. Sometimes the restlessness takes on the velocity of a full-scale gale, upsetting other people, and leaving you nervous and emotional.

You have the first duality of nature to appear in the zodiac, making it difficult for others to understand you. Most of all, you can find life complicated by not truly knowing yourself, since the two parts of your nature can tear you to pieces. Those of you who appear happy, charming, and even brilliant to some, may find that others will see you as a materialistic pessimist. Neither will be correct, for you're truly a mixture of all these characteristics. But your nature is so chameleon that you'll usually project that part of yourself which you think will make the best impression on the other person. This is due to the mercurial content, which your ruling planet of Mercury imparts.

You reflect changes in your environment, circumstances, and emotions, as sensitively as a barometer registering changes in the weather. Although versatility is your strongest attribute, you get knowledge by association with people, rather than entirely by study. You can be a fine student providing you take up a subject which doesn't bore you. You give up once boredom sets in, and nothing will encourage you to go back to it—by this time, some other subject has begun to intrigue you. Although versatility can be your greatest asset, it can also go into reverse and become a weakness. In the desire to relate to and please others, there are periods in your life when you don't dare let go of the image you first used to impress the person. So you become trapped and this can lead to the nervous hypertension you often suffer.

In personal emotional relationships, you're honest by intention, but you have an uncertain element which can loom up, making you very fickle. Certainly, your two halves are very strong and equally wayward. Both demand time to show themselves. You can honestly want to love a person and really believe you're in love. Then the other half begins to rationalize and analyze. In the end, one half of you is capable of condemning or eliminating the other, and you can change from one love to another in hopes of finding some semblance of security.

Most of all you need to find an identity. This is the most difficult part of your life. The cohesion of your two parts can be your life's work, and you always need help from other people. Yet inability to accept criticism may hamper your acceptance of help. No sign can be more easily understood or hurt than you, even though you really want to be in love and to receive love.

Financial instability can have a particularly bad effect on you, even though the appearance is deceptive. For you may appear like a butterfly, without a care in the world. But the desire to have enough money for your many wants is always in the back of your mind. Not being particularly practical, you can mistake your wants for your real needs, and you're not too good at making things easier by sitting down and trying to economize.

Your imagination is prolific. You accentuate difficulties without consciously trying to accept the solution—going from one person to another, eager to have advice, but usually discarding it. Making decisions on your own is never easy because you can always see two sides to every question. This can lead to procrastination, because few real problems—that is, problems which are not products of your imagination—can be walked away from. Reality has an uneasy habit of catching up with you. This creates traumatic conditions, again playing havoc with your sensitive mental and physical make-up.

It's not easy to talk about a positive or negative type for members of your sign. Individual Geminis seem to have within each of them both positive and negative traits. This is understandable when you realize that your symbolic zodiac sign is the Twins.

Try to use the inherent versatility bestowed on you by your ruling planet Mercury; channel your good intellect and ability along positive lines. Stay with a project, a job, or a lover, long enough to really understand them. If you really can't reconcile yourself—and there'll be many times in your life when you can't—then you must go on to something else. But think before you act. Remember there's no gain in jumping from the frying pan into the fire.

Sometimes the most negative aspects seem to be in your easygoing nature and desire to please. This can be overdone so that you lose the respect of the very person you want to impress. Worst of all, you can develop feelings of guilt. You can offset this by trying to face reality. Study the facts. Try to put both halves of yourself together, and ask yourself if the person you wanted to impress just couldn't cope with both halves of you? If the answer frightens you, then you simply have to forget and go on to something else. Fortunately, you do not find it hard to forgive and forget. This helps make any new project alive by your own enthusiasm to try something new.

Your remarkably good mind can be relied on just as much as your charm. In conversation, you can be witty, easily captivating anyone listening to you. But you like most to mix with people who are foils to your versatility. When others upset or bore you, you don't like to hurt them and prefer to jab lightly rather than inflict deep wounds. You are capable of gentle but effective sarcasm but try to remain charming even at these times.

CANCER ♋ JUNE 21st-JULY 20th

As the first of the water signs, you're under the rulership of the moon.

The moon is the swiftest-moving of all the heavenly bodies, taking 28 days in its orbit, showing four distinct phases of itself from the waxing or growing of the moon to its full light, to the waning or dwindling away of the light. It also affects the tides of the waters of the world. Everything under the rulership of the wayward and fickle moon is subject to these periods of ebbing and flowing. You feel its effect in your own swiftly changing moods—making you emotional, sensitive and highly romantic, and even tearful.

You have a vivid imagination. Everything in life becomes personalized to you. Read a novel, see a play, and you immediately relate to some character in it. However, if you read it or see it again, it doesn't mean that you'll relate to the same character. With so much ability to absorb all the people you meet, you should use great discrimination in choosing your close associates. Your curious nature, which is also sympathetic, draws you to all types of people. This isn't always good for you, because it's people who affect you most. They can drain much of your energy when they come to gain your readily sympathetic ear for their troubles. You tend to take on their problems, although you're better at sympathizing than at offering solutions. When anyone near to you is sick, it's as if you can absorb their symptoms by osmosis, and this again can be very bad for your own delicate system.

You're sensitive to all things concerning your family and have a deep love for the comforts of your house. Your constant need for change can be upsetting to people close to you. They sometimes wonder why the things that pleased you yesterday don't please you today. Indeed, it's a hard job keeping pace with your whims and fancies and you're not very easy to understand. For this reason, you may find that there's a constant coming and going of friends in your life. This also applies to your romantic life; it's not unusual for you to have three husbands or at least several high-powered love affairs which you'll terminate just as swiftly as you started them. Many Cancers, with their fine intuitive force, are interested in occultism—sometimes only from curiosity.

One of your most positive attributes is a retentive memory helping you to remember even small events from the past in exact detail. Often you indulge in childhood reminiscences, your career, or the lives of your children when they were small. Conversation comes easily, providing it's not limited to any one subject. Certain negative aspects come through when you're bored, and sometimes you become a compulsive liar. This is rarely done with the intention of hurting anyone, but rather to draw attention to yourself. Fortunately your retentive memory helps you, and you're able to cover up any lies later on with a massive coating of charm—or even contriteness if forced into it.

You have idealistic ambitions, always wanting to do your best. Sometimes you fall down on good intentions because of your change-ability. Ceremonies and rituals of all types impress you—be they weddings, religious services, or funerals.

In real estate, business, or even in buying your own home, you can be remarkably shrewd. Sometimes your air of childish innocence is deceptive, and you use it to advantage to bring off deals which would put more experienced people to shame.

You have an excellent sense of values when you want something for yourself or your family. The watery content of your sign makes you over-generous in large things, but you can appear quite mean over items no more important than a postage stamp. Personal possessions mean a lot to you, so that you tend to accumulate things. If you give something away, chances are you add two more things to your closet. General tidiness isn't your strong point except in matters of personal appearance. You love to be admired, and you certainly take time enough to prepare yourself for admiration. Providing you have plenty of personal possessions around you, a little untidiness doesn't upset you, but it's a trait which often distresses others in the house. Your generally kind nature, however, often inspires others to help you in mammoth cleaning-up operations—but this is a sporadic rather than routine action.

When the positive trends of your imagination are chaneled into artistic work, you can achieve success, especially in the field of fiction or painting. When there are too many negative trends, you're apt to become easily hurt, imagining that people have upset you and dwelling on personal hurts. Most of you resort to tears rather than to temper which become the outlet for frustrations and any emotional hurt. You'll rarely suffer any personal insult in silence, and often this can cause those of you who are negative to become apathetic.

Your symbolic animal in the zodiac is the Crab—peaceful enough if allowed to have its own way, but able to inflict hurt if forced to do so. The crab moves erratically, and this is somewhat reflected in your own way through life which rarely takes a straightforward, easy trek towards its goals.

LEO ♌ JULY 22ND-AUGUST 21ST

You are the second of the fire signs, under the rulership of the life-giving force of the sun.

You delight in all the vital spheres of life, and if you can live on a grand scale you're much happier than when trying to make ends meet. Limited finances upset you more than anything else, for you have an inherent ability to enjoy the best of this world in food, drink, your home, or other pleasures. You're gregarious enough to want to share your life and its delights, but often this is done in order to impress others and develop a "hail-fellow-well-met" type of character.

You can be very proud—especially of your birthright and ancestors —passionate in your emotions and professionally ambitious. If you're able to fulfill the high potential of your sign, you're a born leader, capable of exercising authority and excellent at organization.

In this century we're seeing many of you who have the capabilities for success but not the opportunities. For this reason, many of you know the frustration of not being able to take your rightful place as leaders. Many of you will have worked hard and diligently, yet often be forgotten when promotions or salary raises have gone to others. You're prepared to fight for your rights, which often leads to the idea of the Leo being overbearing and pushing. When successful, you can be domineering; you expect everyone to know who's in command and will rarely tolerate inefficiency or lack of respect. In the most positive members of the sign, the overbearing, domineering traits soften to create a warm-hearted, sociable, generous, cheerful person, completely sincere in relationships.

You belong to a sign noted for its longevity and resilience—its ability to recover from illnesses with little time for convalescence. Your strength of mind and body, and the vital and intense feeling you're prepared to put into life, can be an inspiration to others. Praise is necessary to you, but you're prepared to earn it and not accept cheap flattery.

Once you're disillusioned about a person or project, the more negative qualities assert themselves either by temper or a complete contempt of the situation or person. You don't use subtle measures to show this, and are quite capable of throwing out an unmistakeable insult if provoked. Because pride is necessary to you, there are many degrees in which it manifests itself—varying from personal pride in yourself, family and possessions, to haughtiness which may be a defense mechanism. Boastfulness and a supercilious air can alienate you from casual acquaintances, but will be understood by friends.

You like to get to the root of any matter without beating about the bush. In business, you can be intensely practical and hard-headed but still capable of expressing warm-heartedness to people who work for you. But before this happens they have to go more than half way to prove their loyalty and efficiency. Thereafter, no employer can instill better relationships with employees than you.

Although pride's the defense weapon which may sharpen your tongue, you can forgive easily—without going so far as to fully forget. Frequently, you can strike back again when the memory of an old wrong or an attack rears its head again, even if it's many years from the time of the original quarrel.

You accept the good things of contemporary living with forthrightness, which is characteristic of your direct way of thinking. You thrive best in an atmosphere of luxury, good clothes and expensive homes. If you've too many negatives in your personal horoscope, there can be a marked lack of taste in choosing clothes like a flamboyant tie for a man or too much costume jewelry for a woman. You wear what suits you and "the world can take it or leave it" becomes your attitude. You sometimes become more conservative when you have enough money and don't feel financial pressures—although you never seem to feel you have quite enough to keep up with your real needs, and desires.

Providing you have more positive than negative qualities, you'll stick fast with your principles, defying anyone—even if you have to suffer from taking a firm stand. It's not unusual for people of your sign to walk away from a good job purely on a matter of principle, although you'll cling to a marriage long past signs of its being shaky.

You can endure anything for a long time whether it be a job, personal relationship, or involvement with a pet project, probably in community and civic life. Yet you can say goodbye dramatically when the occasion arises, and nothing will tempt you back. The main impetus for leaving is nearly always hurt, personal pride, or a case of principles. When you leave, you do it dramatically, so that no one doubts your reasons. The orthodox religions attract you, especially those with colorful ritual and ceremony.

Your symbolic zodiac animal is the Lion, who must know a form of personal freedom if he's to show his main attributes of fearlessness and strength. The lion is respected by his fellow animals—they may not understand him and many will fear him, but he's mainly left alone.

Mankind has become the main destroyer of the lion, either by killing or capturing him. The same feelings man holds toward the lion are sometimes also expressed by man toward people born under the sign of Leo. Given freedom of will and action with respect, no one is more dignified, regal, and capable of behaving like royalty, than you are. Deprive you of freedom in any form and you become the equivalent of the restless caged lion in the zoo. If you've ever seen a lion in a circus, you may have noticed that he'll perform his tricks at the demands of the trainer. But there's always an air of apprehension through the audience—an awareness of the lion's potential strength. Sometimes lions revolt against their trainers, and this is the position in which many human Leos find themselves during this century. You can be cajoled but never teased and prefer to perform to the best of your ability without the sound of a whip cracking in your ears.

You feel that your freedom and that of others is something worth fighting for and, generally, you're right.

VIRGO ♍ AUGUST 22ND-SEPTEMBER 21ST

As the second of the earth signs, you have some of the better qualities of Taurus, the first earth sign. But you're much more sensitive as an individual and in your approach to others.

Many crude edges seem to have been removed from your make-up. You're shrewd, discriminating, and so quietly active that much of your work may not be fully appreciated or even attributed to you. You have a strong inclination to be reserved, and when this reaches a negative state, it can be difficult to understand. Any harshness on your part really disguises a nervousness peculiar to your mercurial temperament, influenced by your ruling planet of Mercury.

There are times when you may want to be sympathetic but you're rarely able to express this in words while doing something "behind the scenes" in order to help the other person. You have a great deal of personal insecurity, a desire to be needed which can never be expressed. Most of your friends are those who can see this need and tend it tactfully and discreetly. With a nucleus of hand-picked friends (who may choose *you* rather than you choosing them) you can gradually bolster your need to feel secure and confident.

Your mental capacity is high (again influenced by Mercury), and many of your I.Q.'s will be far above other signs of the zodiac. Being on an intellectual plane can make you feel remote and alone, for you don't have time to waste on trivialities or even social small talk. Applying method and logic in your own life, you appreciate and expect the same of your friends. Your greatest danger to personal popularity is a biting sarcastic tongue and a tendency to analyze everything down to bare bones. Even constructive criticism isn't always welcomed in others' personal affairs. When combined with a cold analytical approach, it can make people think you're much more destructive than you really are.

Sometimes it appears that warmth and normal outgoing types of friendship are abhorrent to you; this again reduces the number of people who can feel they really know, understand, and like you. Of all the signs in the zodiac, you're the ones who do little to encourage affection, although you need it. There can be a masochistic quality in your determination to reject love and affection by normal standards.

Once over this barrier, however, associates will respect you, and you'll show them a great degree of stability. Once a friendship is established—although for you this is always a slow, painful process—it will stand the test of years. Especially if your friends understand in time that they'll have to go more than halfway to meet you.

Respect comes to you much more easily than affection, generally more for your mental qualities rather than for your grace and charm. You do have these latter attributes, but rarely exploit them to their full advantage as others would. You can always be relied upon to improve on someone else's ideas since you're the perfectionist of the zodiac. You function well behind the scenes rather than in the limelight but you do expect credit where it's due.

Your most negative trait is found in vacillation, showing a lack of self-confidence. All negative traits result in digestive disturbances: many of you, especially in the last twelve years, will have had periods of illness rooted in psychosomatic pressures. You can literally worry yourself into any illness you've heard of, but it aims for your stomach and the solar plexus—the seat of many fears. Great care should be taken in all partnerships, and you have a built-in awareness of this. The danger is that many of you let opportunities for business and personal partnerships pass because you try to analyze many things out of existence. In a desire to produce the perfect rose, some gardeners fail by pruning the plant too much.

The positive Virgo, aware of negative traits in his character, can eliminate them by the same ruthlessness which makes him study his friends under a microscope. Lone periods of self-analysis are essential to you if the positive qualities which can lead to positions of responsibility and success in life are to emerge. It's not easy to turn your thoughts inward and to determinedly strip away any negatives, yet you're prefer this to having anyone else dare to point out your failings. Should this happen, you're ruthless and point out flaws in the well meaning friend —which, again, doesn't help make easy meaningful relationships for you.

Your symbol in the zodiac is the Virgin, which relates to the harvesting of the earth's crops and which is generally shown holding an ear of wheat. If you plant seeds and take meticulous care in spading and tilling, you expect to reap and share a rich harvest. You're able to do this in your own life, watching your brain-children grow and mature into business activities. But, generally, someone must supply you with the life force of the seed. This is only possible when you can accept personal or business partners for what they are and not insist they be what you wish them to be.

LIBRA ♎ SEPTEMBER 22ND-OCTOBER 22ND

This second of the air signs is one of the most refined, elegant, artistic, and intuitive signs of the zodiac—providing it's capable of living up to its positive characteristics.

You can make comparisons and criticism and then deliver a considered thoughtful opinion, earning you the respect and gratitude of those who appreciate your judgment. This ability, however, is far more acute when you're making an assessment for someone else. In your personal life, you tend to put off making decisions. Therefore it's essential for you to have a partner who, without appearing to be domineering, can help you to make up your mind. With a compatible married partner, you can achieve great success in realms outside the home. In fact, no one in the zodiac can benefit so much from married life as you, but should it become disrupted, you can be remorseful and regretful to the point of getting ill.

The positive members of your sign have great curiosity about everything, including the lives of friends and associates. They don't like to feel left out. It's always better to tell you anything that may concern you than let you discover it from someone else. When the negative aspects dominate, this insatiable curiosity can be mistaken for prying, but once you discover a secret, you rarely gossip about it.

You hate to be involved in any quarrels, even in a remote way. If they intrude on your personal life, you feel debilitated and soon lose your grasp on everyday things. It takes very little to upset the balance of your zodiac symbol, the Scales—and the same applies in your life. Your nervous system is delicate and can be easily thrown off balance.

Your airy, versatile nature is influenced by the planet Venus, symbolic of all that's good and beautiful. This is the balance you strive for in your life—to be with harmonious people in pleasant atmospheres, surrounded by artistic décor and works of good taste. Obviously, money will always be necessary for your happiest existence, but you're mentally well-equipped to earn a good income from your creative talents. This can be most possible if you have a strong-minded partner providing the drive and energy you may lack. It would be wrong to say that you're lazy, but you do tend to project a rather languid attitude, proceeding slowly in all your projects.

Your attitudes toward friendships seem to change every eight years. Such a shift isn't often dramatic— simply a drifting away from people who were once friendly with you, and you're quite capable of picking up the strands of friendship several years later. On the other hand, once a friend has gone from your personal orbit, you're not inclined to write and check up. This can happen even to people you once felt close to and can be of some concern to close friends. You may try to behave as if nothing had happened, but most people like to receive a card or a letter in the interim. It's not unusual to find your curious nature probing into the depths of E.S.P. and occult matters, but more in the manner of a student or critic than of one with a desire to be involved. Your own E.S.P. can be high, but you ignore it, preferring to read about the exploits of others in this field.

When more positive than negatives appear in your personal horoscope, you appreciate music and enjoy following all artistic pursuits with frequent visits to the opera, ballet, and concerts. You can also partake actively in artistic careers such as designing or anything to do with beauty—hairdressing, cosmetics, interior decorating. Sometimes antiques attract you, and you prefer the most elegant periods in history such as Eighteenth-Century French furniture, the Impressionist painters. In the higher professions, the law and architecture can attract you, but you can easily be a dilettante in both professions, if you have enough money to indulge personal whims.

Your symbolic sign of the zodiac is depicted as the Scales, meaning the scales of justice. You do, indeed, have a strong sense of justice;

the danger is that you may act as the critical judge before you have analyzed yourself. The Scales are always depicted as being slightly off-balance—showing that perfection for man, who is less than God, isn't possible. You can, of course, always strive to maintain a close-to-perfect balance in your own life, and the majority of people under your sign conscientiously struggle to do so.

Many are surprised that a seemingly contented and placid Libran can show signs of being militant when the occasion justifies it. Once your sense of justice is outraged, you can become very militant: more professional soldiers are born under your sign than poets.

SCORPIO ♏ OCTOBER 23RD-NOVEMBER 21ST

You are the second of the water signs and now the water which started in Cancer becomes deep and turgid. So are the depths of your character, which is very complex.

The old astrologers saw you as capable of the greatest and lowest in achievement—which means that within your sign there are many who can fulfill high positive attributes and an equal number who have a negative approach to living.

Your magnetic personality can influence friends for good or evil, according to your motivations. You can be determined, critical, shrewd, cautious, and intensely secretive—all at the same time. There's always a watchful, wary air about you—sometimes as if you're deliberately looking for your associates' Achilles' heels. This wariness is really a shield—you want no one to completely probe the depths of your dark, mysterious, brooding nature.

It's not easy to become a close associate of yours because of this wariness. Your innate sense of dignity is a form of defense, just as the horny body of your symbolic zodiac animal—the Scorpion—is well protected from attacks. No one's permitted to take liberties with you, or you're capable of retaliating with a sting as malicious as the Scorpion's itself.

It's been said that people under Scorpio combine the "head of the eagle rising toward the Heavens with the belly of the snake, content to crawl in the undergrowth." There's truth in this. It manifests itself in the deep characteristics which can make you an enigma to those you meet. According to the positive and negative, whichever dominates, you can be highly uplifting in thought and action or equally content as part of a corrupt underworld.

Your strongest characteristic is being strong-willed, bold, and self-confident combined with a masterful temper, displayed at the slightest provocation. You're capable of the most biting and withering remarks, leaving no doubt as to how you feel.

You have many of the qualities of your preceding sign, Libra, but can lack the elegant quality which makes the most critical Libran bearable. Where they'll make the subtle sarcastic remark, you'll be outrageously outspoken, not caring about effect. You have a compulsion to hurt when offended or upset, and this can alienate you from many who'd like to help you. This isn't so much a lack of consideration for others as a determined desire to show that you have a defense mechanism. The biting quality of your angry tongue has no equal in any other sign of the zodiac.

Most of all, you never forget a wrong and can spend years nursing a grievance, constantly resentful toward the person who inflicted it. This tenacity can make it certain that you'll never go through life without making enemies; it also seems that you need this to goad you on to prove you were right and the other person wrong—even if it takes a lifetime to do so. When negative aspects are more in evidence, this hostility can dissolve in self-pity and make you carry a chip on your shoulder.

Although you dislike others taking liberties with you or probing into your personal life, you enjoy unravelling others' secrets. You're the natural detectives of the zodiac and can often use this talent professionally.

Few of you can escape a highly emotional, traumatic love life, since you're always swayed by intense emotions toward the other sex. When love affairs go wrong, you're dehydrated and like to go off and brood. The brooding rarely takes into account any thought that you might have made a mistake. The wound-licking does you good, and you can eventually emerge still retaining your dignity. A tremendous strength of character always enables you to put up a facade to hide the sensitivity you fear might be construed as weakness.

You have little sympathy with illness, whether your own or anyone else's. Fear of illness can be more devastating to you than illness itself, for your vivid imagination enables you to fear the worst.

While you'll spend money freely upon yourself, you're not noted for being overly generous to associates and family. You like to have things on our own terms, dictating and controlling the way friendship and love must go, if they are to survive. It's important for you to have a flexible type of companion who'll appreciate your own strength and allow you to mould his way of life. When crossed in business or love, you react violently.

Your mentality is complex, subtle, acute, and shows to its best advantage when unraveling mysteries or dealing with complications. The positive members of your sign use their personal magnetism, invincible will, and executive ability whenever they can. Once ambitious instincts are awakened, you have a great capacity for clinging tenaciously to the project and can accomplish the seemingly impossible. Your negative aspects show pride (which is not entirely justified), selfishness, violence, and a complete inability to forgive. There are few ways in which you know how to compromise.

You have two ruling planets, one of which is Pluto, the planet associated with the unexpected and often called the dark planet of mystery. Not enough is known about Pluto, but it seems to fit in very well with the complexity of Scorpio. Mars is the original ruling planet attributed to you. This can influence the drive you have in getting the most from all areas of life, but it has many aggressive qualities to guard against.

SAGITTARIUS ♐ NOV. 22ND-DEC. 20TH

This third and last of the fire signs can contain the best of the two previous fire signs, Aries and Leo. Many of the imperfections found in the two preceding signs are less evident in yours.

You're independent, honest, loyal, and always active. You almost always have philosophical ideals, and your intuitive powers can take you into the realms of prophecy. Throughout your life—even without consciously looking for them—you'll attract people who need your help and guidance. Always ready to spend time giving advice, you also like to see the advice carried out. You'll go out of your way to make contacts, practically carrying other people's burdens forever on your back. There's always an element of sincerity in your desire to help friends in a practical way, and you offer much more than sympathy. Many of you are the natural teachers of spiritual and material affairs, being able to combine both with ease.

In contrast to these characteristics, many members of your sign are rebels and extremists. Despite your good nature and desire to help others, life seems to offer more than a fair share of burdens in your personal life. Sometimes there's an elderly relative to look after, or an invalid married partner. When negatives dominate, you become slaves to convention, relying on your outer sense rather than the intuition which is really one of your major assets so long as you are guided by it and not rebelling against it.

While the positive members are sincere in all they do, the negative ones can adopt a hypercritical attitude, finding fault with new ideas without trying to understand them. Often rebellious instincts, personal trials, and turmoil in other people's lives, can awake your stronger inner self. Then an awareness arises which can make you able to follow the traditions of some of the world's greatest teachers.

Your honesty can become a byword and shining example when you follow your heritage to guide and uplift rather than to destroy and cast down. Your opposing sign of Gemini is very similar in its contradictory nature. The difference is that Gemini will deliberately maneuver toward changes, while you're launched into change without contriving.

Sometimes honest qualities can lead you to speak without thinking and then you're likely to hurt someone. This outspoken quality is as much influenced by environment as by your ruling planet of Jupiter, one of the most benevolent of the planets. Jupiter is remarkable for its qualities which manifest themselves to you in the broad spectrum of friends and acquaintances with whom you like to surround yourself. You enjoy group living and are rarely at your best leading a lonely life, unless by special choice with some project in view. You may not always understand others' sensitivities, mostly because many hard kicks have led you to philosophical thought rather than sensitivity within yourself. You have an almost stoical belief that you must tread a hard road through life, but you're strong enough to surmount difficulties even if you get bruised on the way.

All the fire signs are capable of temper, but ignite for different reasons. Your temper is likely to explode more when an injustice is done to someone else than if done to yourself. Then you'll use all your means to right the wrongs, even if you have to go through many channels to do so. You're not shy about using strong language in attacking your opponents' Achilles' heels.

Although strong-willed and always ready to work hard, many of you don't achieve personal success professionally or emotionally until after middle age. Being gregarious, you need the companionship of others, even if all too often it's the other person's needs which drive him to you. After middle age, there's often a change in this: friendship becomes more equal, with each party appreciating the other.

Long platonic friendships, generally born of a bond when you both face trials, abuse, and tribulations together, are not unusual. Inevitably, when you shed one burden—such as looking after an elderly relation—you miss the burden, and will avidly seek someone else to look after. The need to be wanted expresses itself in many ways, not always in the desire to achieve love, but to be of use to others.

Your symbolic animal in the zodiac is the Archer, the half-man, half-centaur who is shooting his arrow into the air. When you're positive, all your arrows have a habit of finding their mark. When negative, a lot of energy is drained away; the target is missed and the arrow also lost; but the centaur-man is tenacious enough to start all over again and, by middle age, can generally reach his target.

CAPRICORN ♑ DEC. 21ST-JAN. 20TH

This last of the three earth signs symbolizes the earth after the first push of spring in Aries and the harvest in Virgo. It notes when the earth becomes dry and barren, often lying fallow to await the touch of warmth which will generate life again.

You're practical, persevering, cautious, and economical. Many of you eventually become self-made people, doing well in business, but not without some bitter lessons. How well you have learned the hard lessons, though, is the measure of your success and happiness.

When you live up to the positive trends in your sign, you're impressively faithful and thorough—always showing an industrious approach to life. Yet you can have a ruthless quality, never softened by mercy or the kindness of your preceding sign, Sagittarius. You'll always give good value for money to employees, but you rarely feel any warm emotional bonds with them. You expect to give your pound of flesh, but you also expect to receive it when negotiating. In many ways, you're the most practical and sensible sign of the zodiac—unless extremes are reached, where so many negative and unlikeable qualities creep in.

In your sign are found a dry, unemotional approach to business, a tendency to care more for money and climbing the social ladder than the nuances of tenderness. Although you can have a subtle wit and the ability to tell a good story, there's little that's brisk and dashing about you. All your effects are contrived, rather than spontaneous expressions of *joie de vivre*. You like to think before you speak and then take time before going into action—which is premeditated to the extent that you falter or run away from anything outside the norm.

Often you lose much by not venturing out to fulfill a project on your own since your cautious nature dictates to you. Very often the early part of your life is a series of lost opportunities which you regret. But you rarely learn from past experiences in this way. You'll still meditate, look for a long time, and then forget to leap. Changes occur in your life when you're catapulted into them by certain planetary patterns which leave you with no choice.

Your ruling planet is Saturn—the teacher and taskmaster who moves so slowly that major changes rarely occur more frequently than every 26 years. When they do, you're not always resilient enough to absorb them, and can become bewildered by even the *idea* of change, which is never looked for and so must be caused by wills other than your own.

When the negative aspects are dominant, you can be soured and embittered, discontented with your lot, but not consciously capable of making any effort to improve it. You can slip in and out of the slough of despondency which is one of the traps Saturn lays for you. Depression isn't unusual all through your life, and you have to make a very determined effort to use the abuses of Saturn so that profitable lessons are learned from it. Then you can succeed and pull yourself up by your shoestrings.

Sometimes you're considered introverted or self-centered, but this is a defense mechanism to protect your own interests; you're sure you can't trust anyone else to do so. You make little attempt to share responsibilities with associates.

The gap between the female and male Capricorn is not only one of sexual differences. While the male can become soured and more introverted, the female has a degree of patience that can make her one of the most downtrodden of housewives—or the most perfect, when she deliberately strives to please. She wants to do her best for her family, and finds no sacrifice too great. That she's not always appreciated is another Saturnian affliction, but she doesn't ask for praise or appreciation, being quite content to do her best without hope of material award. Often, unless she's partnered by an understanding, compatible sign, she's not given many rewards of affection either. But when given affection, she's at her best, never seeking the limelight but happy as the power behind the throne.

You're happiest when exerting control over someone else, and can be excellent in positions of responsibility where others rely on you. Although you're capable of making friends of sometimes unusual characters, friendships are always limited either by your own desires or the will of your partner in both business and marriage. Once they're admitted into the inner sanctum of friendship, you expect newcomers to maintain their dignity. Respect is much more desirable than other forms of affection —at least on the surface—but many of you have inner feelings that demand love, though you dare not venture halfway to meet it. For this reason, many frustrations build up as Saturn acts as a restrictor and creates obstacles for your desires.

As you need to win respect, you're also capable of giving it. Anything that's unconventional or unorthodox makes you worry, and you're not averse to taking steps to rid your life of non-conservative elements. This is more of a duty than entirely a wish, for the secret part of yourself is always in conflict with the dry image you show to the world.

You struggle to preserve the past, preferring it to being an innovator of new ideas. Environment and upbringing influence you a great deal. Many of your most bitter childhood memories can lay the foundation for the reserve you have in meeting new people and your suspicions of any overtures of affection. Although you can be judged as self-centered, sacrifice in the cause of duty is not unknown to you. You take refuge more in being respected than loved, more in being feared than liked.

Your symbolic animal of the zodiac is the Goat, climbing upwards along the rugged path of life and determined to reach the summit. Many of you do, indeed, succeed against tremendous odds, showing your tenacity.

You're one of the signs which can expect longevity. If the youthful period has been bleak, after middle age it seems that Saturn relents a little and gives you a second chance to see if you can still learn from his lessons.

It's rarely a consolation to know that success and the things you struggled for in youth are delayed until old age when much of the zest for living has been diminished. Still, many of you are capable of enjoying a very happy old age with the cares and bitterness of the past merely a memory.

AQUARIUS ≈ JANUARY 21ST-FEBRUARY 19TH

This third and last of the air signs contains the accumulated characteristics of previous air signs of Gemini and Libra, with the addition of philosophical thought.

You have a deep understanding and feeling for humanity on a broad spectrum that reaches beyond the home. You have plenty of personal magnetism, and are likely to use it to influence groups of people without being conscious of it as a form of personal charm. You can be very inventive; many of the world's most famous inventors were born under your sign. While not all of you can be geniuses or well-known, the same basic quality shows itself in the way you can devise ways and means to carry out a plan.

An idealistic attitude soars you above any materialistic conditions, and you're quite likely to contribute funds to good causes even when you haven't too much money yourself. Your inquiring mind interests you in the past as well as the future, and you may like to study social conditions from the past in order to understand the way the world is going.

Gemini has the curiosity of a child. Libra is curious to know how to extend his own ambitions. But you have an insatiable curiosity to gain knowledge in order to tell others about it. You always feel capable of improving someone else's life. When the humanitarian instinct is strong, you're very happy to be a leading light in projects which stretch out into other countries.

When negative aspects are in evidence, eccentricity based on fads shows, and you'll have lightning flashes of temper. If you can't have your own way, you can lapse into long periods of silence, and an unjustified arrogant kind of independence. Your negatives, however, are not as hurtful to others as many of the negatives in the other signs where distinction between positive and negative seems much more marked.

When positive aspects dominate, you are highly intellectual, thoughtful, and enormously resistant to fatigue. Providing you're convinced you're right—and you rarely do anything unless this seems to be so—you can work long hours, never expecting good conditions. Often this is injurious to your health. All too often you ignore a deterioration of your own health, although you're most solicitious when a member of the family shows even the slightest symptoms of not feeling well.

Once your health deteriorates, you can go to pieces very suddenly. This is a characteristic of your ruling planet, Uranus, the planet that acts swiftly and without warning. This is a contrast to Pluto, the other planet concerned with unexpected happenings. But Pluto rumbles and groans, giving warning before striking.

You're always so sure that what you have to do is right that there's a tendency to resent advice or anything interfering with the project in hand. It's difficult for members of your family to understand that you have to move quickly and can never truly relax. In contrast, they have difficulty also in understanding that you also need time to be alone without giving any reasons. Although fond of trying to help others (always on the grand scale), you can fail to see bad conditions in your own family circle until it's too late to help. When you learn that your family may be suffering, it has the Uranus impact of being a surprise.

You're exceptionally good at reading people's characters. You may suffer disillusions afterwards, however, since your main idea is to consider people likeable until they prove otherwise. This characteristic of wanting to see the best in everyone is excellent in theory but, in actual living, conditions can lead to sudden letdowns when even small flaws appear in another person.

Although you're ultra-sensitive, it doesn't often show. You can be easily hurt, especially by people you love the most. Yet when in love, no sacrifice is ever too great for you to make. You can be faithful even under platonic circumstances, and many of your happiest moments are with friends you love on a platonic rather than a highly emotional basis.

Love on the married basis often comes because you believe you can help your partner, rather than from an exciting, romantic feeling. Unless your partner understands the terms of your love from the beginning, your marriage may run into difficulties. If you're an Aquarian man, you prefer to be the dignified father-figure to the romantic lover, and are generally attracted to women much younger than yourself.

Although every Aquarian has a curious mind, open enough to want to explore areas of life which you don't understand, many of you are skeptics. Few of you accept such things as E.S.P. or occultism on face value. Nevertheless, you investigate, read, and then decide for yourself whether or not they're valid. In no area can anyone make up your mind for you. This is part of your independent heritage.

Your symbolic figure in the zodiac is the Water Bearer, a man kneeling with an upturned vessel from which water pours. So it's in your life, as part of the human race, that you want to give something of yourself. Water is one of the essentials of human life. (A man can live longer without food than without water.) Why don't we always see that the Aquarian likes to allow the milk of human kindness to flow from him to the world? Because your interest in philosophical thought, the kneeling figure of the water bearer with his bowed head, is also symbolic of the humility the true philosopher feels.

PISCES ✕ FEBRUARY 19TH-MARCH 20TH

The zodiacal circle ends with Pisces, the third and last of the water signs. It seems to include all the characteristics of every other sign, as well as the accumulated ones of the previous two water signs—Cancer and Scorpio.

Because of this, you present a variety of types to the astrologer and show a duality of nature even among each other. So many complicated characteristics of the other signs seem to go into the make-up of every individual in this group that there's rarely a "typical" Piscean.

You can give an astrologer a major headache as he spends a long time probing the patterns of planets in your horoscope before he can come up with patterns that explain you. Every positive and negative in your sign has tributaries of para-positive and para-negative. Some of you show the more positive attributes to some of your associates, and then show a different side to others. Part of this is due to the resilience of your nature, making you all things to all people—letting them see what you wish them to see at the time.

You can be sympathetic (sometimes carrying it to the extremes of emotional sentimentality), patient, generous, and hospitable. When you say "my house is your house" you mean it, and leave nothing undone to make guests comfortable. In contrast, many of you become recluses. When this happens, few people see you in your own home and you don't encourage visiting or go visiting yourself. Mainly, however, because of an interest in other people, especially those less fortunate than yourself, you're gregarious. You're ultra-sensitive, too, and this can lead to some painful experiences in personal and emotional relationships.

When your positive trends occur, you can combine the practical with the theoretical. Generally, you're well-informed on a variety of subjects. Your literary ability can reach high standards, and many of you have professional interests in music and ballet. You can attain success and enjoy it in a completely uninhibited way, often building one success upon another, *or* you may despise everything that success and popularity has to offer. In everything, you go from one extreme to another under the influences of the diverse members of your sign.

Your more obviously negative signs are a complete contradiction to everything. In conflict with yourself and those around you, you can go from pillar to post, buffeted by circumstances which you seem powerless to control. You can also show signs of complete dissipation, taking no pains to do anything about it and refusing help from others.

The majority of you love beauty in all forms and lean towards refinement, disliking and running away from anything crude. You can have a passionate love for nature. Many famous psychics are born under Pisces, which seems to draw one into the realms of occultism and all mysterious forces of life. Sometimes you accept mysticism without asking questions about it, and this can lead to involvement in strange cults.

In business, you thrive best in a partnership—especially if the partner comes from one of the earth signs—Taurus, Virgo or Capricorn. Such types will supply a balance, keeping you from getting too dreamy-eyed or overly optimistic about projects. Enthusiasm is excellent, but it should have some reality. Many of you are very happy to spend much of your life in a dream world. Although you're considered easygoing, you can be excellent in business if handled with tact by partners and not driven too hard.

Your ruling planets are Jupiter—the kindly, expansive planet—and Neptune—which can bring elements of treachery and illusion into your life. It often seems that the benevolence of Jupiter is especially good to you, preventing any of Neptune's drastic efforts to destroy you. This is probably why many of you can get away with outrageous things in personal and business life and still come up smiling. Many other signs would be destroyed by the risks you seem able to take without being put in danger.

There's always a double aspect to you—two distinct sides to your nature, two planets to influence you. Your symbolic zodiac figure is that of two fish. With so many alternatives, so many variations on the theme of being Piscean, is it any wonder that you present everything within your own sign?

You have the ability to carry on two professions, which many of you do, being successful in both. It's not unusual for you to have two loves which you're capable of handling so that no one gets hurt. Generally, you have your best successes when you move from the land of your birth and work in another country. Traveling always intrigues you, and you have little qualms about packing up for short one-day excursions or trips halfway round the world. You're adaptable to any surround-ings, not through fickleness, but because philosophically you want to make the best of each day. Your greatest detriment is spreading yourself too thin by dissipating your energies in too many channels. Yet there's always a compulsion to tackle the impossible, and the challenge offered against odds is generally the impetus you need to succeed.

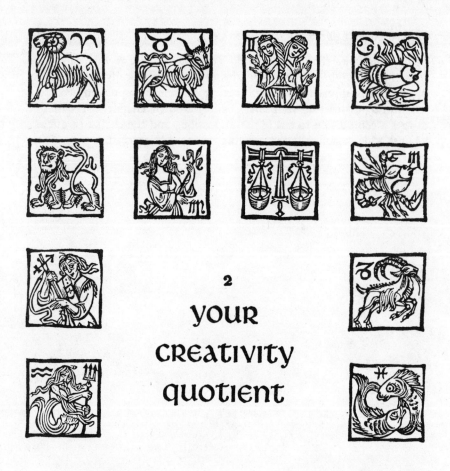

2

YOUR
CREATIVITY
QUOTIENT

ARIES ♈   You're happiest involved in constant physical activity and leading a busy social life.

This highly charged Mars-motivated design for living can defeat
your creative instincts. Your curiosity and drive—always looking for
new activities—can often lead your artistic nature to run riot. Unfortunately, creative intentions come in spurts. You're likely to have unfin-
ished paintings, sketches, pottery, or knitting scattered around the house.
You rarely go back to complete your work. Once you've put them away,
they become part of the past. Involvement with social life, generally, is
the cause.

If you can bring yourself to pinpoint some form of creative endeavor—enamelling, jewelry designing, metal work—allow yourself
time to finish it. This could bring you rarely experienced satisfaction.

Before starting a new activity, try to master the one you've begun. Sometimes this is more easily done if you join a group of creative people where conversation can lighten the creative intensity. Almost always, a competitive quality behind the group activity can be the impetus you need to retain interest and go on to completion of your project.

TAURUS ♉   You're not noted for spontaneous bouts of creativity, but with the Venusian influence you are attracted to art in many forms. With the ability to work hard, you'll always attempt to conscientiously master anything you make up your mind to do. Creativity in music—such as playing the piano, violin or taking singing lessons—sewing, and writing are creative forms which will appeal to you.

You can be very practical with your hands. If you're engaged in some home dressmaking, you'll get added satisfaction from feeling you're helping the family budget. This also applies to being thoroughly interested in making drapes, cushions, or lampshades for the home. Once you've made a decision to go ahead, you're conscientious about reaching your goal and take pride in completion.

You prefer to organize your creative activities—rather than being revolutionary one day, putting aside housework, and concentrating on "The Great Masterpiece." You're sensible enough to realize that creativity can be just as satisfying if done in your spare time, after the usual household chores. You'll work towards a finishing-date and almost always achieve it before going on to anything else. Moving slowly and methodically shows good results at the end of the year. You really finish things and get them into use while many of your friends are still talking about their creative efforts.

GEMINI II   Because you know a little about literally every subject under the sun, you're one of the world's best conversationalists.

It's difficult, though, for you to concentrate on any one subject because you prefer to scratch the surface rather than study in depth. The duality of your symbolic sign of the twins compels you to be involved with two projects at once.

You're capable of accomplishment in many areas without becoming a master of any. You can be particularly creative in anything requiring paper. Japanese origami and mobiles can provide enough variety for your creative drive, as no two pieces really turn out to be the same. Writing and musical composition—if you have had any training—also come easily to you. Since you're most comfortable with two projects going at once, try to settle for one which keeps your mind busy and one which keeps your hands busy and then you're quite likely to accomplish both. Nothing pleases you so much as getting the best of both the materialistic and the imaginative worlds.

CANCER ♋   You're a great home lover and find the most contentment in working at making it more attractive. The most ambitious of you will enjoy studying interior decoration to the point where you can become professional, or use it yourself, or be able to advise your friends. Many of you are addicted to collecting antiques, which easily extends to a creative interest in restoration. Such work can be a form of relaxation that will both satisfy aesthetic needs and appeal to money-saving instincts.

Practically everything you create can become a conversation piece, especially as you have a childlike desire to be praised for your work. Praise being part of the impetus to further efforts, there's a danger that you may become so inspired that you don't know where to stop. But the surplus lampshades and the many pieces of bric-a-brac that you've restored and then stored always come in handy as presents.

You rarely count the time you spend in any form of creative endeavor. As people heavily influenced by the moon, you're subjected to fantasies which, if channelled creatively, can produce some extraordinary results. The world of poetry and fiction sometimes opens up to you in this manner. Collages and your instinct to decorate just about everything that you can find—from wastepaper baskets to closet doors—also result from your fantasies.

Yet the moon, which influences you to be creative, also means that you become easily distracted by people around you. Try to remain true to your original goal and desire. Express your own creative forms without allowing other peoples' ideas to superimpose themselves on yours. It's also good to sometimes stop sharply and see that creative efforts at home can add up to paraphernalia cluttering your rooms. Streamline your efforts much more. Add a dash of realism to your creative efforts by understanding that you can't possibly use everything you make in your own home. If you're in business, this profusion of expression can be excellent.

LEO ♌ Your love of the dramatic suggests that you develop your creative talents in acting as well as production and stage management. Displays of all kinds—dress design, cooking, metal work—are areas where you can work confidently and let off some of your fiery creative drive.

Most people like to be praised when they've created something, but for you there's the danger that even with talent and hard work, you'll not always attain the success you expected. Through disappointment, many of you brush aside ideas which could be creatively satisfying without professional involvement. But you can get immense satisfaction from a profession that puts your creativity to practical use. Do not be the eternal dilettante. Listen to friends who may say that you try to do too much too quickly.

A number of you are practical around the house, being able to make the extra carved valance for a window. But for creativity at home, you need to be bolstered up and inspired by someone you're trying to please. It's as if you can't get the ultimate satisfaction in doing anything creative unless it's a means of communicating with someone who will praise both you and your work. The satisfaction is in the end product rather than in the actual time spent in creation and unless someone else is there to applaud and encourage you, there's a chance that frustration and even bitterness can erase the original creative drive.

VIRGO ♍ Although spontaneous creative activity doesn't come easily to you, many latent talents can evolve from your powers of reason derived from the influence of Mercury. When your Venus is well-placed, you show great love of beauty and full appreciation of others' efforts, even though you're also critical. Because of an analytical ability, you often miss opportunities to experiment with your own creative talent, feeling it may not be worthwhile or up to your high standards.

Very often you lack ambitious drive. If you can overcome your timidity and tension, you can become proficient in many areas. Music, research for writing, and detailed drawing of a technical character all require the sensitivity and meticulous discrimination which are so much part of you. Some of you add your knowledge and skills to the work of others—retouching photographs and generally giving careful, final, perfect touches.

You're the perfectionists of the zodiac, but finding fault with ideas before putting them into creative action can often dampen your enthusiasm for beginning anything on your own. With the right encouragement to help you eliminate these first fears (often unfounded), you have a wealth of creativity to tap. But you need to accept that many creative efforts go through experimental stages before they're regarded as final.

Don't allow your creative brainchildren to die at birth. Give them a chance to mature, coaxed along by constructive criticism, not spoiled self-abjection. It may help to realize that you may have to consult others and, also, to help them with their work. But don't let your "service to others" attitude deplete your own creative energy in any way.

LIBRA ♎   With Venus always accenting your craving for beauty in all forms, your own creative instincts are apt to show up in everything you do, whether at home or professionally. Painting, sculpting, interior decorating—on any scale you desire— are within your creative reach. It's your inner struggle for harmony that can harm your creative talents. Your sensitivity and emotion and inner awareness of beauty can lead to some spellbinding inspiration. Yet the instincts which cause the inspiration can also bring about nervous tension and it can become emotional agony to decide on a specific point. If you use your creative abilities professionally, there may be tension because you have too little time to enjoy your own home.

Learning to adjust and maintain the vital balance necessary to your happiness is as much an achievement as the actual creating of an idea. When completely inspired, you have to become moderate in your social life. This sometimes means sacrifice, because you draw a great deal of inspiration from company and the interchange of ideas. Let your excellent reasoning power make a compromise between pleasure and creative activity, and you'll find you've gained the best of both worlds, satisfying your material need to be surrounded by beauty, and satisfying deep emotional needs, too.

SCORPIO ♏ You have all the dynamic energy given to you by Mars and the mental agility necessary for creative originality—especially in literature, music and poetry. Pluto gives some of its better influences by encouraging many of you in avant-garde types of creation.

However, you're under so many opposing influences at times, with Mars driving you very hard, and Pluto planning the unexpected, that you tend to use your energy alternately for construction and destruction. This can be shown, perhaps, when you create an art form and then deliberately destroy it, either as the result of your own or someone else's criticism.

Let your iron will power give you self-understanding and the control needed for putting your energy to work creating new and positive ideas. Leave them for a while, but then go back to them before becoming too critical.

Once you've made up your mind to begin a creative project, you can get results quicker than any other sign in the zodiac. While so many of the others signs get tremendous satisfaction from creative effort, you rarely do, and so much is lost when your project is finished. If you can rely on admiration from your friends, chances of destruction are eliminated. But there's always your fear of rejection, so that much of your work is kept secretive unless being used in a professional field. You both fear rejection and use it as the catalyst to a form of depression but —given time—you'll recover your good spirits and go on to other successful creative projects.

Self-deprecation is justified only if you're not skillful and need to reassess the work you've done, wondering, perhaps, where you can improve on it. But you're capable of carrying self-deprecation to extremes, and it takes little to reduce you to wondering if creative endeavor is worthwhile. It certainly is, if you can become more objective. In your need for your work to be admired, remember that even the best of friends are not always good judges and, at worst, they can be jealous. Only you can truly know what you're seeking to produce. Once self-confidence is established, you can be one of the most prolific people in many creative forms.

SAGITTARIUS ♐   You're assured of some success because of the benevolent influence of Jupiter, your ruling planet. This applies to many of the creative ideas which interest you. Jupiter also gives you a reflective ability to learn from past experiences, trials and errors, as well as successes.

You must be careful not to wallow in contemplation. This can sink you into an unproductive inertia where it's just as satisfactory to dream as it is to actually do something. If you can avoid this pitfall, you can achieve outstanding results in philosophical writing, poetry, music, and many dance forms.

You'll achieve your best results if you allow yourself enough time to work in your own style and concentrate on your chosen endeavor. Don't try to copy other people's work at all, even though you may find that you make mistakes. You're courageous enough to take criticism from people you consider qualified to judge.

If you're working professionally in writing and music, try not to procrastinate. You'll probably have a deadline, and although all forms of creative work require inspiration at the beginning, there comes a time when you have to get down to putting ideas and plans into action. Social life often has to be cut down in order to do this, but you're often saved in the nick of time by realizing that you have a duty to meet a deadline.

Persuade yourself that your deadline is earlier than it actually is and you won't lose your initial spurt of inspiration or feel that a creative effort has turned into a chore.

CAPRICORN ♑   In his taskmaster guise, your ruling planet of Saturn may prevent any truly creative work in your early years because of financial problems. If you can link your creative endeavor to something like a commissioned work, you can outpace the obstacles Saturn puts in you way, and go on to create your work of art without feeling that you're wasting time, money, and energy. Try not to be over-cautious though, or you may not recognize security when it's reached.

Few of you will get a deep personal satisfaction from artistic work unless it is practical—like upholstering furniture or dressmaking. Yet you have a direct potential for research and writing. Try to understand that time isn't wasted if you're doing something you like to do rather than going out to work. The therapeutic results gained from creative work in your spare time cannot be measured. They certainly could help to offset the depression that comes from strong Saturnine influences.

Although you're inclined to be secretive about your creative work (at least while you're doing it), a great deal of satisfaction can be gained by working in a group. Encouragement and the interchange of ideas can spark off your energy, should it wane. Try to take others' advice as well-meaning, and don't make the mistake of thinking that advice is a negative form of criticism.

AQUARIUS ♒ You're the visionary people of the zodiac, with a pronounced flair for originality and inventiveness given to you by the influence of your ruling planet of Uranus. Your creative talent always flairs up unexpectedly. A dash of Saturn gives you strength, and you can use it to enforce ideas as inventors, creative writers, composers, as well as style-setters in fashion and design. True, some of your most inventive ideas may be ahead of their time, but there's a great deal of satisfaction in leading the way for others to improve on your efforts.

You're not afraid of any form of creative activity, and with the determination which comes naturally to you, you can easily produce valuable results. You lack a sense of business because your mind is so agile. It goes swiftly from one project to another, often allowing someone else to profit from the work which you thought of first.

Being so thoroughly independent by nature, if you use your creative talents professionally, it is often best to have a partner. This can give you more freedom to experiment. But the same independence which creates the creative urge is always wary of partnerships—perhaps feeling that they may impede your ventures. But one who could benefit you in marketing your creative ideas could be advantageous to you. Often you'll think about a partner, but your inherent wisdom makes you wait until the right person presents himself.

Once you've conceived an idea which may seem impossible, you'll proceed with dogged determination and patience—giving no thought to the time needed to produce it. Other ideas may flow freely, but you're capable of carrying an idea through to completion without being distracted by new ideas.

PISCES ♓   You've made vast contributions to the
artistic world in the past, and this trend is likely to continue.
Even when you've been beset by the bad influences of Saturn, you've
always allowed your creative talent full rein, surviving many obstacles,
and coming up with some massive examples of talent in many spheres.

Most of you are happiest when you're able to give a great deal of
time to your chosen creative activity. Even if such prosaic things as
housework have to suffer, you're able to forget it and concentrate on
creation. You're highly emotional, especially at the onset of a bright,
creative idea—but this, of course, is necessary for the most truly creative
efforts. There's always a letdown, which can result in depression, once
you've fulfilled your project, and you should guard against this. Often
it's better for you to do something entirely different when the project's
finished.

Your changing emotions mean that you'll often try out two ideas
at once, ranging from music, poetry, and sculpture, to painting, writing
or many of the dance forms. You produce your best work under pressure.
Unfortunately, this can result in a completely letdown feeling, nervous
tension, or in some cases, physical illness.

Take enough time to learn the discipline of your chosen art form,
and be careful that Jupiter and Neptune don't give you unjustified
optimism. You're always a contrast between strength and weakness.
Although it's almost impossible to attain a balance, your resilience can
turn this weakness into a satisfactory creative enterprise.

Ideas flow freely and, with them, a great release of inspiration.
Channelling the ideas to achieve a happy medium between being a
dilettante and a professional—or at least finding a useful purpose for
your energy—is often your problem. So many of you manage to combine
business instincts with creative talent, however, that you can get away
with unorthodox approaches to distributing your handiwork. Once you
achieve professional status, this in itself becomes the impetus for a
further output of work, and there are literally no limits to what you
can attain.

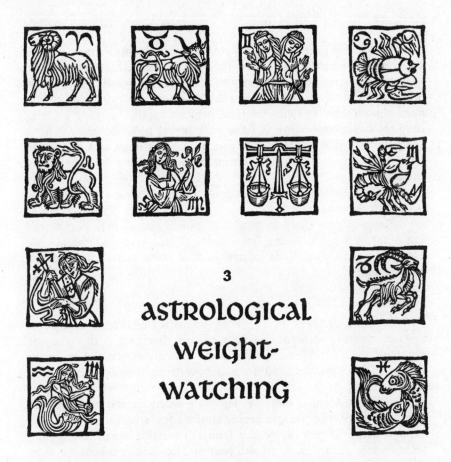

3

astrological weight-watching

ARIES ♈   You are figure-conscious, but often you don't need to go on a stringent diet. You burn up a great deal of body fuel in your everyday life because of that hard driving whiplash from Mars which galvanizes you into great spurts of energy.

Because you're inclined to exaggerate when the bathroom scales move a few pounds over a certain weight, you immediately imagine that middle-aged spread is setting in. A high-protein diet and a determination to eat all your meals more slowly than you usually do, will help rectify minor or imaginary bulges. Learning to relax with breathing exercises will help you through difficult months should you feel your wiry, athletic figure is getting out of hand.

Eat regular meals and skip night raids on the refrigerator. Because of your physical and nervous energy, you may find it difficult to sleep at night. Making your overactive brain run down doesn't always coincide with normal bedtime hours. Compromise with yourself. If you feel like a catnap at any time of the day, try to have one. It's amazing how a few minutes' rest or sleep can refresh you. The more energetic you are, the more you're likely to nibble at food between meals. Learning to relax can help cut down on this. A brisk walk before bed can help get some of the last shred of energy out of you. If you live in an area where you don't like to go out at night, compromise with some deep breathing exercises.

Many members of your sign profit by doing some sort of work at home before going to bed.

Keeping your body in good condition is linked with correct eating, sometimes with dieting, and also with knowing that the air you breathe plays its part. Your interest in most diets wanes after the first few weeks.

TAURUS ♉   Being an earth sign, you're capable of facing some of the facts of life. One fact is that you can never get those hip measurements down as easily as other signs in the zodiac. So don't feel defeated if the diet your friends recommend doesn't have rapid results for you.

If you eat three meals a day with hearty interest, a diet may frighten you even before you begin. Maybe a few slight changes in your eating habits will give the desired results or maybe you can resign yourself to a few extra pounds around your middle. You're one of the signs who can become very irritable unless you feel comfortably well-fed, and counting calories can produce temper flareups.

Exercise rarely rolls away enough fat, but you should try to make a habit of taking a brisk walk each day. Slimness isn't always indicative of good health. It's essential to feel well, too. Remember, too, that you're a sign that enjoys cooking and eating good food, and it can be a form of torture to cook for the family and then try to enjoy nibbling a few lettuce leaves. Better retain your dignity and temper and compromise by cutting down on the *amount* you eat at each meal or adjusting your diet to cut out many carbohydrates. Generally, you enjoy meat. If you can eat this without heavy gravies or sauces, you can keep your hips down to reasonable proportions.

GEMINI Ⅱ   Because you're a sign in which duality plays a great part, you're unable to make decisions and carry them out. You may be mentally in tune with the latest diet, but lack the willpower to start it. You can always find six good reasons for starting to diet and then find six equally valid ones as to why you shouldn't. This can upset the delicate balance of your constitution much more than a little extra weight will do.

Vanity can generally start you off on a diet, but taking this first step is not enough. It's important to check with you doctor to see that you don't suffer from a vitamin deficiency. If you do, stick to those vitamins prescribed and don't let friends tempt you with things which aren't actually necessary for you.

If the doctor gives you a diet, try to keep to it for a specific time. Normally, you're a light eater, tempted to substitute a cigarette and many cups of coffee for a regular meal. Too little food plus too many cigarettes can upset your nervous condition. Guard against this and be firm with yourself from the beginning of a diet. It's a mistake to think that skipping meals will help you. Regard a diet as a form of therapy rather than a waste of time.

Peace of mind is always important to you and certainly so when you're starting on a diet. Don't be put off if you don't lose weight rapidly. Sometimes it's better to drop a few ounces gradually than a lot at one time. Generally, when you lose a great deal of weight too suddenly, it's because of bad health. This also begins to show on your face and not necessarily where you want to lose weight.

CANCER ♋   You have a very happy attitude towards food and can enjoy every meal you eat. Rather than lose this healthy regard for food by dieting, accept advice as to whether you're overweight or if it's just exaggerated vanity. As a water sign, you'll retain water and generally you feel best when well-rounded.

Although you have a delightfully feminine figure when you're young—with well rounded legs and arms—unless you exercise regularly, this puppy fat can turn into layers of fat. As you get older, you're a compulsive dieter, always trying the latest methods. Any adventurous new recipe will soon take your mind off a diet and this can be your downfall, if you seriously wish good results. Limiting your intake of liquids will also help against the tendency to retain water.

If you can keep off the bathroom scales during the first week of a diet it will be helpful, for you can easily become despondent if you don't get instant results. Few diets slough off fat immediately. Remember, it may have taken you a long time to gain those extra pounds and they're not going away any quicker than it took you to gain them. You'll just have to be patiently optimistic.

Because you're susceptible to other people's views, don't go from one diet to another on friends' advice. Consult your doctor and get a diet which is designed for you.

Because the moon rules your sign, your moods are subjected to as much fluctuation as the tides. Start a new diet when the moon is waning; that's when you'll have a better chance of succeeding without ill effects on your health or temper.

LEO ♌   Your housekeeping budget always suffers from strain and it's not wise to follow a diet which isolates you from your family, forces you to cook two different meals, and most likely adds to your expenses. A change of food is generally good for you and it won't hurt your palate to move from exotic dishes to simple foods.

As a fire sign, you use up a lot of physical energy which needs to be replenished by food. It is, however, essential that you eat well-balanced meals. One of the easiest ways to lose weight is to increase proteins and decrease carbohydrates. Your ability to expand energy will help burn up carbohydrates.

You're much more likely to go on a diet because of health than vanity although, as befits any Leo, you always enjoy being in the lime-light. You can get carried away with enthusiasm for anything, including dieting. Once you start on your chosen diet, you have enough willpower to carry on with it. But you shouldn't try to make every member of the family go on the same diet. Remember that repeated conversation about how well you feel on the new diet or how easily you cope with it can be boring. It's your privilege to decide that you want to diet, but everyone is not interested in your views about this.

Be careful not to confuse a well-developed figure with one that's overweight. If, for health reasons, you think a diet is necessary, consult a doctor. You're too independent to be influenced by other people's diets but it's a mistake to think you can work this out for yourself. Common sense is indeed useful even in food. But advice from a professional dietician can solve your weight problem better than you can. Your will-power is enough to make you cooperative enough to follow it through.

VIRGO ♍ Health-conscious, careful, meticulous Virgos have fewer weight problems than many other people but you're always interested in diets even if they're for other people. You're also interested enough to want to keep a slim and youthful figure well into middle age. Luckily, this rarely presents a problem for you. Many of you become professional dieticians, and almost all of you have an interest in health. As fastidious eaters yourself, any change in your food habits has to be thought about quite carefully, and the reasons for making the change carefully evaluated. If you decide that you need a special diet because of health, you'll go promptly to the best professional for advice. You have the willpower to keep to it so that it becomes a normal way of eating.

One of the best ways for you to enjoy food (and when it does you the most good) is when you sit down to a meal with harmonious companions. Quarrels at mealtime can quickly upset both your appetite and your digestion. Spurts of temper, even small ones, usually boomerang back to you by way of minor stomach ailments—more inconvenient than serious. If you go on a diet, remember it's as important for you to eat in harmonious conditions as it is to diet.

Naturally accustomed to the more simple types of meals, the eating habits you establish when you are young generally stay with you all your life. This probably accounts for many of you having slim, youthful figures after middle age.

It could be better for you to take a more romantic interest in food and not always see it as a means of survival. It's often depressing to cook for members of your sign because you lack appreciation for exotic recipes. When you decide to diet, you do it drastically and can rarely be tempted off it by any members of your family. If a diet is forced on you for reasons of health, you'll accept it gracefully and rarely complain of its monotony.

LIBRA ♎ While you can't sustain a rigid interest in diet as far as carrying it out goes, you're always interested in diets—especially those designed to help keep your figure under control. But a diet for you mustn't be monotonous and must allow some semblance of elegance to creep into the main meals. You're noted for your judgment, so you'll go to great pains to find a diet which seems interesting, varied, and still reduces weight. You'll always need a little encouragement from your family to continue with any diet. You find it hard to give up the luxuries—including exotic food—which you regard as part of graceful living.

Be firm about accepting dinner invitations. If you're likely to succumb to temptation because of your hostess' reputation as a fine cook, be tactful and explain that you're on a diet. If necessary, offer to send her a copy of it. It isn't hard to get you to drop a diet for a birthday celebration or some other festive event. If you can't resist, don't be surprised or upset when your weight goes up.

Because your metabolism is delicately balanced, as with most of the signs inclined to duality, it's better not to change from one diet to another too often. If you find yourself doing this, it might be wiser to discontinue rigid dieting and simply cut down on the amount of food you eat at each meal, eliminating things like bread and desserts.

Try taking a walk instead of driving, if you have only a short distance to go. It has a threefold purpose: fresh air and exercise is good for the mind and the waistline, and you save money if you have to take a cab or bus.

SCORPIO ♏   With an inherent characteristic of not trusting anything, you're more likely to give away the bathroom scales when they begin to register more pounds than you believe you should weigh. Keep the scales—but ease your doubts by weighing yourself at a friend's house. If you still show more pounds than necessary, face the moment of truth. Recover from the shock and decide to do something about it.

Because of your secretive nature, you're not likely to discuss diets with your friends or even let them know that you're considering going on one. It's likely that you'll choose a less obvious way of getting rid of those extra pounds—such as eating less food. Best of all, cut down on liquid intake, especially hard liquor. Vodka has fewer calories than many other alcoholic drinks.

As you're a water sign, you retain water and will find that your weight fluctuates every month whether you're on a diet or not. In fact, if you weigh yourself at a particular time, before or during the menstrual period, there's likely to be a rapid increase of up to five pounds.

If you go on a diet at this time, don't delude yourself that you've lost weight when your periods of water-retaining are over.

When Neptune's in your own sign, you'll find that scales play treacherous tricks on you. The main things is to decide if you feel well. If you do, then a little extra weight isn't detrimental to you. If you begin to move more slowly than usual and get out of breath after normal exercise, see a doctor and get a diet planned especially for you.

SAGITTARIUS ♐   So many of you would rather fence than switch to a diet. Since you're generally active and go in for sports when you're young, there's always the chance that you'll begin to feel fat when you reach middle age. Nothing turns to fat more easily than muscles which were once toned up and then not used. Try to keep an interest in sports or at least keep active after the age of forty, even if you don't indulge in strenuous pursuits. Most people who are interested in sports are also health-conscious and with this comes an interest in correct eating habits. Nevertheless, you *can* be erratic in dining regularly. Adjust this, cut down on carbohydrates and hard liquor, and you'll hardly know you're on a diet.

Fencing is an excellent way to maintain a lithe figure. If you've had the advantage of starting young, it is an art you can maintain as you get older. Yoga exercises are also good—as a prevention, not as a cure of fat. Vibro-massages and steam baths are also likely to appeal to you. In fact, any of the variations which will keep your figure trim are likely to be more beneficial than struggling with a diet.

CAPRICORN ♑   Dieting doesn't normally present a problem to your naturally determined nature to be successful and thorough in anything you undertake. Sometimes it needs a suggestion from a friend or member of your family to get you started, but once you've decided to diet, you rarely have any emotional traumas. Nor do you feel that food becomes more boring when associated with a diet.

Use your businesslike mind to make even the smallest meals well-balanced. It is very easy for you to become depressed, and nothing encourages this so much as dull meals with dismal conversation. So, even if you're eating less and not having food that seems very exciting, try to serve it in an agreeable manner. Relax from business worries at mealtimes. You're not likely to bore your friends with conversation about your diet.

It's not unusual for Capricornians to diet to increase weight rather than lose it. Eighty per cent of your sign are likely to have an angular rather than a rotund figure. In all matters concerning food, how you feel and your general state of health should decide whether or not you change your normal eating habits.

AQUARIUS ≈   So many of you have followed fads in eating habits over the past twenty-six years that interest in dieting is not new to you. Now you can sit back quite happily when dieting is on everybody's tongue, knowing that you knew it all years ago.

Be careful not to encourage your friends to adopt sudden drastic changes in their eating habits simply because you, personally, may have found eating nothing but nuts and fruit beneficial. It probably was—but just as you like to retain your individuality and make up your own mind, it's possible that your friends also feel the same way. One man's diet can be another man's poison. You enjoy being an armchair dietician, believing that proper food is the way to health. Often you have little patience with people who are simply interested in losing a few pounds and don't mind how they do it.

As you get older, and you turn your attention to the possibility of a thicker waistline, some of the disdain you felt for vanity-conscious friends begins to leave you. When you're on an unsuccessful diet, your thoughts have to turn elsewhere for the solution. Philosophically, you can understand that as one gets older, there's a natural inclination to gain weight—it's one of the hazards of middle age. However, you can keep your figure at its best by such things as steam baths without too much change in your regular food habits.

With your tendency to poor circulation, there are other medicinal baths which can be helpful. But you should consult your doctor about them. No drastic drop in weight is ever really good for the system as a whole but there are baths and good masseurs to keep you fit and in fashionable shape.

PISCES ♓   Affected as you are by the impact of Jupiter and Neptune on your life, as well as being a water sign
with duality about it, you can often find weight control a problem all
your life.

The mercurial changability of your mind is no help in maintaining
a diet for any length of time. Even when on a diet, you're likely to forget to change your drinking habits. You need a large intake of liquid,
especially if you have anything of a psychic quality about you. But liquids
are a double-edged sword in your life. With liquids, you're likely to
increase your psychic ability. But this will mean that you'll have to live
with a weight problem or, you can lose a few pounds and also lose extrasensory powers.

With a general love for water at any time, medicinal baths are
helpful. But life can be a constant battle against the bulge unless you
realize that even a diet will never completely keep your weight constant.

There are mitigating circumstances. Generally you're so busy, busy
all the time that today's worries about weight can be forgotten tomorrow
as you start on other lines of thought. Try to eat regularly instead of
snacking your way through the day. Eat your main meal in the evening,
at least four hours before you go to bed. It's also helpful to try to exercise more than you normally like. Keeping healthy is always going to
be more important to you than keeping pace with fashion's figure demands.

4

"Beauty
is truth..."

ARIES ♈ Nothing fascinates you so much as new things. You'll always be the first to change your hair style, not always because it's the fashionable one but sometimes just because it's different. You may see a style in an old magazine and try that simply because it's different from anything you've noticed around you.

Although you don't use too much makeup, you're very likely to buy the latest just in case you *might* like to experiment one day. Having deep-set eyes that always seem to look into the distance, you certainly don't need heavy makeup for emphasis. That expectant look—as if something's going to happen (and it generally does)—is part of your wide-awake charm and symbolic of your general alertness.

Because you lead an active life, it's natural that you keep your beauty routine to the minimum—not able to waste time unless for a very special occasion when you're capable of creating an entirely new look. With a fondness of all activities, including sport, the sculptured hair style appeals most to you. And you'll constantly go back to it even if long hair is the "in" thing. When you spend money at the beauty shop, it's generally to get a good cut so that all you have to do is run a comb through your hair.

Generally, you manage to appear well-groomed—more by accident than design. This is an asset in times of last-minute invitations. You're figure-conscious, and your body's likely to be deceptively youthful even after you've passed middle age and successfully bypassed the extra weight associated with later life. Mars, your ruling planet, helps you burn up a lot of surplus fatty tissue without needing to diet.

TAURUS ♉   As one of the truly down-to-earth signs, you're not likely to be carried away by the latest trends in cosmetics or hair styles.

Once you've found the basic cosmetics suited to your personality and pocketbook, you're inclined to use the same brands you used in your youth. The only thing likely to tempt you away from this is someone giving you a present of cosmetics—then a certain thriftiness will urge you to use it.

The same attention to the cost of beauty aids keeps your dressing table practical. It is content rather than pretty packaging that appeals to you: you like good value for your money. Hair of good texture and color is often one of your major assets. You can manage this very well yourself without frequent visits to the beauty salon, but economy may drive you to unbecoming snippings with scissors and also drive your hairdresser to despair.

Your most vulnerable point is the neck and you should pay attention to this when applying cosmetics. Creams will keep the skin supple, and exercise will keep aging and unseemly wrinkles at bay. Don't neglect your figure even if you feel that dieting doesn't completely restore the figure of your youth.

Exercise, even if only taking regular walks, is going to help you maintain a strong, well-developed look. Providing you can escape flabbiness, you can still have a remarkably good figure after middle age even though you may have to work harder at it than many others. Get advice on the right exercises to keep yor hips in proportion with your bust.

You have the determination to exercise with faithfulness once you've been advised. You're practical enough not to expect miracles.

Try to concentrate on your eyes—one of your best features—and remember to baby your work-worn hands. Being so practical, many of you use your hands for gardening as well as household chores and forget that exposing them to hard usage can make them rough and unattractive. Your hands and feet are never likely to be your most attractive features, but you can make the best of them with special attention.

Your natural good features can help you cut down on time spent applying facial makeup. But with an extra five minutes a day your hands and feet will present the picture of good grooming and neatness which you aim at directly.

GEMINI II   Many ladies born under this sign can be proud of their trim, tall figures, many of which can almost rival the professional model's long legs, slim hips, and firm bust. The attention your figure gets from others make you conscious of your legs which you enjoy showing off. Take care to apply makeup when necessary or to keep them evenly tanned in summer.

You seem to prefer the translucent type of facial makeup with matching lipstick, and you apply it so subtly that you never look like a painted doll. Although a naturally good complexion isn't your greatest asset, you're adept at camouflaging it so that any slight blemishes are hidden. Try not to forget that the blemishes are there, however. Clean off all makeup every night, and periodically have a facial mask. A brisk daily treatment with hot and cold water also helps to tone up the skin before applying makeup, but you often don't have the temperament to follow this very simple and basic routine.

A manicure is essential to your beauty routine, so you generally keep your nails and hands in good condition—although many of you, when nervous or emotionally upset, spoil them by unconsciously nibbling at them. Nails and hair always show up badly when you're upset, and they soon get in poor condition. Anything that stimulates the circulation —whether a skin or body massage or brisk, regular hair brushing—will help prevent the nervous condition spoiling your looks.

Because you're very sensitive to touch, all your cosmetics must feel good to you. This sensitivity prevails even when you consider the packaging itself. Being under the sign of the Twins with its overtones of duality in your personality, hair coloring and styles that have a two-tone effect will appeal to you, whether silver streaks, frosting, or wearing a fall.

As you're under the influence of Mercury—a planet with an affinity for electrical beauty gadgets—all appliances of this nature appeal to you. Often you buy them as a child buys a toy—using them for a little while, then putting them in the drawer and forgetting them. It's just another reason you often feel you just don't know where your money goes.

You're much more likely to buy an expensive vibrator to roll away surplus fat, even if it's imaginary, than to go on a diet. There's some wisdom in this, but only if you follow the instructions—which generally rely on regular treatment for effectiveness. Try to use your electric gadgets as you would your electric toothbrush: at least once a day and every day without missing. If your electric appliance doesn't then give you the advertised results, you have to realize that once again you've been reckless with money. Chances are that you still won't have learned a lesson and will buy the next electric beauty aid that comes along. Anything you buy as an extra aid to beauty, such as wigs, should be cared for. You'll not only look better if your wig's well cared for, but you—at least in theory—will save money.

CANCER ♋ Everything that's pretty fascinates you, so you're the advertising man's joy because you buy attractively packaged cosmetics without considering brand names too much. Generally, because you believe everything that's said in advertising or on the package, you're one of the mainstays of the flourishing beauty business. If you finally become disappointed in your pretty packages and find the contents don't live up to your expectations, you throw them away. Then, you begin again, with entirely new cosmetics.

You enjoy and try to buy matching sets of makeup, including bath oils, body lotions, and perfumes but you rarely remember to keep them tidily in your bathroom or to put lids back on. Although you enjoy displaying your beauty treasures, wastage is prevented if the stopper's put back on perfumes or the lid on talcum powder.

Soft romantic hair styles are your personal extravagance and joy, for inside every one of you there beats the heart of a little girl, always desiring to be youthful. Soft babyish hair styles go well with your naturally good complexion which can retain its milk and roses texture into old age if you use cosmetics with discretion. The overall effect of youthfulness can be ruined if it appears contrived or if you forget that even figures that were graceful in youth have a habit of maturing from well-roundedness to plain plumpness. You're always diet-conscious, but being a water sign, you carry more water than many of the other signs. Exercises, such as isometrics, will do more for your figure than constant changing from one diet to another.

There's also the advantage with isometrics, in comparison to diet, that your face will retain its youthful appearance. Dieting doesn't promise that you lose the extra pounds on the hips and arms instead of the face. You have one of the prettiest pair of hands in the zodiac, naturally well-shaped, and you're wise enough to pay attention to them, using nail polish and emery boards. Your teeth can be very pearly in youth, but need extra care as you get older. An electric toothbrush, providing some massage for the gums, is as good an investment as any cosmetics.

LEO ♌   For many of you, it's as important to have a rich, golden tan (as befits the children of the sun) as it is to spend money on makeup. When you do the latter, you're inclined to overdo the treatment. As many of you can be quite dramatic in looks, a toning down of makeup achieves better results than exaggerating your features. Try to wear the minimum in daytime, saving the dramatic look for evening or very special occasions.

Although lady lionesses don't have the luxurious mane of the males, it can still be their crowning beauty if well-dressed. Attention should be paid to the shape of the face rather than to the current fashion and sometimes it's possible to attain a happy medium here. Your style is to have unrestricted hair, appropriate to the freedom most of you strive for in life. If you use color, try to remember that your symbolic animal is the Lion and that the Sun is your ruling planet. Don't aim to look like a raven-haired American Indian beauty. Golden types of coloring will always best suit your complexion and be more suited to your radiant personality.

Most of you have a jungle-like grace when walking, moving lithely on strong, well-proportioned legs, so spend a little time keeping those legs beautiful.

You're conscious of your figure and manage to keep it in good shape by natural exercise, although some of you can keep on a diet and obtain satisfactory results. If you feel that contrived exercise is going to help you, figure out which part of your figure needs the most attention and concentrate there. It's no use making a big all-over workout of exercises because certain areas may then be sacrificed by a buildup of muscles. Let's face it—a strong woman is one thing, but a muscular one rarely looks her best.

Pay attention to regular treatment and conditioning of the hair, and to keeping the nails of both hands and feet in good shape. In your effort to attain overall good looks on a rather magnificent scale, you're apt to overlook the details of small things—like nails and teeth. Let comfort and freedom be your guide to beauty rather than attempting to follow prevailing hair and cosmetic fashion.

VIRGO ♍︎ Although you never strive for the limelight, you love to present a neat appearance of quiet elegance in which well-groomed hair and skin play a major part.

If you have any vanity at all, it's with your eyes—which you realize can be your most startling feature. Many of you have grey-blue or greenish-tawny eyes which would attract attention even without makeup. You're wise to make these your focal point, literally building the rest of your makeup around them. Very few of you can bear to go out day or night in makeup unless it's done with the utmost finesse, looking as if you hadn't spent any time at all achieving the desired effect. There'll never be a time when anyone can accuse you of being overpainted or mask-like. Your attention to detail is part of your meticulous, Mercury-influenced nature.

Because your teeth are often crooked, there's sometimes a tendency to have a badly shaped mouth. You should exert as much care in applying lipstick as you do to treating your eyes. Accent the shape of your lips, regardless of the color you choose, even if you have to do a little building up of one side or the other. Within a few days, you'll achieve the right technique. Not with pouting bow-lips but with long lines that will balance up the smallness of your chin and focus attention, instead, to your good clean neckline. You'll be wise enough to know that no line should show between the facial makeup and the line below the chin. But do be careful not to make the normal swan-like neck too pronounced. Once you've found makeup that suits you, there's little danger that you'll change.

Your hair may be baby-fine and difficult to manage, so it's wise to have it professionally cut. Be in complete command of how you want it styled and set and try not to panic if your favorite operator isn't always available. You're quite capable of tactfully telling a new operator just what you require. Have confidence in her, although you really dislike changes.

Few of you need to worry about your figures—if there's a fault it could be an exaggerated slimness which can incline to scraggliness as you get older. Pay attention to the saltcellars near the collarbone as you get older and, if necessary, ask advice about correct makeup. The same applies to the elbows, which can be rather bony. Arm and leg makeup are equally as important as the face and hair at different times of your life.

You'll probably prefer to do your own nails rather than going to a professional manicurist. There can be something quite soothing about attending to your own nails. Natural or pale clear polish will appeal to you more than the more exotic new colors. As you get older, many of you will like pale grey hair—if you like color at all—and this can be very attractive with your well-lashed eyes and finely penciled eyebrows.

You'll never consciously strive for the youthful look once you're middle-aged, as you accept this change as natural. However, nervous tension can add lines to the eyes and droopy corners to the mouth, and sometimes a little hardness can creep into your makeup as you grow older. Once aware of it, there's no reason why you can't adapt your usual makeup ideas in a way that softens lines and still retains a smart, elegant look.

LIBRA ♎   Under the influence of Venus, the planet of beauty, it's natural that, of all the signs of the zodiac, you're one of the most conscious of personal appearance. Your interest can soar to vanity. Generally careful attention presents a picture of you that's worth looking at.

Good makeup—with time to apply it while considering every detail—seems to give you the confidence to rise graciously to any occasion. Your attention to cosmetics is likely to start at an early age, and you rarely begrudge spending time on yourself, making the most of your best features. Once you've established a routine, you'll never be coerced into any slaphappy methods. You enjoy experimenting with fragrant creams, even though you know exactly what will suit you. But there's a conscious striving to attain perfection.

Take care not to gild the lily. You run this risk generally after middle age in the hope that cosmetics may take a few years off your age.

Yet no one can grow old more graciously than you, and this is the ultimate achievement.

You'll always guard your skin or any part of your body that's exposed to the weather. No sitting in the sun for you without a protective lotion as well as an umbrella shade. You'll prefer to use artificial aids to tan rather than risk the tortures of blistered and raw skin.

Hair can be difficult because of its tendency to lankness. If you live in a humid atmosphere, regular visits to the beauty salon, with conditioning and friction treatments, will produce the hair texture and style which suits you. Wigs or hair pieces can help you keep a well-coiffured look, and you have the ability to wear them without any self-consciousness, providing they're of good quality.

If you have several good planets making a pattern in your personal horoscope, there's little danger that your figure will coarsen, although this does happen occasionally. You rarely work on a slim outline with anything so energetic as exercise, so sometimes you may be faced with rigid dieting.

As you get older, keep away from any makeup around the eyes which gives you a strained, hard look. Finely penciled effects and heavy plucking can be attractive at certain ages, but as you get older, pay attention to more delicate shaping. Keep the lashes in good condition. A nightly application of oil to the eyelashes will help, but always be sure to clean off any mascara with the special pads made for this. Mascara clogs up the eyelashes and is very detrimental to natural growth. It's often advisable to limit mascara to evening makeup.

SCORPIO ♏   Ruled by fiery Mars and the unpredictable Pluto, your approach to makeup always has something of the dramatic about it. Sometimes there's a tendency to over-accentuate your best features. It's very important to know you have naturally expressive eyes. But applying theatrical-type eye makeup for daytime wear can defeat the expression of your rather sultry temperament. Makeup should be an accent for you, but never a magnification, if you want your magnetic personality to express itself. Some fine artists are given to over-painting their pictures and you could easily make this same error with your eyes and lips.

Your luxurious hair is one of your best features. Your sense of the dramatic can be better expressed through a variety of hair styles rather than heavy eye makeup. Discuss latest fashions with your hairdresser. Try anything once, but most of all aim at a hair style suitable for a particular occasion. You wouldn't wear an evening dress to a breakfast party, so apply the same rules to your hair. Having plenty of hair you can afford to experiment, but do choose a beauty salon that's expert with thick heads of hair.

Your most difficult feature can be your skin—often inclined to dullness and poor texture. Lively sparkling skin is not only the result of care and cosmetics but also of correct diet. When blotches appear (as they frequently will) don't just try to cover them up with makeup. Seek the inner cause. Healthy skin needs fresh air and some friction by gentle massage. As you're inclined to heavy makeup, it's important to give your skin a complete holiday from makeup at frequent intervals.

It's sometimes difficult for you to remember that makeup and beauty care are not exclusive to the face. Roughened elbows can be as unsightly as a powderless nose, and you have a tendency to get thickened skin here as well as on the ball of the foot. If you feel it's too much trouble to care for your own feet, find a good chiropodist and visit regularly.

Many of you are oversensitive about your weight, which can be a problem. For you, it can have psychological connotations: you brood over the extra pounds and wince if your friends mention it. Face facts —you generally are an impressive figure, few of you being willowy-wisp slim. You're also a water sign and enjoy good rich food. Steam baths will probably do you much more good than attempting a rigid diet and they're infinitely more pleasant and relaxing.

Do try to make a distinction between street makeup and the more dramatic type which is suited to evening dates. If you can gain the courage (which you have) to experiment with hair styles and spend some time varying your facial makeup, you might find it an interesting adventure with very becoming results.

SAGITTARIUS ♐   You can have one of the best fig-ures of the zodiac without being excessively or fashionably skinny. You generally have a tall, well-proportioned figure with an athletic and dignified carriage. You walk gracefully instead of sloping along. Your natural interest in sports makes figure control less of a special chore for you than for others.

However, you can be very casual about facial makeup. Sunned, weathered skin looks fine on a man but adds little to the attractiveness of a woman and shouldn't be confused with radiant good health. You can benefit from professional lessons in the art of individualized makeup. Get to know the right type and correct application. Although you may hate the idea of putting anything on your face but the usual soap and water, the healthy, well-scrubbed schoolgirl look is all right only when you're young. Very few older faces can go without a suspicion of makeup.

Use makeup to highlight your best features and to subdue any tendency to a heavy chin. Moisturizers will help eliminate dried-looking skin. With help you can find a makeup you won't feel self-conscious wearing. Try to take attention away if you have a full, firm chin by discreetly highlighting the eyes. You'll rarely need do anything more drastic to the eyebrows than shaping them a little. Artificial eyelashes rarely appeal to you, but there are many natural-looking ones on the market, and it's wise to keep a set on hand for evenings.

Being a practical type, your hands take a lot of wear and tear. It's important to use hand lotions and to apply simple cuticle and nail treatments at home. The main thing is to get into a regular routine, giving them extra special care without thinking you're wasting time.

Your hair is so often easy to manage. This can save you beauty salon expenses. Especially if you have a natural wave. A little more than shampooing will probably be necessary if you enjoy swimming, though —so spend some of the salon money you save on a home hair conditioner and remember to use it.

CAPRICORN ♑   So many of you have taut, trim bodies resulting from dancing, physical activities, or even Yoga exercises, that figure control isn't a problem. This should give you more time to pay attention to makeup, but the fact is, you aren't so interested in taking regular care of your face. You're inclined to want maximum results with minimum time.

Sometimes, there's a parsimonious streak in you that makes you feel it's a great extravagance to spend money on cosmetics. In your youth you can get away with this, probably just relying on cosmetic gifts. It's better, however, to decide which cosmetics suit your personality. Today there's such a wide range, with something to suit every pocket. You need not have a guilty conscience as you're not likely to overdo your makeup and a small investment in the right brands can last for a long time.

Generally, you have a naturally well-structured face with good cheek bones, and you can get away with a minimum of makeup. Study your features well—note the good deep-set eyes and concentrrate on these. You're likely to have a good natural hairline over the forehead, so choose a style which emphasizes or at least, makes use of this natural feature.

Home hair treatment is for you except for special occasions, so get your own beauty shop equipment around you. The right types of curlers are important if you want the hair to fall in graceful, natural lines. Your hair is often thin and soft in texture, and may need special shampoos for more buoyancy and a fine, non-sticky hairspray to keep it in place. Back-combing is generally not the answer for your type of hair. An attractive hair piece can be a good investment for days when humidity dooms hopes for a lasting hair style—especially if you have an unexpected date. Take time learning how to put it in place, so that you feel confident wearing it.

Being under the influence of your ruling planet of Saturn, thin hair and brittle nails are often characteristic. You can help the nails not only by manicuring, but by drinking gelatin. But you have to remember to persist. Irregular drinks will do nothing—you have to build up the gelatin forces which will strengthen the nails. Good cuticle oil is as important as the right nail polish color.

The secret of producing a successful all-over presentation to the world, with a neat and elegant appearance, is to rigidly concentrate a few minutes each day on makeup plus extra periods each week on finger and toenails. The youthful figure is likely to be maintained well into old age, but it's no use looking good from the back and then presenting a wrinkled face. Some of the hormone creams can be helpful after middle age. As your ruling planet gives you the Saturnine look, tending to be serious, try to remember that smiles can also contribute their own special form of beauty.

AQUARIUS ♒   People under your sign have two distinct reactions to makeup: you're either for it or completely against it. Being thoroughly independent, if you choose to forego makeup, you're quite happy to present the well-scrubbed look—relying on your good features, such as a fine bone structure and an excellent profile, to carry you successfully along. Or you begin to use makeup at an early age and feel naked without it—even in the early morning. When this happens, you're likely to continue buying the brands you first used, rather than spending time browsing around cosmetic departments shopping for the latest.

Your complexion is, fortunately, one of your best points, and perhaps there's some wisdom in not overloading it. There can be a happy medium in this if you accent the best features, such as your deeply set grey or blue eyes. Proper use of eye shadow can be very alluring, especially if you use a darker shade nearest the eyelashes and then lighten it off towards the eyebrows. Keep the eyebrows well-shaped, but full enough to be interesting. Thinly pencilled brows are not for you.

You generally like your hair swept up, not hanging around the shoulders. You may have to experiment quite a bit before finding the style you feel expresses your determined independent personality. High, bouffante styles, or the French twist, have been popular with many members of your sign, the latter not so outmoded. Try to be a little more adventurous with your hair, even if only by reversing the way the twist goes. A chignon, either with your own hair or an artificial piece, is great for showing off a fine profile.

False pieces may not appeal, but they can be the greatest boost to the morale of a busy person such as you are likely to be. Once you've gotten over the prejudice barrier, one or more hair pieces can save you time.

Your legs are your vulnerable area, sometimes being too thin to be truly beautiful. But you can help this with various leg exercises designed to firm them up without making them fat. Something in your psychological makeup can keep you from spending regular time on your legs and hands, but they're important to any woman who wants to look her best.

Too often, you're content with the quick dab of facial makeup and forget to polish your nails. With short skirts, leg makeup becomes just as important as the usual facial cosmetics. Keeping the circulation in good condition is important, too. So try sitting in positions which don't induce cramps. Walking helps, of course, as do proper types of health-giving baths. Time is always your enemy when doing anything for yourself, but if you can brainwash yourself into understanding that time spent on makeup can also lead to relaxing your nervous system, it may persuade you to settle down to it.

You're rather clinical about washing your face and cleaning your teeth. Carry over this thoroughness by giving yourself the extra ten minutes you need to complete makeup, plus spending an extra five minutes every day on the nails.

PISCES ♓   Being a water sign, you have a tender skin that generally benefits from using some of the delicate herbal cosmetics now on the market. The use of these can also help the esoteric feelings you're likely to have. Often stores don't carry a full range of herbal cosmetics, but you can buy by mail order if there's no health shop in town.

Rarely are there any of you who don't have beautiful, very expressive eyes, so let the soulful look speak for itself. There's little need to exaggerate them—delicate eye shadow, rather than the dramatic ones, will be more in keeping with your complexion. Many of you are fair-haired and fair-skinned, and you look best retaining the pale, translucent look with maybe a tiny, subtle touch of rouge to offset any pallor.

Your hair is plentiful and grows quickly, so a hairdresser who can style and trim it well is a good investment. Leave it shoulder-length rather than aiming at the sculptured look for you can have a fleshy face. The high hair styles are often too stilted to suit you. Also, as you're inclined to have a short, plump body with fairly short legs, it's not always possible for you to be as dignified as the high sculptured hair styles demand. You're rarely the Greek Goddess type.

Figure control can be your greatest beauty problem as you have little inclination to stay on a rigid diet. Exercise will do little more than tire you. You may have to learn to live with a figure that becomes a little more plump each year. But the well-rounded figure can be attractive: your best bet is not worrying about it. Offset it by making the most of your hair and paying a lot of attention to the hand and toe nails. Keep a good stock of nail polishes: shade the nails well and use hand lotions if you're bothered by work-weary hands. You'll often be engaged in creative work using your hands. Besides, you rarely talk without using them as fluently as your tongue.

Those of you born in the first ten days of this sign can be extremely feminine. This is the image to maintain with makeup. Eliminate hard lines. Keep to the pale look, and you'll always command attention from men. Those willowy Greek Goddesses can get some competition from you once you can forget your plump figure and let your personality come through.

Those of you born in the latter part of the sign are likely to eschew makeup. But the days when any sociable woman can go out with a face untouched by any cosmetics is really gone. Body lotions, perfumes, and bath oils will always appeal to you as much as an exciting array of facial cosmetics. Try to get harmonious perfumes that won't make war with your paint and powder.

5

ENTERTAINING

ARIES ♈   Although you thrive on being invited to
large cocktail parties, you're conscious of the difference between being a guest and entertaining. In your own home, you prefer
giving small dinner parties, although not necessarily formal ones. You
choose your guests for their conversational ability and have the common
sense to know that you're best at concentrating on a small group.

Try to work out a definite plan of action so that you don't have
to spend too long in the kitchen. You really want to enjoy your guests
and you can do this best by spending as much time as possible out of the
kitchen. Eat at an early hour so that you have plenty of time for conversation afterwards and, as you're often argumentative, it's better to
argue on a full stomach than an empty one.

As host or hostess, try not to drink too much even if you supply plenty of drinks for your guests. Too much liquor can make you thoroughly loquacious but sometimes aggressively argumentative.

TAURUS ♉   For you, a formal dinner party for about eight guests gives opportunity to show off your talent at preparing menus. It's also enough to be called a real party yet not too costly—so your housekeeping budget won't suffer if you plan carefully.

You'll always choose your guests with discrimination, taking care that they know each other and are likely to get along. Because you're a marvelous host or hostess and enjoy entertaining at home, don't attempt meals that exhaust you and take you away from your guests. Remember, they want to enjoy your company as much as your food and drink. Be gracious enough to accept help, if they offer. This will let you spend more time talking and is one way in which a guest can thank you for what's generally a memorable meal.

When you're visiting, don't immediately announce that you have to be home at a certain hour. This can embarrass a sensitive host.

GEMINI ♊   Thoroughly enjoy giving cocktail parties with lots of people drifting in and out and often have parties spread well over the usual one hour. No one will need to have dinner after one of your mammoth cocktail parties and you're good at supplying foods for all tastes. Keep extras of hot dishes. Guests who have been told to "drop in any time," deserve hot as well as cold canapes.

You always make too much food and buy too much liquor. The last doesn't matter as liquor doesn't spoil—but too many canapes are almost as bad as too few—better to make less and use emergency supplies of nuts and crackers if you run short. Decide early which dress or what tie you're going to wear and don't keep guests waiting while you dress. Prepare ahead of time so that you can enjoy your guests' company. Mix well with each group but be careful not to get so deeply involved in conversation with one special friend that you forget the others. Being adaptable and easygoing, you'll have no difficulty coping with a lot of people at one cocktail party.

CANCER ♋   Although you're the most hospitable of hosts or hostesses, any emotional turmoil before a party can upset you and you're apt to worry long before the party begins. Try to relax and guard against worry by planning your food and drinks. See that as much is done as possible before the first guest rings the bell.

A buffet dinner relieves you of a lot of work (unless you have additional help) and it allows you to serve some excellent dishes. Be sure you have enough chafing dishes to keep food hot. An advantage of the buffet dinner is that you don't need split-second timing and any late guests can still enjoy eating. Keep your conversation light and cheerful and don't talk to your guests about any hard time you may have had getting ready for them. Enjoy being gracious and everyone will have a fine time.

When you're being entertained, try not to be late. You can help yourself by having clothes and jewelry planned ahead of time and not by deciding to wash your hair a few hours before party-time. Don't talk about your illnesses or operations. Even old friends become bored with these subjects.

LEO ♌   You love any excuse for a big celebration but often like to take your guests to a restaurant. You're generally well-known in the best restaurants in your area and can make a party into a personal occasion by calling the restaurant and discussing the menu and arranging for a good table. When you entertain at home, you like it to be in the grand manner and go to unusual pains to make everything splendid for your guests so that they enjoy themselves and you, also, enjoy hearing them express appreciation of your efforts.

You're not always discriminating in grouping compatible people because you're generous and you may impulsively invite someone to your party who may be having a private feud with another guest. Although most people are too well-mannered to quarrel in someone else's house it can, nevertheless, make conversation strained.

When you're entertained, you like to feel that people have made some special preparations for you and don't like casual impulse-invitations on a "drop in any time you're passing" basis.

VIRGO ♍   Although you always seem to have a busy schedule, there are times when you feel a party can fit into your life and you'll take great pains to make it a pleasant occasion. You don't especially enjoy large groups. A dinner of familiar guests suits you best. You're always at ease when organized and you'll doubtless make preparations well in advance—inviting your guests several days ahead of time and even calling to remind them of the exact time.

You don't like to delay eating if one guest hasn't arrived and this can be almost traumatic for you. Having taken your own time to make sure that no possible emergency can arise, you're likely to become fretful if the improbable does happen. Yet, although it upsets you emotionally, you're really able to cope with even an extra guest. Realize that you're your own worst enemy, so control your nerves.

You're not too happy when visiting others unless you know who will be there and you're generally one of the first guests to leave, even if you're having a good time. Your habits are so set that you rarely let entertaining or being entertained upset your schedule for retiring at night and can be quite tactful in marshalling guests to the door when you consider the party over.

LIBRA ♎

You like to have plenty of time to plan a dinner party and are especially conscious of things like the correct flowers, porcelain and silver. This is just as important to you as arranging the menu and inviting exactly the right people. You're wise enough to allow plenty of time to dress, arranging to have your hair done and having all personal chores completed, leaving you free to be the gracious hostess. Libran males prefer entertaining outside the house, although if they arrange a small dinner party at home, they're perfectly able to do their own cooking.

Your ability to arrange elegant parties and your careful selection of guests make you a popular hostess. When invited out, you like to be formal, rather than casual, and are never really thrilled at impromptu parties or outdoorsy poolside affairs.

SCORPIO ♏

You're capable of being very expensive when planning either a cocktail or dinner party. But the essential thing for success is that you start off in a good humor. If you're feeling over-tired, it's better to forget it—even though it may be a necessary business party—or to take your guests to a favorite restaurant. Always plan your dress and jewelry as thoroughly as you plan seating arrangements at your dinner table. You're very good at dealing with emergencies and, indeed, seem to thrive when the souffle is left too long in the oven—passing it off lightly so that your guests are hardly conscious of the mistake. Once involved in a party, you rarely allow anything to upset you. But it's fatal to start the evening off in a temper. You like people from the theater, literary and artistic world and thrive on dramatic conversation as much as you do on food.

When going out it's again essential that you start off in a good mood. Otherwise, it's better to make an excuse and not go at all. So magnetic is your own personality that your mood often passes on to the other guests.

SAGITTARIUS ♐

You have periods during the year when you feel a compulsion to have a party. Then you can go for months without doing any entertaining at all. But you love to be entertained.

A dinner party allows you to cook and male Sagittarians love to show off their prowess at barbecues, producing excellent meals. You love outdoor parties and rarely worry if lots of people arrive. Although you're a tireless worker and can cope with large groups on your own, if you have an indoor party try to do as much work as possible before the guests arrive so that you can sit down with them. You sometimes forget to maintain a balance between being hostess and cook. This is why the freewheeling barbecue party allows you to be at your best.

When a guest, avoid controversial conversation and try not to out-stay the other guests, even if you're enjoying yourself.

CAPRICORN ♑

You're not the world's best host or hostess unless you have a small party. Large crowds worry you and even if you have help for an outdoor party, you can still get yourself tied up with nervousness, wondering if everything's going to be all right. Invite friends you feel comfortable with although most of your parties are given for business more than social reasons. Whatever the occasion, it's important that you feel at ease. If you enjoy dressing up, do so. But if you don't, your friends who know you won't be surprised to find you neat but not especially festive-looking. Your secret of success is feeling comfortable.

When invited out, the same rules apply, as you rarely accept invitations from people unless you know them well. Male Capricorns are more likely to want to dress up for a party than the females. Both sexes like to do the best they can and even if not financially well-off, you can give a party that will be interesting and appreciated.

AQUARIUS ♒   You like to be organized even though at times you may seem quite the opposite. But, remember, there's no need to check everything twice over. You're rather insecure when it comes to giving parties, wondering if you've invited the right people or forgotten to invite someone you should have. Your best plan is to get help from some member of the family or one of your many friends. Discuss the basics with them and divide the work so that both of you have individual jobs to do and there is no question about supervision. Just plan and then go ahead!

As you generally have many friends, a cocktail party is better than a small dinner party. You can entertain everyone at once, fulfilling obligations acquired in accepting invitations from others.

When going to other people's houses, check the time and date and don't arrive late.

PISCES ♓   If you're having a dinner party, you're happier with old friends than trying to make small talk with new acquaintances. You're more at ease if you entertain casual acquaintances in a restaurant than in your own home.

It's not unusual for some emergency to crop up at your dinner parties but you can generally pass them over and no one's inconvenienced. Since you enjoy taking care of arrangements yourself, plan well in advance. See that you have all the shopping done and check simple things like having enough dishes, salt and pepper—for it's in the small arrangements that you can make mistakes. Have an early meal, leaving plenty of time for conversation or music afterwards. Just clear the table, forget the dishes until after the guests have gone, and you'll always be thought of as a charming hostess.

When invited out, plan such things as baby-sitters or leaving the office in good time, so that you arrive promptly without anything worrying you. Try to forget the telephone exists as this can be irritating to the guests as well as to yourself.

6

love
and
courtship

ARIES ♈ With fiery Mars energizing you in every
way, it's natural that love affairs play a great part in your life.
Sometimes you don't know where to stop: should one violent love affair
come to an end, you take little time to recover from it. In a short time
you're ready to embark on the next emotional adventure.

For you, love is an all-encompassing thing which can lead to your
showing the least attractive part of your nature. It's very easy to fall into
the quagmire of jealousy and impatience which lead off into temper ex-
plosions. You rarely have a love affair without stormy periods between
you and your partner. You're always willing to forget, but sometimes
the partner is unable either to forgive or forget. This is generally the
reason why one love affair fades away as quickly as it begins. Many of
you have a destructive quality—even in love relationships—because it's

difficult to meet people who understand the volatile temperament that's so much a part of you. Even if you who arrive at the point when—intellectually—you know you must be patient with your loved one, you can rarely achieve this. And then the fireworks explode again. A relationship with members of your sign is never dull, but it's rarely romantically poetic or peaceful.

The most compatible sign for you is Libra, but you enjoy the witty conversation of Gemini. Leo can provide you with a violent affair but it's apt to burn itself out as you're both fire signs and like to have you own way.

Sagittarians can be very harmonious, if you both realize that you shouldn't brood over the inevitable quarrels. Once you can find a happy medium in this relationship, it can provide a lively adventure through life, with both profiting from the experience.

All your love relationships can prosper and provide added zest for life. But you may have difficulty in sustaining them and enjoying their ultimate potential unless you can curb your jealousy and fiery temperament. You expect loyalty, but you must also be prepared to give it. Once you can master the art of going even halfway to meet the requirements of your partner's temperament, you can be an exciting lover.

TAURUS ♉ The Venusian qualities which dominate your sign enable you to hold onto a love affair or a marriage more successfully than so many other people. You have a phlegmatic attitude towards love, realizing that you may have to tread a stony path before you reach the bed of roses—and you can do this without losing any of your interest in the loved one.

Sometimes you're content with long courtships, and this isn't always pleasant for your partner unless you can explain the reasons for it. Often the reasons are monetary ones, wishing to have financial stability, if you are male, before marrying. The ladies under this sign like to feel they have a partner who can supply them with a home, but they're willing to work and make contributions to comfort. To both sexes, the idea of a home is paramount and gives you a sense of security without which you can never be truly happy.

There's sometimes a danger that, while you need constant reassurance of love, you may not always be so free in giving the right word of endearment at the right time. Few of you ever forget things like birthdays and anniversaries, but you're inclined to feel that once you've made

a declaration of love, it should be accepted and not need constant reiter-
ation.

Libra is a very compatible companion—especially if the relationship begins with a strong physical attraction. A Taurean male is often
delighted to supply the material needs which Libra loves, providing the
partner is emotionally responsive. You're also attracted to Scorpio, but
after the first exciting flush of love begins to fade you often may find
you've married a partner with the same stubborn streak you have. The
Taurus-Scorpio marriage, however, can last through reasons of con-
venience and, occassionally, manages to revitalize itself through a common interest in children.

GEMINI II   Emotional pressures leading to nervous
            tension can wreck many love affairs for you. If this is allied
with financial difficulties, even the best of love affairs suffers to a point
where you're likely to let go of it. You can be the most loyal and devoted
of lovers if your partner makes a determined effort to encourage and
sustain the first love interest. Without this, you can easily give your
affection to someone else, often without completely relinquishing your
relationship with the other partner. This state of affairs is not conducive
to relieving any of your nervous tension and can at times become a
habit from which you can't extricate yourself.

You don't seem able to help yourself when love begins to run into
difficulties, seeking to move away from it, rather than face your partner
to talk matters over in an adult manner. The only person who seems to
get hurt is you, despite efforts to maintain your butterfly existence. It's
most essential that your partner understand your fluctuating Mercurial
temperament with its variation of moods and not mistake any casual
attitude on your part for a breakdown in love.

There's a great deal of immaturity in your love affairs, often due
to your first attempts to please, strangely enough. At the first slight, you
cease to be concerned with this and begin to make other arrangements.
Many of you will find a compatible partner from the signs of Aries and
Leo of they're older than you. You can be enchanted with the ardor of
both these signs, but it has to be maintained and always sustained by
constant physical attraction as well as sweet words.

It's characteristic of a certain section of Geminis, born in the second ten days of the sign, that business partners or associates often become your marriage companions. This happens, no doubt, because you

can build up a feeling of security with them which is at first divorced from an intense physical emotion. Love is generally at its best for you when tension is removed from the relationship. For this reason, the steadiness of an elderly Sagittarian can become your ideal mate after a period of experimenting, which is inevitable until after the age of forty.

Your main danger is that you may enjoy experimenting for so long that the idea of a permanent relationship may seem to threaten a loss of the freedom you love.

CANCER ♋   There'll be many times in your life when you need to sit down and quietly analyze what you believe to be your needs for happiness in love. Many of you are very demanding in your requirements, but the trouble is that the moon's influence can cause those requirements to vary. There's always some conflict between wanting a highly social life and one in which security plays its part.

In youth, through many experimental love affairs (and probably at least two marriages) you may be quite certain that you can sacrifice security for more romantic interests. After middle age, financial security will mean more than physical attraction—although a "little-girl" part of your nature will always enjoy being petted and pampered, even when you're old. Capricorn can be a harmonious companion at this stage, but rarely does this relationship provide you with enough excitement when young. It's much better after middle age, since, by this time, the thrifty Capricorn can have reached a point of financial security. There can, however, be an illusionary effect in this if the Capricorn is *too* thrifty and finds your demands too extravagant.

Your most romantic associations are likely to be with Pisceans, and these can be lasting affairs resulting in marriage. Although Scorpios will always appreciate your sensitivity, you may find this partnership too demanding after a while, especially in marriage, although it can result in some dramatic love affairs. Rarely will any of you get through life without having a series of affairs. Many of them will leave scars, but you're resilient enough and imbued with enough optimism to believe that the next affair will be *the* one.

Children play an important part in your life, but sometimes there's a transference of affection from your lover to the children. You can go through life without being conscious of this or ignoring it until the partner realizes that he wants more attention. If you're unable to return to the first flush of love, even after trying a second honeymoon, you'll go back to being a doting parent to your children.

No sign can show such a variety of emotions as yours when it comes to personal relationships. You always remember past loves and can indulge in romanticizing them, for the moon allows you to have full play with your always-fertile imagination.

LEO ♌︎   You like to have your love affairs with people you've met many times. This is a contrast to the fiery nature of your sign dominated by the life-giving sun. You rarely love a stranger, for despite the passion you can generate when in love, it has to start with a degree of casualness and then fly up into a highly combustible state. You often attract others because you show a degree of strength, but while you'll lend a shoulder to cry on, you don't regard this as a basis for love.

You have a very real need for harmony in your personal life and will thrive best when your final partner comes from your own social circle. You like to show off the object of your love, and this sometimes means that the partner finds difficulty living up to your ideals. You need your love to be up on a pedestal, but you can be very jealous if someone casts even an innocent but admiring glance at the pedestal. Only constant reassurance of love sustains the original passion.

You seem to thrive best with your opposing sign of Aquarius. You can relax with them and they indulge your own extrovert nature while retaining the dignity and independence you like in your partner. The love of your life can rarely upstage you without running into trouble, even though you'll always try to make up for this when you're alone. Aquarius will understand this trait and not make the same mistake twice.

You're always attracted to Aries, though relationships may be short-lived when the two fiery personal ties clash. You can literally talk yourselves out of love. Both of you are good conversationalists, but Aries enjoys arguing. Libra companions can be harmonious to you, especially when it's the Leo male interested in the Libra female—who'll generally present a serenely beautiful picture he can admire. The danger in this is that both of you may be too extravagant. The clash can come through financial difficulties with both of you feeling you have the right to buy the things you like without consulting the other. Libra will take it because she thinks *she* is entitled to it. And you will take it because you also feel it's your right. This is offset by Libra being able to find enjoyment in mental activity as well as being the object of physical pleasure.

It's not unusual to find two members of your sign enjoying a long love affair in which passion is generated by both parties and a mutual interest thrives in the upbringing of your children.

VIRGO ♍   Although you thrive under the banner of the sign of service, you're inclined to be arrogant in love. Sometimes you bring up the shortcomings of your partner by analyzing them too closely.

Your partner in romance will always have to be very understanding and sympathetic to your needs without being overly sentimental. You're not likely to rush either into love or marriage and sometimes miss opportunities by waiting too long before approaching the object of your affections. In courtship, you show respect and kindness with little passion, and this can be accepted by so many signs simply on its face value. Once you've reached the point of marriage, you can be a very loyal and understanding, but you can easily slip into a routine which, while satisfactory to you, could produce a feeling of dullness for your partner.

This can be eliminated if you have joint intellectual interests which will long survive any physical attraction. For this reason, it's important to choose your partner very carefully—although always remembering that you can wait too long and find yourself left at the post in the marital stakes. Few of you are ever likely to die of a broken heart when this happens. You're good at disguising your feelings, perhaps because they're not generated by passion but have their roots in respect and devotion.

Taurus is highly harmonious to you if you decide to marry young; most of you will have had at least one love affair with a Taurean. You're also attracted to Scorpio, especially if you meet in business and allow the romance to develop as secondary to the business. This, however, is generally upsetting to the volatile dramatic Scorpio nature. Also, you may not like the scenes which Scorpio can throw, for any love affair must not be embarrassing to you or detract from your dignity. Probably the most ideal partner is Pisces, who can supply the understanding which you need even more than outward signs of affection.

While you have an inward desire to be loved, you sometimes forget that to attain this, you also have to be loving.

LIBRA ♎︎   Although you enjoy a social life, it's hard
for you to adjust to new relationships on an emotional basis.
The partner has to make most of the advances, following them up with
every known attribute of the lover. You enjoy the courtship when there's
a prelude of roses, discreet, tasteful dinner parties—everything that goes
towards the big romantic adventure.

Perhaps you find it difficult to adjust to a love affair without these
preliminaries because you're easily hurt. You are the most vulnerable
of all the signs, and a love affair which leads you to expect so much,
and then doesn't reach maturity, can make you physically ill. Unfortunately, you're likely to have at least one unhappy experience that you'll
never completely forgive or forget. This generally happens when you're
young. For this reason, you feel much more secure with a man considerably older than yourself. The Libra man likes the companionship of
women a few years older than himself who have retained their looks
and figure.

If there's sufficient financial stability, you find Aquarians very
compatible. They can represent the father figure which seems as important to you as a lover. Without the right financial security to give you
a good background—a house and the right clothes—you're rarely happy.
No one needs love and admiration more than you—but not necessarily
through a single marriage. Because you look for perfection, you may
have to experiment through several affairs and marriages.

A Leo man can be very compatible to a Libra woman, but this
partnership isn't so successful for the Libra man and Leo woman—the
latter being too domineering for the Libra male. If you can find an
Aries who understands your vanity and won't be impatient if you keep
him waiting while you finish off your toilette, you can find him a charming and exciting lover.

Sagittarius can be helpful, but more as a business partner than a
romantic one. Should you be attracted to one who can fulfill both needs,
you can generally look forward to a successful relationship.

In all love affairs, there'll be many times when you have to sit
down and examine your own emotions—particularly the reasons behind
them. You can attract anyone you like, but it's in the *holding* of him
that you are apt to fail without realizing that you may have contributed
to the failure as much as he has. While you always desire to be fair in
so many spheres of life, in romances your usual good judgment can be
faulty unless you're aware of what you're doing.

SCORPIO ♏   You have to be careful in your romantic
involvement, for you can become obsessed with the idea of
love itself, forgetting that many practical things have to be talked about
if it's to lead to marriage.

You have enough energy from Mars to be a passionate lover, but
you also have to contend with the erratic Pluto and its ability to fling
you into unexpected situations. The hurts that occur at this time can
bring out destructive qualities in you. Seeking revenge on a partner who
has defaulted is not unknown to Scorpios. You can also be very jealous
and possessive. The greater the love, the more this seems to come out,
and neither jealousy nor possessiveness are conducive to transforming a
passionate love into a happy marriage. You have to learn to be tolerant
and not imagine the worst if your lover is late or has to break a dinner
date. You can show a great deal of brooding resentfulness about such a
mishap, and although it has its roots in missing an opportunity to be
with your loved one, it doesn't add to easy reconciliations.

Sometimes you appear to be domineering because you demand so
much from love—even though willing to give a great deal of yourself
at the same time. After the initial attraction to your magnetic personality, the opposite sex can withdraw when evidences of domination
appear. In love, there can be something quite cannabalistic about you,
giving the impression that you would sooner see your lover destroyed
than lose him. It's essential to find a partner who understands your
love's dramatic needs and general personality and who won't flinch from
responsibilities. The truth is that your domineering attitude is generally
a defense mechanism—you're quite capable of being guided carefully
if your partner is strong enough to see this.

You can be very happy with a Taurean, providing he's on a par
with you intellectually, and if you meet when you're both young. Should
the Taurean be older, he's more likely to be set in his ways and unable
to adapt to you any more than you are to him. The Cancerian—although
of a much quieter nature—seems able to fulfill many of your needs,
inasmuch as patience and appreciation of your own vulnerability helps
to offset any weaknesses.

With Pisceans you can have some torrid love affairs. Both of you
can be hurt or hurtful, but at least the Piscean quickly tries to make
amends and doesn't resent being the first to make up after a quarrel. So
strong can your nature be that pride prevents you from apologizing, even

if you love a person tremendously, and know in your heart you're in the wrong.

Few of you go through life without tempestuous personal involvements, seeking for an understanding partner as much as a perfect love.

SAGITTARIUS ♐   Desiring forever to widen your mental horizons by philosophical reading, you're also very eager to understand your fellow human beings. This can lead you to some strange emotional situations which rarely benefit you in any satisfying personal manner. For this reason, love on a permanent basis often comes after middle age. When young, you can mistake sympathy and other people's need of you for love. You're more likely to be reckless and impulsive after forty.

The females of your sign can have a fortunate love life if they remember that an intellectual companionship is more likely to last than a highly romanticized and dramatic love affair. The men of your sign are so intent on being kind to maidens in distress—even if they've married when young—that they can find themselves in a strangely complex web of intrigue not of their own making. The constant offering of a shoulder to cry upon is often the preliminary to a romantic situation that can leave you bewildered when your kind and sympathetic intentions are mistaken for something deeper. Extricating yourself from such situations can take up a great deal of time and often deter you from following up more meaningful relationships.

Your opposite sign in the zodiac, Gemini, generally provides your most harmonious romantic companion, bringing a bright, witty relationship and the art of laughing you out of your most serious moods. Leo can also be compatible—especially when there's a business interest as well as a romantic one.

A Libra woman is slightly more satisfactory if she's matched with a Sagittarian man, but this isn't so good when the sexes are reversed. The Libra female can often bring out the most tender feeling from the Sagittarian male, but the Sagittarian female often doesn't have enough patience with the Libran lover and tends to seem to want to dominate. This is a situation which the Libran man will soon resent although he's probably quite capable of providing more romantic interest than the Sagittarian female needs.

CAPRICORN ♑   Most of you like long discussions on a very business-like basis before considering marriage—although, all too often, the males pursue a series of extra-marital relationships. Secrecy is part of their technique, since they're always anxious to maintain a respectable public image. Once it becomes likely that the romance will be talked about, they'll find reasonable ways to forget all about it.

You're so highly introverted that you fall into dark depressions, rarely wanting to talk to your companions about the reasons. Saturn, your ruling planet, can be very destructive to love affairs. It can bring such pain to your companion and such dark moods to you that the path of love is all too often strewn with obstacles. For this reason, Virgo can be a good partner for you, if you both remember that loyalty and devotion can exist without a great exchange of words. But it's not often an exciting romance, generally finding its basis on financial security.

You can find lasting relationships with Taurus, but again, the romantic interest is surpassed by a business-like attention to details—arranging budgets before marriage and deciding what work each is to do. Aries seems able to supply an emotional impact as well as a business partnership—Aries takes the initiative and you follow, a little fearfully.

So many of you like to have decision-making taken out of your hands. A business-like approach to love sometimes upsets the other person, and you should try to speak of your intentions without upsetting your partner of the moment. It's not a waste of time to be both romantic and business-like but a sense of proportion should be maintained. You're not very good at timing, and if your partner's in a romantic mood, he or she will hate being brought down to earth by a discussion of the family budget.

A Cancer partner will love making a delightful home for you—not always in a neat manner which can upset your methodical nature—but at least she'll give the impression that she wants to please. She can match you at being business-like in a shrewd way if it's a middle-aged relationship.

AQUARIUS ♒   Many of you miss out in a fully romantic partnership because you can't take an interest in the many small details which may please your companion. You demand a lot of freedom in all personal relationships, hating to feel possessed and rarely jealous if the other person shows independence, too. You prefer being in control of the situation, enjoying being solicitous to the point of being fussy. Should you be unable to keep an appointment, you're likely to expect your companion to understand, without asking why. This can lead to friction, especially in the early stages of a romance. It's just another expression of the freedom you must have if you're to be happy.

Your attention to physical comforts and providing a home doesn't extend to relieving your companion of worries which can come from your erratic moods and movements. There's also a compulsion to exclude your loved one from any of your business affairs, as you tend to worry in silence without realizing that your very silence causes your companion to worry.

Leo can be a most compatible sign, romantic in courtship and happy in marriage, especially when there are children. You can take a mutual interest in their welfare, and Leo-Aquarius parents can be among the best in the world, prepared to make sacrifices for their children, and basking in any success they may achieve in later years.

An alliance with Gemini can supply an exciting love life on a physical and intellectual basis. This also applies to Aries, who can provide some of the drive you lack.

PISCES ♓

All too often your ambitious drive in creative work has to be linked with a romantic interest. You like to feel you're killing two birds with one stone. (Even if you don't always succeed, at least you have a lot of fun.) So often, without this dual interest in romance and work, you become vulnerable.

It's often difficult for you to make up your mind in affairs of the heart, preferring a strong partner who can guide you. But you'll run away if the partner uses a domineering manner. Your best love affairs are those with a touch of the iron hand in the velvet glove. Some of your companion's strength can rub off on you once you have confidence in him or her.

You love freedom, but you also love to be in love—whether the romance leads to marriage or not. This is most significant to females of your sign born in the first ten days and the romantic interest can dwindle to negligible qualities as the sign gets nearer to Aries. You always have the problem of letting small worries interfere with your romance and, at this time, the tactful partner should murmur sweet words of comfort.

It's essential to bolster your confidence in your own ability to love. You're quite likely to prefer being possessed to being possessive.

Broken romances can upset your creative drive and injure your health, but you're rarely resentful—simply hurt enough to want to be alone. Many doses of romantic music and reading poetry can bring you out of the dazed stage more quickly than friends' well-meaning advice

A relationship between you and a Cancerian almost always endures, as you can both understand your mutual variations of mood and are both highly romantic. You're attracted to Libra, but it's likely to be a short-term affair. The most congenial partner is Virgo who—although he may cause many moments of unhappiness in the early uneasy stages of the relationship—seems to have an enduring quality. Generally, the Virgo is there when needed and is interested in your creative efforts. Survive the criticism and you can discover many areas where your outlook on life is the same. This is more likely to be when a Virgo man is older than you are.

Many of you have a great settling-down period after middle age, keeping your romantic instincts, but being less demanding on your partner.

What to expect from a date

ARIES   Loads of energy and action—and that includes a rapidly moving romance.

TAURUS   A definite courtship period, and a good deal of thought given to serious subjects such as setting up house and joint finances.

GEMINI   An on-and-off romance. When you may think your date's fickle, he's actually just making comparisons among various girls. You could call him the type who shops around first before making a decision. You'll probably have to give him quite a few talks to straighten him out and let him know that no one can compare with you.

CANCER   He'll want you to keep pace with his moods and whims, and he'll be hurt if you can't. At least give the appearance of trying!

LEO   Laugh at his stories, even if they're slightly ponderous and long-winded, but never laugh at *him*.

VIRGO   Always expect him to be punctual and to have the date well-planned. If you discuss in advance what you want to do, he'll be reasonable and eager to cooperate. But once the plans are made, he can be difficult about changing them.

LIBRA   Expect him to be dressed for the occasion and assuming you'll be the same. If he indicates that you're not doing something in good taste, don't commit the same outrage twice. Be prepared for him to change his mind but also to be very reasonable in explaining why he may be late.

SCORPIO   He'll like to give you murder mysteries to read and take you to movies with a highly dramatic flavor (rather than merely a romantic one). If he's in a quiet mood, don't try to kill time by small talk or you can expect some stinging replies. If you feel ultra-sensitive, he has a habit of finding your Achilles heel and applying pressure, although he'll make up for it afterwards. Be prepared for arguments and stand up for yourself.

SAGITTARIUS   He'll expect you to tell him your problems and will do his best to help. Remember, though, that he can become hurt if you discuss your troubles with someone else and he hears of them in a round-about way. Let him know you appreciate his offers, but remember his eagerness to help may not match his ability. Take out double insurance by giving him the opportunity to help and then cooperating with him.

CAPRICORN   You may have to start with the realization that he runs on an austerity program, preferring to eat in places where the food is good enough but where he doesn't feel he's also paying for lush surroundings. He'll be secretive about his finances, but curious about yours. He'll give you a line about two being able to live as cheaply as one and expect you to manage living up to it.

AQUARIUS   He'll forget dates unless you remind him, and then be apologetic. Accept his apologies graciously. Always check to be sure he has the theater tickets or offer to look after them yourself, always letting him think he's a capable arranger. Never embarrass him by making a scene in public.

PISCES   He'll enjoy looking after you, but be prepared to express appreciation for anything he does or plans. Look forward to post-mortems after going to the movies, ballet, or theater. Keep up with the latest books and news of personalities connected with esoteric matters. You may have to go through a period of attending yoga or ESP classes together.

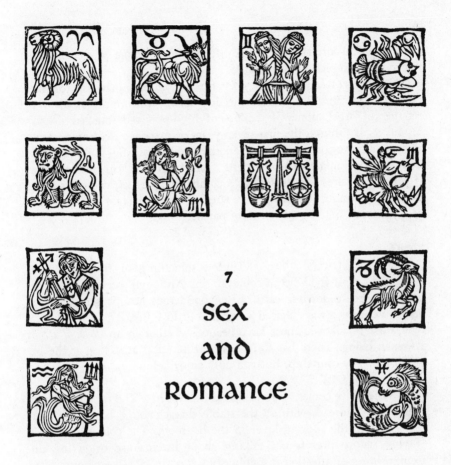

7

SEX
and
ROMANCE

ARIES ♈   True to the character of your symbolic animal, the Ram, you don't like spending time on long courtships. You have a very healthy, down-to-earth approach to sex; you're
not likely to be an ostrich about it and generally accept it as part of
courtship. Slow, ponderous love isn't likely to appeal to you and you're
likely to reach an understanding about any relationship in quick time.
You prefer being the hunter to being the hunted one. Quite likely, you'll
be the one to make the first move in a friendship, always drawn by
physical attraction.

     Sex is as important to you in married life as the romantic courtship
is with wooing, soft lights, sweet music and flowers. You rarely enjoy
public affection but, like most of the fire signs, you can be an ardent

lover. Physical attraction and sex life has to continue in marriage or you're likely to seek favors outside.

Money's often one of the great forces holding a marriage together after the first flush of excitement dies down. But you're headstrong enough to forget money if the fire of high-powered romance doesn't sustain itself through the first seven years of marriage. In leaping from one love affair or one marriage to another, you fulfill your zodiacal birth-right—being impulsive and leaping from the frying pan into the fire. If your sex desires are satisfied by a compatible partner, you can survive many of the other hazards which wreck some marriages and can be a happy, loving, intelligent, exciting partner.

TAURUS ♉   There's something of the lotus eater about you when it comes to sex. Although you have the repu-tation for being down-to-earth, often ponderous and conservative, the planet Venus is always alerted towards your love life.

First of all, you must have beauty, whether in an *objet d'art* or a human being. There has to be a strong physical attraction at the be-ginning of any courtship. But you only enjoy belonging to an attractive person.

When love comes, you often lead a secret life. The facade of being thoroughly Taurean, with all the stable characteristics, has its counter-part in being the adoring lover in the bedroom. The conservative part of your nature prefers not talking about lovemaking or giving un-seemly shows of affection in public. But you can be a most uninhibited lover with a partner who understands your sensitivity.

You need a companion who enjoys being an object of adoration, for you can literally shower affection on such a partner, never demand-ing too much in return. In marriage, you're prepared to be faithful and you demand fidelity. Jealousy plays a part in the early stages of a Tau-rean romance, and this probably encourages a Taurean to become an excellent lover with emphasis on sex.

Any suspicions about your partner's fidelity can result in displays of temper, sulkiness and irrationality. Should your suspicions be justi-fied, Taurean stubbornness comes into force. Though there's rarely a chance of reconciliation, you always want to be scrupulously fair when it comes to monetary considerations. In cases of divorce, you gen-erally try to keep ownership of the home—sending the offending partner on his way with anything that can be legally proven his—but never a dime more.

Once you've survived the early periods of jealousy and begin to feel secure, your love has an undying quality, making your marriage happy and durable.

GEMINI II   Although it can be confusing to a partner, you're generous enough to want to show that you do indeed belong to a double sign. The sooner your partner learns that he's fallen in love with two often distinctive types, the better he'll settle down to being a satisfactory lover.

Your dual personality can bring him a two-edged sword; two love affairs for the price of one. There's a dangerous quality in your sex life because of your constant love of change, and you're perfectly capable of having two highly emotional love affairs going at the same time. Your perverse sense of humor takes most of the sting out of your relationships, but you definitely find it hard to settle down. There never seems to be an easy transition from courtship to parading down the wedding aisle.

How deeply the emotional experience of love affects you is only known to yourself—at least to ONE of your selves. One part of your dual personality can often dance along its accepted butterfly way, leaving your twin to dance with a few tears in its eyes. Sex is only important as a way of expressing one of your many moods; sometimes it becomes no more than an extension of conversation and is probably easily forgotten. You unabashedly long for the fun that goes with a love affair, and if sex is part of that fun, you accept it readily.

When someone comes along and sees beyond your butterfly half and takes time to understand your changeable foibles, you stand the best chance of being happy. Such relationships rarely get off to an easy start, and much depends on the perception and tenacity of your partner. If he lets go of you easily, you can shrug your shoulders. If he can take your tantrums and still be kind and considerate, the excellent reasoning power given you by your ruling planet of Mercury comes into play and you begin asking yourself a few questions. Generally, the replies either frighten you—so that you try to escape from what could be the best and safest love of your life for fear of being trapped—or you settle for it and stand a chance of living happily ever after.

It all depends which twin is in control on the day it all happens.

CANCER ♋   Your love life is all too often a three-
or-more-part saga starting when you're quite young and attracting attention with your charming girlish ways. The second stage
is marriage—sometimes with sudden fear and disillusion that life isn't
the rosy path you thought it would be. This leads to childish tantrums
or frustrations, and you begin looking for ways out, often via the divorce
courts. Your sign has the highest potential for going through the divorce
courts twice. This brings you into a new era of life where you tell your
friends you're a much wiser woman. Then you disprove it by making
the same mistake again with loneliness your great enemy.

Love is more important to you than a highly exciting sex life and
you can easily spend the first forty years of your life experimenting with
love. Because you look for the big romantic dream, the knight in shining
armor, with yourself the beautiful maiden forever wishing to be rescued,
the illusionary quality appears again and again in your life.

The erratic course of the wayward, fickle moon affects your emotions more than any other sign. The White Knight can change into
Black Jasper almost before the first dawn of the wedding night. After
forty, and probably with a record of two or more divorces, wisdom does
indeed set in, and you begin to associate romance with security based on
a solid bank balance. This is probably your best period, the time you
stand the best chance for finding personal happiness. The truth is, you
love security and a home, and enough money, as much as a child clings
to its parents when it's very young. In these days, sex life doesn't end at
forty. But by now you've learned that even dashing cavaliers like to
relax.

Male members of this sign don't go through quite such traumatic
love and sex experiences. They prefer to cling, even to the shreds of
married life—even when they're aware that they've married someone
who's not as compatible as they thought. Rather than run the risk of going from bad to worse, they'll cling to the idea that the devil they know,
even though an unsatisfactory wife, is better than the devil they don't.

Both sexes can enjoy romantic experiences mentally just as easily
as the actual physical adventure—for to you the trials seem to outweigh
the pleasures.

LEO ♌   You have the lion's share of astrological
publicity when it comes to sex and love. Ancient astrologers
frequently affirmed that "if one had not been loved by a Leo, one had

never known love." Leo's reputation as a great lover comes down to this day probably because so many male Leos have a courteous yet braggadoccio air of gallantry to the opposite sex. Presumably, they're able to carry through with this in a romantic attachment.

It's not so simple for the female Leo, however. She attracts attention but may be cooler emotionally than her companion imagines at first. Once married, the female lion of the zodiac is capable as much of duty as of a compelling passion.

With the lion as your symbolic animal—tawny, brave and golden as your ruler the sun—an aura of warmth exudes from so many of you that this can be mistaken for a greater interest in the opposite sex than you really feel. Beyond the warm interest, the majority of you are almost prudish in the matter of sex. Promiscuity is really a matter of exaggerated rumor rather than fact. Once married, you can be the most faithful of lovers, eager to protect your partner and generally willing to administer to his or her welfare.

There's always a physical attraction, heightened by personal magnetism, when a Leo comes on the scene. It's easy to see how rumors start about you, because you can be a considerate escort to many girls, always treating each well and making each feel very special. This can boomerang on you unless you come to a firm understanding with your companion early in your relationship. With no intention to deceive any innocent females, you're still likely to have a series of angry young ladies swearing you're a wolf in lion's clothing.

You are attracted by the opposite sex and they are attracted to you, but motivations may be quite different. That adds both to the glamor of your friendships and to your reputation as a pseudo-Lothario.

Almost all female Leos like to be treated royally, with respect and general admiration. They also like being in command of all situations and can firmly decide whether this is to be a romantic relationship or not.

VIRGO ♍   There's a lot of pride in you and you expect worshipful admiration from any suitors. You're not the sort of woman who encourages young men to sow their wild oats and you can survive long periods of courtship without being unduly anxious to rush to the nearest marriage license office.

Your ruling planet, Mercury, gives you a delightful mind, and you're blessed with good looks which rarely deteriorate with age. The opposite sex is naturally attracted to you, but some strange quirk in your emotional makeup generally makes you repel this natural attraction. While many other signs have a great deal of fun in sex and love, you view these things with somber intensity. A lot of your life can be spent in a hassle, trying to keep from being emotionally linked with anyone. But when you decide to indulge in courtship, and finally marriage, you have a strong sense of duty. Many Virgos in past years haven't found married life a bed of roses. But they adapt themselves to the thorns with resignation.

A companionship based on intellectual compatibility generally survives and is more common to Virgos than a hectic full-blooded romantic relationship. You also like to be in a position of financial security before venturing into marriage. It's not unusual for mutual interest in work to be the bond which is important to your marital happiness.

LIBRA ♎   Rules by the planet Venus influencing you to enjoy beauty, influence your actions in sex and love. You enjoy being the focal point of special people who are tender, courteous and never coarse in speech or action. The ancient astrologers saw the female Libran as the love goddess of the zodiac while the male members were noted for their courtly charm. Beauty and charm demand acknowledgment—they are possibly the most obvious assets for attracting love.

While sex has its part to play in most love affairs, its constant repetition as an act is not so necessary to you as the repeated evidence of love by thoughtful acts. Love to you is not, in the words of the poet, "a thing apart," but sex can be. You're generally happy with love manifesting itself in many small ways—the unexpected gift, consideration for you as a person, the desire to pelase. Sex is often used as a reward for such things. There's not often the healthy animalistic approach such as Taurus, also ruled by Venus, feels. Your approach to sex is often well planned rather than spontaneous—the planning varying with your environment, upbringing, and mood at the time and is always associated with a sense of luxury.

As advocates of gracious living, you can carry this right through to the bedroom. When young, you're capable of making mistakes in love affairs and if marriage ensues, it can leave some tragic overtones—chiefly due to the distaste and disillusionment you feel. This probably accounts for your reticence in marrying again. Many Librans, having had one love affair or marriage go astray in youth, content themselves with a series of affairs, managing to keep a good reputation so that they're rarely accused of being a butterfly or libertine. It's simply a matter of regaining your balance and treading warily on the dangerous ground of sex and love. Few people can be as discreet as you while having a romance.

SCORPIO ♏   It's all too easy to dismiss members of your sign as having characteristics based on "sin and sex." You can love with passion but always after deciding whether the person is worthy of the emotional drain a love affair brings. When you find a compatible person who understands the depths of your nature, you can be one of the most exciting companions.

You see sex as a necessary force of life. When your partner is responsive, you can be uninhibited. Although you enjoy being the center of romantic attention and love to dramatize it, a compatible partner will see that this is a defense mechanism. You need to feel that you're in command of any affair and often fight your partner until he or she has earned your complete confidence. Then the drama of sex and love settles down into long periods of satisfactory fulfillment. When this happens, you're at your best and those of you who are creatively inclined may find that a love affair is the catalyst that inspires you to write, paint, or sculpt. Equally so, should a love affair end disastrously, some of the fountain of inspiration dries up and life seems its most dismal and melancholic.

For you to be happy, sex and love must go hand in hand. All the intellectual companions in the world, all the kindness and courtesy in the world, will never completely fulfill your need without a sex interest, too. Your mind is versatile enough to demand an intelligent companion, but it's not always easy for you to find the right mate unless there's a strong dash of an exciting lover as well.

You don't expect marriage to cause any lessening of physical interests and can enjoy sexual activity even as you get older.

SAGITTARIUS ♐   There is a libertine element associated with the last of the fire signs despite the facade of philosophical thought. Your ruling planet encourages expansion and this, combined with an interest in people, naturally leads to your being interested in possible romantic episodes. Like so many of the fire signs, you're inclined to rush in where angels fear to tread when it comes to romance, and, unless you're careful, the passionate fire can burn itself out into smouldering embers.

If you're fortunate enough to find a soul-mate who enjoys a sexual life as well, the fire can be sustained for a long time. But if your partner is not responsive, you're very content to be an exceptionally good friend. Every fire needs added fuel to sustain its flames, and you want your partner to go more than half the way, constantly adding fuel.

In courtship, males can be very determined—especially when there's just a touch of the damsel-in-distress, which alerts your humanitarian instincts. Sometimes one wonders how you would react if the damsel were rather plain?

Your zodiacal sign represents a creature that is half man, half beast, aiming an arrow at an invisible target. Presumably you have your target in view, in which case nothing will prevent you from wooing and winning the fair lady even if she protests too much.

The female archers are equally determined. But characteristic of your sex, you're a little more subtle—although no less determined in your pursuit. Both sexes are prepared to wait—and sometimes the romantic hunt is better than catching the chosen prey. After marriage, you're apt to forget some of the foibles of courtship, but you're adept at keeping out of the divorce courts. There's generally a very healthy approach to the subject of sex even if the frills of romance get lost in the pursuit. But once reminded of the fact that you can be forgetful in such things as birthdays and anniversaries, no one can try harder to remedy it.

CAPRICORN ♑   If Saturn, your ruling planet, specializes in providing barriers to your ambitions, it's felt most virulently in the realms of romance. You're rarely able to help yourself and can disguise your feelings so well that your best friends hardly dare to offer advice. Many of you are forced to suffer from unrequited love, putting a brave face towards the world, even to the point of denying you're capable of deep and romantic love.

Both sexes have a remarkable knack of making unsatisfactory marriages, all too often going to the altar for materialistic reasons rather than for love. Sometimes it's a brave attempt to forget another person you love—because the desire of your heart doesn't realize you exist or doesn't care. Few of you are happy if you marry young and go through the divorce courts. You never escape without some secret embitterment.

Yet, in the male Capricorn, there's an intense desire to have a full sexual experience as part of an adventure in love. But circumstance, the blocks of Saturn, social conditions, and the desire to appear as an upright citizen, enables you to disguise this very effectively. You're adept at secret liaisons, but are rarely truly happy with them, resorting to them out of loneliness or desperation. Frequently, by the time you're a little beyond middle age, you can look back at a string of love affairs which never really materialized into anything special—yet left their mark on you.

In marriage, the female Capricorn can be one of the most dutiful wives of the zodiac, but she's rarely motivated with passion. You can be content to stay out of the limelight, attend to your household meticulously, and make whatever contribution you can to your husband's work. There's always an element of martyrdom in your sign's experiences with love. How well other planets are placed in your personal chart decides the degree of happiness or frustration which you may feel.

Generally a quiet form of marital happiness comes very late in life, which accounts for the yearly newspaper articles about men in their seventies suddenly leaving their wives or marrying young girls. Saturn, despite its bad reputation as a heavy planet intent on grinding down the individual, always relents if its subjects live long enough. Sometimes it presents opportunities for happiness at an earlier age, but the subject is too mistrustful to open the door or seize the opportunity for a new life.

AQUARIUS ≈ Vitalized by your ruling planet of Uranus, the planetary progenitor of all electrical and offbeat original things, it's not exceptional to find you with partners who defy convention even venturing into the bizarre.

There's nothing flighty about your approach to life, but after a bad love affair before the age of twenty, you adopt one of two attitudes: you become ultra-discriminating, or you look among the rare and unusual for your next romantic adventure. If a few experimental flights of fancy are indulged in, your good mind rationalizes that you're seeking perfection. Sometimes you have to consider how much perfection there is within yourself. But your spirit is so independent that you often can't face this stringent self-examination.

Male Aquarians generally marry women younger than themselves. Probably there's something safe in presenting a father-image rather than a lover-image, and youth can often make age feel very superior. Aquarian females generally look for someone who follows their own humanitarian instincts. Some very good marriages occur when both parties have dedication to an ideal or cause outside themselves. How marriage survives with this dedication as motivation rests with the pattern of other planets in the joint horoscopes. Sex is not merely a joyous romp, but aimed at the production of a family in which the Aquarian female desires to feel pride.

In many Aquarian relationships, there's an element of selfishness towards offspring, generated by desiring that they have a good start in life through education and knowing right from wrong at an early age. Logically this should work out very well, but rarely does in practice. The children, too, may have desires to be individuals and not merely the reflected images of their parents—even though the parents are good, upright, idealistic people. Ideals vary as generations succeed each other, and this is hard for you to understand. No one is more dedicated to the pursuit of truth, but it is a sad thing that one of your best attributes when carried to extremes can become detrimental to you, especially in the case of your own children.

In love you can go from the extremes of being completely idealistic (expecting your partner never to slip from the pedestal on which you like to see her) or you can become casually libertine and advocate such things as free love. The main thing is that Uranus, the planet of the unexpected happening, certainly produces some remarkable liaisons among members of your sign.

When friends and relations say "what does he see in her?" it rarely matters to you. You have the ability to see beyond physical attraction. Given time, you stand an excellent chance of finding the missing part of yourself—your soul-mate.

PISCES ♓   You have practically all the other signs of the zodiac at your mercy when it comes to romantic episodes. Once you become bored with a companion, you can say goodbye quicker than anyone else. On the other hand, you're romantic enough to want beautiful moments to last forever and are quite capable of idealizing the object of your emotions. When they say goodbye first, you're hypersensitive and can literally retire from the world after a romance gone sour. Until next time, that is—for all Pisceans, whether they understand it or not, are generally saved—with time healing even the most frightful of Cupid's wounds. You're resilient enough to recover with very little bitterness and go on to the next love affair with an intensified desire that *this* time it is for real. Optimistic right into old age (that is, if you're born in the February part of your sign), you're capable of attracting love well into old age. For those born in the March period, the love life is not quite so good.

There's a courtsean quality in the female Pisceans born in February, and so diverse are the members under the sign of the fishes that the March signs can go to the extreme of the love stakes, renounce the world, and seek life in one of the meditative religious orders.

As lovers, you enjoy sex but always desire the full romantic treatment well after the wedding bells stop ringing. No one can be hurt so easily or recover as swiftly as you. Your two ruling planets, Jupiter and Neptune, seem to give you the best of all worlds and you're quick to seize on any advantages offered. If Neptune, in its treacherous aspect where romance is concerned, causes a love affair to come to a tragic end, the good expanding nature of Jupiter supplies another love to heal the wound. Despite a few anguished cries, you can fall into the river of romance, almost drown, and then surprise your friends and yourself by coming up with a bouquet of roses.

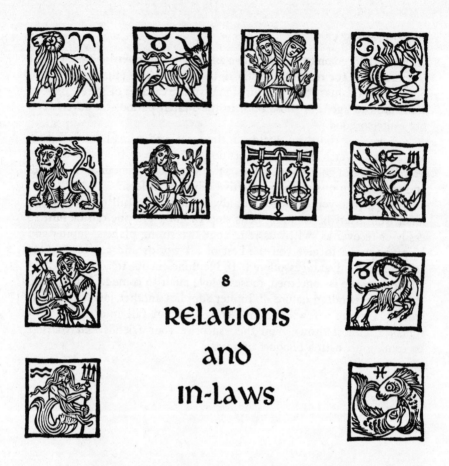

8
RELATIONS
and
IN-LAWS

ARIES ♈ Those born under Aries sign never come for the weekend and stay the proverbial month. Certainly they are never boring you, and should any of the usual family quarrels arise, there's little likelihood that they'll be resentful or bear any grudge. Aries have the enviable ability of forgetting domestic disputes. An Aries mother-in-law may, at first, appear somewhat overbearing. She'll certainly talk too much, usually starting with advice on how to look after her child who's now in your care. But once the novelty of your being newlyweds has worn off, she'll become less trying. A busy, active person herself, she's never likely to dwell on one subject for too long—even anything as important as you.

If you have an Aries father-in-law, he'll hope you maintain a good standard of living, dress well, and aim to improve your family status each year. You can have a very satisfactory relationship with Arian relations, chiefly because they're interesting and interested people who like to keep involved in life. The only danger is that they may find you dull —in which case be assured they'll limit visits more and more.

TAURUS ♉

Your Taurean relations will always insist that you can count on them in any emergency—and you should accept them for the staunch, dependable, loyal people they are. But they'll expect you to be financially secure, and their offers to be helpful don't always extend to banking problems. In times of grave emergency, and in order to save face, they would certainly be prepared to loan you money, but they would stop respecting you at the same time.

You can rely on them to help in such things as home decorating and gardening. When children arrive, you'll have devoted, utterly reliable grandparents who'll never mind baby-sitting or taking the children for holidays.

Taureans in-laws like to visit, but they expect to find an orderly home not very different from the one they try to keep. Advice will always be forthcoming, and as Taurean relations become older they're inclined towards lengthy dialogue, often reitering the same theme. Still, they'll expect you to be patient with them.

If you become involved in trouble likely to reflect on the whole family, you can expect their thorough disapproval—however, this won't necessarily affect their loyalty to you as a person. Make the best of your Taurean relations. Extend courtesy and patience towards them and you'll find them very good, sound people.

GEMINI ♊

Your Gemini relations will always be busy and expect you to be the same. If you visit them when they're involved in their latest project, don't expect them to drop everything just because you're there. The best way out is to express an interest in whatever they're doing and then gently try to divert them by discussing some project of your own. They'll almost always be interested. If you have a one-track mind, they won't hesitate to criticize it and wonder how you can be so dull.

Gemini grandparents become intensely attached to their grandchildren and are inclined to spoil any visiting children. You may have to be tactful but firm about this, emphasizing that junior has a few candies a week and doesn't eat them between meals. You may have to explain some basics about children's meals in general, for your Gemini relations will be erratic in their own food habits. But once anything is brought to their attention in a reasonable manner, they respond well and genuinely try to be of help.

Most Geminis retain a youthful mind and spirit, even as they grow old, and are able to relate very nicely to younger members of the family. The generation gap is reduced and often non-existent. Your relations will love to entertain you, but like to be paid in kind when they visit you. Be prepared for them to arrive unexpectedly and to leave just as suddenly.

CANCER ♋   Your Cancerian in-laws will display a great interest in your family background, and this may be trying in the days of courtship. It's not because they want to prove you may not be good enough for their offspring, but rather that they have a natural interest in family trees. They'll enjoy talking freely about their own background and expect you to do the same. If you don't, then they'll probe.

Be prepared for large gatherings at which they can show you off: family reunions go over big with your Cancerian in-laws and they rarely give up this habit. They can become very hurt if you don't attend. As time goes on, it may be boring to go to the yearly reunion, but it's better to make the effort if you want to keep peace with your in-laws.

A Cancerian in-law who feels hurt and neglected can turn into a trying relation who'll forever be on the phone or paying visits, always probing to see what's wrong or "what mistake did I make?" They'll say that they've "always tried to do the best they can." In the end, if you're sensitive at all, you'll begin to feel like a heel.

Your relations will always take an interest in your house, in the way you serve food, and how you bring up your children. Try to realize that Cancerians may have some disturbing habits, but are basically good, kind, generous people who are also extremely sensitive.

LEO ♌ Never take your Leo relations for granted or think you can get away with sloppy housekeeping when they visit you. They love to be paid a great deal of attention, and will expect, in fact, to be treated regally. They have a great desire to be liked, but most of all, they want to be respected. When this need is satisfied, there's literally nothing they won't do in return. A Leo father-in-law may seem ponderous until you get to know him, and his lengthy stories may make a young person impatient, but at heart he takes pride in his newly-found family.

You'll find all Leo relations generous to a fault—especially when your own children arrive—but they also become possessive, due to their basic love of children. Since Leos themselves are rarely blessed with large families, any new baby becomes a focus for the adoration they'd have lavished on any children of their own.

They'll expect you to keep up a good standard of living and love to hear that you're going up in the world, whether professionally or socially.

Never forget to tell them the least bit of family news; they hate to discover in a round-about way their nephew has been promoted. You can rely on them to spread any good news, just as they will hold back any information which might be detrimental to you.

VIRGO ♍ Because of the critical Virgo nature, you may have difficulty in adjusting to any in-laws born under this sign. No use thinking you can get away with an untidy household if your Virgo mother-in-law is around. She'll express disapproval, although she won't mind trying to help you clear up the chaos. Often she'll be content to spend a visit clearing out closets and drawers. Unfortunately, she'll expect to find the fruits of her labor still in evidence on her next visit, for she's determined to be an example of neatness and isn't merely offering her services. To keep the peace, see that the house is tidy when you expect visits from Virgos.

They will rarely visit relations unless invited. They'll rarely drop in unannounced, generally giving a precise time of arrival and a notice as to when they intend to leave. Don't expect them to express affection in words; they prefer to do something for you. They like every day of their visit to be planned and expect you to keep to the schedule. Spontaneous, alfresco entertaining isn't for them.

They accept children but without too much enthuiasm, always expecting young people to be well-mannered and orderly.

LIBRA ♎︎   Relations born under this sign have great
tact and seem to know intuitively how much or how little
advice they should offer. They have little inclination to dominate the
life of any newlyweds, but will offer advice when asked. If unable to
help, they'll be cooperative and find someone who can. When it comes
to decor or any artistic matter, your Libran relatives can be very helpful
and companionable, taking a personal interest in what you aim to do
but not seeking to superimpose their own personality.

It's difficult to find any reason to quarrel with a Libra in-law, for
they will never become a willing party to domestic differences and generally will disappear quietly until harmony is restored.

Librans take an interest in their grandchildren, often helping with
their education—particularly so if any artistic talent is apparent. Then
they'll give practical assistance to the child in its early days and later
make efforts to find the right instructor.

Your Libran relations prefer to be specifically invited than to have
a "come anytime" invitation. When they do arrive, they expect well-
planned meals and a pleasant visit. If you're in the middle of private
worries, it's better not to bring them out for discussion. Perhaps Libran
relatives prefer to live in a world where they see only harmony and
beauty, but remember that they are quite able to cope with their own
affairs and give you credit for being sensible enough to do so, too.

SCORPIO ♏︎   You can expect your Scorpio relatives to
know more about you than you're aware of. In most cases,
they understand you better than you may understand them. They have a
curious nature, however, and if they feel, intuitively, that you're in trouble, they may arrive on the scene just as you're in the throes of the di-
lemma. It's rarely wise to try to put them off, for they have probing
natures and won't rest until they get to the bottom of the trouble. Never
reject offers of help, for Scorpios are sensitive. Once they know the truth,
you can rely on them to do everything they can, often in the realm of
financial assistance as well as through their own time and energy.

When visiting, they can adapt to whatever life you're leading, even
if used to a totally different style of living themselves. Honesty within
the family circle means a lot to Scorpios, and if you deviate from this
code, you can expect the rough edge of a very sarcastic tongue. The
female of the species is more dangerous than the male in the use of this
weapon.

While Scorpio grandparents enjoy young people in small doses, they're always willing to look after younger children—though they may not suggest it themselves. Unless there's an emergency, they tend to want to be asked to do things.

Scorpios thrive on trouble, so you'll always have a well-steeled ally when you need one. The stubborn trait of Scorpio in-laws is also noticeable and, if a mother-in-law says she'll never come to your house again, you had better believe she really means it. It'll be up to you to make advances of reconciliation. Scorpios can be faithful to relations, but never suffer them just because of blood or marriage ties.

SAGITTARIUS ♐   There are rarely any Sagittarian relations—let alone in-laws—who are selfish or lacking in generosity. Indeed, they're often overeager to help and seem to enjoy carrying the burdens of a second family. If you're a working wife, you can rely on a Sagittarian to offer to look after the children or clean the house. And they rarely expect thanks or material recognition.

They also like to keep abreast of what's happening in the community. If you're looking for a new job, chances are that your Sagittarian relative will know about it and be very quick to tip you off if something is available.

Expect your in-laws to be active and energetic and very tolerant with you, even if you're not so inclined. They'll rarely desert you, even if you've been guilty of some escapade that would normally shock people. There's a friendly companionship about Sagittarians which, if responded to, can make any family happy. They take great interest in children, especially if the little ones are interested in sports, and are equally comfortable and reliable about baby-sitting or looking after family pets while you're away.

CAPRICORN ♑   Never talk against your Capricorn relations, especially if some other member of the family is about, for they cling to their dignity and whatever prestige they may have attained. They'll also like to see you gain recognition in your community. Any form of scandal is abhorrent to them and while they'll be on hand to do what they can, they prefer to do it so that other people aren't aware of it.

They have a compulsion to live long enough to see their children and children-in-law successful and are quick to point out where their own mistakes have prevented them from achieving their own life ambitions.

A Capricorn mother-in-law is interested in running a household and may be a little too forceful in explaining that she knows the best way to cook a dish or in expressing disapproval of food or decor. This disapproval is rarely energetic, but rather given in an obtruse manner which—until you're used to it—may trouble you as appearing sneaky. Just take it for granted that any advice or disapproval isn't offered with any malice, but with a genuine concern for what they consider your best interests.

Your Capricorn in-laws may not appear overly friendly when you first meet. They are wary of new people, and you may have to exert yourself to get to know them. Generally, a Capricorn male relative is very practical and can be relied upon to have the right tools for jobs around the house—and he's quite eager to do them himself.

Neither sex shows a marked enthusiasm for young children. Capricorn in-laws are often happier with children between seven and fourteen than they are with babies.

AQUARIUS ♒   So many Aquarian relatives are interested in the world at large that it may be difficult for members of their family to get close to them or even to be on visiting terms. They are not very "relative-conscious," often stating that they can choose their friends but have to put up with their relations—a remark not guaranteed to inspire a new daughter-in-law to go to her in-laws for advice or even to try to become acquainted.

Being firm believers in independence, your Aquarian in-laws will strive to maintain their own independence and leave you free to do the same. Once a chick is out of the nest, their attitude is that it learns to fly and, if it makes mistakes, it should profit from them. In times of stress, little sympathy or practical help can be expected from Aquarian in-laws. They'll treat you as responsible adults and expect you to live up to this. A relationship with Aquarian in-laws is based more on friendship than on family ties and, unless you can accept this, you may find your family drifting apart. Once a friendship has developed it's usually based on worldly discussions, and rarely relates to family or domestic matters.

The birth of young children makes a difference to Aquarians who generally like to discuss future educational plans and prospects even before the child is out of diapers.

PISCES ♓ Your Piscean relatives will genuinely want to like you and will try to to establish a harmonious relationship almost on sight. Beware of trying to get them involved in family controversies though—most Piscean relations come visiting hoping to find peace and harmony. Some may need this because of their own difficulties. Though no one can lend a more sympathetic ear than a Piscean, they'll rarely want a long list of your troubles immediately on arrival.

Piscean in-laws are alternately gregarious—seemingly wanting to visit you and be visited—and moody, during which times you may not hear from them for months. This period of retirement is necessary to them and can also be helpful to you—the not-too-frequent-visits being something to look forward to. They're apt to spoil children because they need to show affection in a positive manner. There's nothing obtruse about a Piscean who expresses his likes and dislikes.

Your Piscean relations can be unpredictable in their own life and so are very much in tune with you when you don't conform to social conventions. They believe very deeply that everyone has a right to do "their thing"—providing it doesn't hurt anyone else.

Short cuts to making friends with:

ARIES   Praise him.
TAURUS   Trust him.
GEMINI   Keep pace with him.
CANCER   Indulge him.
LEO   Let him talk.
VIRGO   Be reasonable.
LIBRA   Supply his incentive.
SCORPIO   Don't ask questions.
SAGITTARIUS Accept all offers of help.

CAPRICORN   Don't try to talk him out of moods, leave him alone at such times.

AQUARIUS   Cooperate.

PISCES   Be kind and sympathetic.

9
ZODIAC
SHOPPING
GUIDE

ARIES ♈ Shopping for everyday things often bores you. You tend to be impatient with sales people, forgetting they may be limp already from several dozen customers as impatient as you. You enjoy being served by anyone who's bright and enthusiastic, and while you rarely need help in making up your mind, you appreciate a chance to talk about your purchases while still getting quick service. Efficient packaging and goods delivered on time also please you.

When repairmen come to your house, you tend to tie them up in conversation. Being one of the world's most voluble talkers, you forget that their time is likely to cost you money. To keep the bill down, either learn to do small repairs yourself or keep your conversation and advice down to a minimum.

TAURUS ♉   One of the most determined shoppers of the zodiac, you rarely go out without knowing exactly what you intend to buy. You're prepared to continue your search if necessary and no amount of sales talk can persuade you to settle for a substitute. You're an unusually amiable shopper and get along well with bank tellers and liquor salesmen. In fact, such associations started on a business basis often develop into friendships. While you're shopping, remember that working people's time is valuable, so cut down on any small conversation.

When you have a complaint, try to be discreet about it. Be sure you're talking to a person who's able to rectify the problem. Try to keep your temper under control.

Many of you can be quite handy around the house and save money by doing repairs yourselves. Be sure you know what you're doing and aren't motivated merely by thrift. Sometimes, in the long run, do-it-yourself jobs can be more expensive than calling in a professional handyman. You expect prompt service, so call early in the day to allow the workman to schedule his time.

GEMINI ♊   You enjoy browsing leisurely through stores and can window-shop happily without buying anything. This can irritate shopkeepers unless you buy something, even a small item. Yet you get along very well with sales people because you're generally pleasant. You can get very conversational, but try to remember that you're on the floor of a shop, not in a public forum.

When you *do* have a specific shopping goal, figure out in advance what size and color you want so that you won't have to return the merchandise. You don't like spending time on repairs for your own car or house, so make it a painless experience when it becomes necessary. Try writing down exactly what you think needs to be done, check with the service, and be at home when the serviceman arrives. You should try to make a supreme effort to keep appointments with professional people.

CANCER ♋   You're always interested in people, including those who help you, serve you, or sell you goods; and often you get on friendly terms with them. Be careful not to probe their private lives too much, although you can of course lend a sympathetic ear. Although shopping's one of your major joys, your nature is so changeable that you're not always satisfied with your purchases when you get home. When you have to exchange goods, use your Cancerian charm and admit that you made a mistake. Many women of your sign hate to admit they've grown plumper and insist on a size 12 when they honestly might settle for a 14. You can be very hospitable to visiting repairmen, offering them coffee and conversation, but do let them get on with their work.

LEO ♌   You're one of the few customers who really appeal to salesmen, for you're a lavish buyer and never want to bother comparing prices. You like to feel you're receiving special treatment from the sales people and will try to shop mostly in specialized boutiques. However, you may lose your temper if you don't feel you're getting proper attention. Take pains to be patient, especially with your bank teller. It's not her fault if you've overdrawn your account because of your expensive tastes. Organize your finances so you can pay your bills promptly and keep on good terms with the people who serve you. You may be too trusting when you need the services of a repairman, so ask for an estimate before he starts work. This will save time and energy and possibly avoid arguing about the bill later on.

VIRGO ♍   As a member of the sign whose greatest trait is service, it would seem logical that you'd understand the trials of those whose livelihood depends on selling their goods and services. But your desire for perfection keeps you from compromising. If your favorite brand of cigarettes or hose isn't available, you can adopt a very pained, accusing attitude implying that the sales people are at fault. A great bargain hunter, you can become very irritated if your plans to buy a piece of Waterford glass at a five-and-ten-cent-store price are thwarted. Because of your high standards, you're not at ease with repairmen, and generally mistrust anyone who's able to do something you can't or don't understand. You need to accept that you need such people. A cheerful face and pleasant attitude will get you the best results, and also make people more eager to wait on you.

LIBRA ♎   With your temperament keyed to artistic and pleasant things, shopping can be irksome unless you shop at quiet times. The rush and tumble of crowds so upsets you and you're likely to be drawn towards more exclusive shops where the staff has more time to give you the service you appreciate. Such salesmen often talk about themselves, and you may have to learn to be courteous and seemingly attentive.

It's not easy for you to cope with repairmen; in fact, you're inclined to treat them with some degree of arrogance. Make things easier for everyone by stating what you want done, get estimates, and don't mind if you get some extensive advice.

SCORPIO ♏   You're excellent shoppers. Difficult though it may be, you usually find what you want because —apart from household shopping—you can think up weird ways to get the things you are after—even things out of fashion.

You tend to get grocery and other basic shopping out of the way with one huge expedition, after which you feel free for pleasure shopping. Sometimes you're aggressive if shopkeepers are slow or don't have what you want—this can be especially noticeable when you're in the beauty shop and expect a certain hairdresser. Try to relax and get all the pleasure you can out of any shopping expedition. Also, plan your time so that you don't dash into shops just as they're closing. Most sales people want to please the customer, but they, too, become tired at the end of the day and may have long trips home ahead of them.

When you call in a repairman, remember that you asked for his services. There's no reason to be irritable to him because you blew a gasket on the car or the television picture tube burned out.

SAGITTARIUS ♐   Your natural curiosity makes shopping an adventure for you. You're never a dull customer, often telling jokes to sales people. You always like to have some conversation going on while considering what to buy. Many staff members enjoy this, but be careful to keep away from controversial subjects, such as religion and politics, since it's often difficult for them to express their honest opinion when there's an employer listening. It's no use berating one political party when the salesman is afraid to offer a valid rebuttal.

Repairmen often appreciate your happy-go-lucky attitude towards their work, but be careful not to be too trusting. Check whatever work's been done and be sure to get estimates before assigning the job. Pay the bills on time, if you expect good service in the future.

CAPRICORN ♑

You need to lead such a well-ordered life that your shopping simply has to be planned in advance. You're never very eager to shop unless absolutely necessary. You like stores that are efficiently run, up to the high standards you expect, and where you can find everything with a minimum of effort. Although always courteous, you may sometimes appear arrogant, rarely able to show warmth to people offering you goods and services.

Although you're handy around the house, occasionally you'll be forced to call in a workman. Don't be disturbed if he isn't as tidy as you or even if he arrives late. Be patient and try to understand these small and momentary inconveniences.

AQUARIUS ♒

Not naturally a happy shopper, it's sometimes better for you to consider buying by mail or phone. In person, you tend to be upset by small irritations. When forced to shop, your natural concern for humanity should extend itself to the individual serving you. Be patient. Keep calm. Don't lose you temper. Remember that sometimes you may be talking to a sales clerk who's going through his own nervous moments. You prefer small, specialty shops to department stores. In order to get something quickly, you may put too much faith in a salesman's recommendation, for you're apt to forget brand names. Sometimes you get a sales pitch thrown at you, so don't be surprised if what you took to be literally true was a slight exaggeration. When you need a repairman, realize that you can't know and do everything yourself despite your inclination to be independent. Repairmen can be useful if only to cut down on your household worries, so let them do the job. Always check to be sure you're getting the right man. Hire your repairmen on a friend's recommendation and you'll be much more confident and happy.

PISCES ♓   You're a facile and happy shopper, but
sometimes have trouble making your own decisions and trust
others' recommendations a bit too much. Be friendly but firm; make up
your mind. Then you'll have only yourself to blame for any mistakes.
While you can't help but use your charm when shopping, try not to become so friendly that every excursion turns into a human drama with
sales clerks crying on your shoulder. It's important to keep your mind
on what you really want to buy, since you can easily be sidetracked. Keep
necessity purchases separate from pleasure shopping.

You may be emergency-prone and, since you aren't naturally handy
at repairs, keep a list of repairmen's names and phone numbers handy.
Then you'll be less harassed and bewildered when an emergency occurs.

10

INVESTING
BY THE
STARS

ARIES ♈   Being naturally impatient, you're drawn
compulsively towards speculative types of investments. For
every dramatic coup you're able to bring off, it's likely that at the end
of the year you'll be lucky to come out even.

If you can resist the temptation to gamble or borrow against future
earnings, your excellent mind may lead you to beneficial investments.
Unfortunately, if you come into contact with friends with get-rich-quick
schemes on the stock market, you're easily tempted. Rather than run risks
with unstable fast-risers, you'd be better off curbing this impulsiveness
and seeking advice from professionals about slow-growing stocks with
dividends.

Also, try to keep calm when funds get low; you're apt to panic at
the first sign of bad luck, fearing you'll have no money. Yet from past

117

experiences, you should know that you can weather such tempests in a teacup very effectively. Nothing seems to calm you down and make you think as when you're short of money. Don't rush to the bank to withdraw funds. Use loan services or cash stocks to meet any pseudo-crises that probably aren't as bad as you imagine. With Mars as your ruling planet, your best investments are likely to come from hard metals, but you'll rarely be lucky with a gold mine.

TAURUS ♉   Because you have a respect for money and realize it's a necessary evil, you're one of the most fortunate signs of the zodiac. The basic respect for money makes you prudent in handling it. You're not likely to be tempted by get-rich-quick schemes. You may be overly cautious at times, but better this than being reckless. Impulsive buying usually succeeds only when there's no real pressure to make money.

Your first thought is to live within your income before trying to expand it. It's a fine idea to keep this in mind and only borrow money for investment after much thought. Many bond issues satisfy your desire to dabble in the stock market, and you'll get just as much satisfaction from a steady 7 percent on your outlay.

With a reasonably stable bank balance to cover your overhead and allow for investment, you're likely to make as much money investing in real estate as on the stock market. Being an earth sign, the idea of owning your own acre appeals to you and is often the reason you buy stocks and shares.

GEMINI ♊   Once you can realize that great oaks grow from little acorns, you stand a chance of being fortunate in investments. You're always conscious of money as the means of getting many of the luxuries you enjoy, but don't jeopardize the luxuries you already have. The stock market seems to attract your basic urge to gamble as much as the desire to gain great profits from it.

Even before you invest, study your income and budget. If there's a great gap in these, forget the investments until you've managed to save just a tiny nest egg. If you receive any "easy money," such as an inheritance, curb your gambling instincts first, even if it's a considerable sum. When investing large sums of money, it's often a short cut to success to get the advice of an expert. With small sums, in your case, it's better to follow your intuition than to take advice from friends who probably know less than you do. Besides, when you discuss money with friends, you're apt to become emotionally involved. It's better to be detached when considering financial investments. Your most spectacular success could come with any stocks and shares connected with movement —such as airlines, communications, radio, and TV.

Many members of your sign in this later half of the twentieth century are obtaining good financial returns from investments in electronics. Another sound investment, compatible with your ruling planet of Mercury, is with any company specializing in paper products, from stationery to publishing.

CANCER ♋   In your financial affairs you're so often saved from what could be drastic mistakes by a rare type of intuition. If anyone is capable of withdrawing from the brink of financial disaster, it's you. This streak of good fortune works in another way as well. You're quite likely to make a blind investment due to the capriciousness of the moon, and then surprise the professionals by making a financial coup.

This isn't something you should rely on, however. If you could combine your intuition with a study of the stock market and time your investments, you can produce a steady increase in your income. However, you tend to procrastinate and can easily be diverted from your original plans by other people's wild ideas. If an idea is different to the point of being wildcat, it arouses your inherent curiosity.

You can obtain good returns from oil, the wine and spirit industry, or any investments concerning the ocean.

LEO ♌   You're always so impressed by other people's way of life that if you're mixing with people who are persistently making investments, some of their enthusiasm passes on to you. Unfortunately, they don't always pass their knowledge on to you and rarely tell you about the mistakes they've made, so it's easy to see investing and the manipulation of money as more glamorous than it really is.

No one can enjoy money more than you, but the desire to make money quickly can often sabotage the things you already have. If you're fortunate enough to have a good income and are relieved from financial pressure, you're likely to prosper with investments. But if you already have financial worries, your good judgment becomes impaired.

In the past few years, Saturn has taught many of you a lesson which should encourage you to be prudent with the money you've managed to save. Consider well before making investments and always seek professional advice. In the excitement of hearing that certain stocks and shares have made rapid growth, you may forget that there are such things as brokerage fees to be taken into account.

Real estate and stocks involved in automation of all types could be your best financial speculations.

VIRGO ♍   You're one of the most careful people of the zodiac. One of the easiest ways for you to be happy is to feel financially secure. Where some signs are impulsive and invest without a second thought, you may take so long to make up your mind that you miss out on the best market trends. It's just as much a fault to be over-cautious as it is to be reckless, for there's a time for standing still and a time to move. Once you can find the happy medium between these, you can be one of the luckiest investors.

You have the ability to analyze the financial status of the market, study its trends, and make meticulous notes of the rise and fall of stocks and shares. The future, from 1970 onwards, is going to be much better for members of your sign making investments, large or small, and you should take advantage of the beneficial influence of Jupiter in your sign. Mercury, your ruling planet, aids your intellect; Jupiter can use the intellect to advantage.

Not only can members of your sign make fortunes by judicial investments, but opportunities open up to use money in many exciting ways without threatening your need for security. Long-term investments, such as planning a personal business venture, are likely to appeal in the next few years, putting stocks and shares into the background. This could be profitable, especially for personal business ventures involved with paper.

LIBRA ♎   You frequently have to make major adjustments in your financial status as money has a see-saw effect on your life. This is brought about by your natural inclination towards personal luxuries and lack of thought of the future.

When it comes to making investments, you have to learn to be much more self-sufficient, relying on your own good sense, rather than the advice of well-meaning friends. Your way of life, however, may take you among financiers. You may be able to profit from any tips they pass on.

In the past few years, you've been under the influence of Neptune, luring you into investments, then turning treacherous, causing you to suffer monetary and emotional disappointments. Now your ruling planet of Venus counteracts this illusionary influence. Those of you who wish to expand financial activities will find the path much less fraught with dangers. Save and invest whatever you can until 1972. But limit yourself to businesses dealing with beauty or art. Things like hairdressing, the world of design, or personal areas of creativity, will be more advantageous in the long run than speculation on the stock market. So leave Wall Street to financiers who are more used to it.

SCORPIO ♏︎   Because Saturn, the trouble-making planet, stirred up mischief with your health the last few years, you find yourself somewhat fearful of adventuring into financial affairs. You hate failure of any kind and the ephemeral quality of the stock exchange doesn't seem as tantalizing and glamorous as it does to so many people.

When certain planetary patterns are right, such as Jupiter taking over from the grim aspects of Saturn, you find yourself delighted to come out on the credit side of any business deal. You're always likely to maintain one or two modest investments which offer small but regular dividends, and then be content with a dramatic plunge every few years. Investments in household equipment stocks may not sound exciting, but you could do very well in such financial ventures, where steady returns leave you free to find adventure in other spheres.

SAGITTARIUS ♐︎   Since 1967, many of you have found a lessening of the burden which you've been forced to bear for many years. This represents a major change in your life and also affects your financial situation—to your advantage. With a little more money available, it becomes easier to let your gambling instincts carry you along in a modest way. Spending money without wondering where the next few dollars come from is a form of freedom which you haven't experienced for so long that buying a few stocks and shares is yet another experience to be added to your book of life.

You will, of course, give some thought to your investments but as you're in a fortunate cycle for making money, the speculative type of stock won't represent too many dangers for you. Be prudent enough to see that you always have some money in your savings account—perhaps spending half at once on investments and not touching the rest until you see how your investments are going.

Your best investments will be made in imported commodities—also in travel agencies, especially if you have a personal interest in one. All transport stock interests you, but it's better for members of your sign to stay away from airline shares. Local ventures generally prove disappointing unless you have a personal share in them.

CAPRICORN ♑   With Saturn, your ruling planet, constantly setting up obstacles, your chances of success rest with how well you've learned lessons from the past and how well you can survive difficulties and turn bad events into good ones.

Throughout your life you have many opportunities to assess your financial situation. Sometimes you miss good chances by being over-cautious. For this reason, when you have money to invest, you're more likely to buy blue chip stocks or bonds, yielding small but regular dividends. Even with Saturn creating difficulties, few of you miss having opportunity knock at your door during your lifetime. But you have to learn when to open the door and go along with the opportunity.

Only you can release yourself from inward fears. It's never good policy to invest money unless you feel justified in being optimistic. If withdrawing savings sets up inner emotional difficulties, leave your money in a savings account rather than speculate. Sometimes your best venture with money is in a partnership—as help from someone else gives you confidence. Stocks and shares involving transport engineering communications—such as a telephone system—generally cause you less pain than other investments.

AQUARIUS ♒   Many of you lead an exciting enough life, but as each year ends you find yourself wondering why you've worked so hard and still have such a small bank balance. You're not the most fortunate of investors, as you can be carried away by spend-

ing money on the products of your own inventive mind. It's a sad thing
that so many of the world's greatest inventions have been made by members of your sign with others making money from them.

Personal involvement with work is perhaps reward enough and,
in the long run, probably achieves more than small flutters on the stock
market. Yet when certain planetary patterns are right (such as Jupiter
rising towards your midheaven to join your ruling planet Uranus)
new cycles can influence your financial situation and make life more
interesting as your bank balance grows. Personal partnerships in business, where you can keep an eye on your interests, are likely to be more
successful than stocks and shares.

The only beneficial land investment is usually your own house as
it can make you feel independent. This is a major form of happiness to
you. Sometimes many of you extend this idea into buying two houses—
one to live in and one to rent. This appeals to your logical mind but, in
practice, it's rarely a success and can often produce another financial
hardship.

Small investments in electronics, made at the right time, can be
beneficial.

PISCES ♓   You're no stranger to financial setbacks
and generally manage to accept such things with a remarkably philosophic attitude. With your full life, you can always rationalize
and count your blessings, even if you can't count your dollars.

Jupiter, your joint ruling planet, offsets the ups and downs which
Neptune inflicts on you. When you're forced to see that money is a
necessary evil—even to a creative person—you pass the turning point
and can begin to study such things as investments. Most of you work
by intuition with stocks and shares—even buying a stock for no better
reason than the fact that you like its name. Professionals are amazed
when you score a bull's eye. There's a certain childlike quality in the
way you can dabble in business and literally get away with it on the
credit side.

Many of you do have psychic instincts that seem to alert you to
dangerous investments, and this saves the day. It doesn't pay to push
your good fortune too far, however. You need to think constructively,
working out such things as your yearly income, setting aside a specific
sum for investment, and not being tempted to gamble with housekeeping money. Several small ventures are more likely to appeal to you than

one grandiose splash on the stock market—unless you have a very good income. You enjoy the adventure as much as the end product, even though your optimism sees investments translated into increased dollars. Stocks in travel or those concerned with liquids often yield the best results for you.

11
Gift
Giving
and
Receiving

ARIES ♈   You love the unusual so much that receiving a prosaic present showing little imagination on the part of the buyer can reduce you to expressing the smallest of polite thanks and little enthusiasm for using the gift. However, such things as a set of road maps with a built-in transistor light for easier nighttime driving, or a clock with unusual mechanism will appeal to you. You like gifts associated with movement. Anything for the car, sports, or of a mechanical nature, such as clocks or kitchen gadgetry, is likely to be well received.

When giving presents, you, too, can be guilty of not taking your friends' tastes into consideration. You often forget dates, such as birthdays, and rush around shopping at the last moment. Plan your present-giving even if it means shopping long before the official date. This will save you time and energy and generally result in selecting a gift most suited to the person receiving it.

TAURUS ♉   Your practical mind expresses itself when buying gifts and you generally have a happy knack of knowing just what your friend may need. If it's practical as well as attractive, you'll be delighted. Your giving-away tastes run to such things as pretty pieces of glass, sets of drinking glasses, table napkins. As you grow older, you can become forgetful and may give a constant succession of glasses to the same friends year after year.

You like to receive any type of leather goods, especially handmade bags, tooled leather desk equipment. Female Taureans can be delighted with handmade jewelry. If your friends ever wonder what to buy you, a well-stocked food hamper or a gift-wrapped package of table wine or liquor will be happily received.

Trivial gifts never appeal to you for giving or receiving. You'd rather receive one gift a year—something you really want and can enjoy for a long time—than lots of trivial presents for every occasion on the calendar. It's not unusual for you to combine birthdays in your own family (should they be near a holiday, such as Christmas) into one splendid present. But you must take into account the kind of person you're giving this double present to. Children, for instance, hate to have two occasions combined into one present.

GEMINI ♊   You have a natural tendency to buy lots of small gifts. You can never quite make up your mind what to choose and so settle for several presents at once. Even when packing gifts, you're apt to slip some extra goody into it rather than face up to making a decision. You often pick up gifts round-the-year—especially jewelry—to give at a later date. And you like to receive up-to-the-minute gifts. If psychedelic jewelry is in, that's what you collect. The trouble with your buying presents well in advance is that you may forget where you've put them and have to search for your cache or end up giving your present late.

You're always delighted with small gifts at any time of the year whether they are for a special day or not—books, jewelry, theater tickets —and you also appreciate a well-wrapped present. The gift-wrapping evokes just as much pleasure as the thrill of opening it and finding a surprise.

The art of giving you a present is, indeed, to give you a surprise, and any husband who asks his Gemini wife what she wants is likely to get some black looks. Make it a surprise, or forget it, if you're to have ultimate enjoyment from it. This element of surprise is carried out in your own giving, and you take a childlike pleasure in other people's enthusiasm for what you have given them.

CANCER ♋ Cancer women are easier to find presents for than are Cancer men, but both love to give presents. You like to receive very feminine things, like perfume, bath essences, jewelry, as well as lingerie, yards of Italian silk or other luxurious material. After-shave lotion, cuff links and tie clips always appeal to the male Cancerian.

When giving presents, you're often motivated more by what you like yourself than what you think the recipient would like and this can lead to some moments of disappointment. You like your gifts to be appreciated because you're also appreciative of anything given to you. Try to buy presents after reviewing the likes and dislikes of your friends.

You really enjoy giving presents, not only to members of the family or close friends. Perhaps that's why your generous nature sometimes makes mistakes about the tastes of others.

Cancer men love personalized gifts—monogrammed handkerchiefs and expensive-looking ties—but care should be taken in going beyond accessories. He will definitely prefer buying his own shirts and socks.

LEO ♌ Big packages intrigue the larger-than-life children of the sun. You'll spend a long time making up packages or having them gift-wrapped and you like your gifts treated the same.

You're an impulse-buyer, rather than a thoughtful one, but also very generous. When you like someone a lot, you rarely consider how much you want to spend on a gift. You find something you like and then try to forget how much its costs. It's essential to you to give gifts not easily forgotten as you like to impress your friends. Because of this, any gifts you give must look expensive even if they've been picked up as a bargain. Yards of rich material, costume jewelry, matching sets of monogrammed towels, will always appeal to you. The male Leo also likes jewelry and something that seems to have been designed for him. It's safe to buy replicas of lions or anything with a lion motif for either sex.

VIRGO ♍   You're not the most generous of people when it comes to giving presents. But when you buy anything for a friend, it'll be in good taste, bought after careful deliberation as to the friend's needs. You're the recipient of many books and prefer them to personal presents such as clothes—especially if you are male—because you have very definite, conservative tastes. If you decide early in life that you prefer grey suits or pale blue or white shirts, it's no use for a friend to give you a mad pattern or a mod style shirt. You'll put it away and deliberately forget to wear it.

The safest present to give both sexes born under this sign is a gift certificate with which the recipient can buy something to his own taste. You are apt to buy gift certificates yourself, often feeling that present hunting takes up time you'd prefer spending otherwise. You're always conscious of birthdates but don't really get hurt if someone forgets yours.

LIBRA ♎   The female members of this sign enjoy presents which are beautiful or made for attaining beauty, so all types of cosmetics or a gift certificate for a special beauty treatment will be gratefully received. Pretty bric-a-brac appeals to both sexes, also antique jewelery.

You're meticulous gift-buyers yourselves, buying what you feel will be exactly right. You can slip up if your friends tastes are very practical, as you enjoy buying pretty things as well as receiving them. You take time to pack your presents in an attractive manner and choose sentimental birthday and Christmas cards rather than the modern fun-cards.

Should a friend forget your birthday, you can become very hurt although you may not show it. But you rarely take anyone off your Christmas card list if they don't send you a card, perhaps being wise enough to reason that there must be a good reason for it.

SCORPIO ♏ You're not easy to please because of a complexity in which sensitivity and the need for dramatic impact come in conflict with each other. You like to feel that a present was chosen exclusively for you and can get upset if you feel that your friend didn't spend lots of time looking for it. You also like a present to be noticed by friends, for there's not much of the shrinking violet technique in your approach to life.

You like gifts that last a long time and are constant reminders of friendship, just as you like to have a love affair in which your partner reiterates his love.

Male Scorpios love to receive science fiction books or very personal gifts of clothing or things for the house. Female Scorpios enjoy fine pieces of glass, bottles of wine or exotic dinners added to the present. Also gifts that last as reminders of a happy occasion. I once knew a Scorpio girl who ended up with a large collection of stuffed animals because, in her childhood, her happiest present had been a fine stuffed poodle. She associated the childhood poodle with love and so, every time she had another stuffed animal, the feeling of well-being was with her again.

You like to make present-giving a big production number with beautiful packages and the air of an occasion to be remembered. Dinner, or perhaps a visit to the theater, can be as much a part of present-giving as the actual gift.

SAGITTARIUS ♐ You're generally so sports-loving that it's very easy for your friends to give you something you need as well as desire. If you play golf, there are numerous gifts ranging from spare clubs, sets of balls, to subscriptions to clubs or gift certificates for so many rounds. The same principles apply to most sports. Male Sagittarians love heavy knit Irish sweaters or sweaters knit by any girl friend or wife who has the patience to make one. It's safe to repeat the same present to many Sagittarians as you have a habit of mislaying or losing such things as key rings, powder compacts or gloves. You're quite easy to buy for and the list of gifts suitable for you is endless.

The trouble comes when you buy gifts for others because it's hard for you to know what your friend may really enjoy. If they're inclined to sports, it's no problem. But many of the male Sagittarians have wives who are golf widows and abhor sports. Try to consider the wife or girl friend as an individual, not as a reflection of your own likes and dislikes. There are few wives who can get enthusiastic about handmade fishing supplies; they'd probably prefer two dozen pairs of fish net hose.

You can be very generous but not entirely thoughtful. This can make you feel hurt if your gift doesn't fill the recipient with obvious joy. So take time when a birthday looms on the horizon. Consider the individual for whom you're shopping.

CAPRICORN ♑   As an earth sign, you're practical and gifts should be bought with this in mind. There's always a need for replacements in the house so things like towels, linens, drinking glasses are welcome. The male Capricorn also appreciates things useful in his professional life—desk sets, a new brief case, anything for his car, books, magazine subscriptions.

Capricorn women are as happy with a present for the house as they are with a truly personal present. It's often difficult to choose very feminine gifts for them as they dress conservatively using little jewelry or perfume, and are inclined to keep such presents for a "special occasion" which doesn't always come. Consequently, presents may lie for years unused.

You're meticulous in giving presents on the right occasion but like to make a little money go a long way. You shop well in advance, spending time choosing the right present at the price you can afford.

AQUARIUS ♒   Most of your close friends will understand that you love antiques and bric-a-brac so it's inevitable that you'll get gifts eminently suited to your taste. Trouble starts if less interested friends give you a reproduction. This offends you and makes you quite ungracious in accepting it. In fact, if your tastes lies in collecting genuine items, a reproduction can almost produce trauma in you and take the pleasure from the gift.

You choose your friends' gifts very carefully but should be careful that your own good taste for things of the past doesn't take over. If you have a young daughter or son, they may like a psychedelic butterfly or something which actually offends your tastes, but pleases them. However, you're rational enough to know that it's better to give presents which please the recipient than those which you'd like for yourself.

You're always receptive to gifts of books, magazine subscriptions or even tickets to club activities.

PISCES ♓   Nearly all members of your sign enjoy traveling, professionally or for vacations. So, a present of lightweight luggage, folding slippers, cosmetics, bags, train cases, writing sets will be practical as well as pleasurable. If you're female, you enjoy luxuries you may not be able to buy for yourself—expensive perfume, extra jewelery, or household luxuries such as table lamps, cut glass dishes. Male Pisceans love anything having a foreign flavor— wines, foods or craftsmanship from some exotic island—perhaps imported Italian silk ties. Pisceans value the time spent finding "the right gift" as much or more than a gift's price tag.

You're the most generous yourself, often not waiting for a special occasion to buy a gift. You enjoy giving friends anything they admire around the house, providing you're sure it will be loved and literally have a good home. You enjoy collecting things having a romantic connotation and when you give anything away from your personal collection, it's generally a sign of real affection. Hopefully, your friends will appreciate this trait in you as much as you love giving to them.

You always remember birthdays and special days but are sometimes disappointed when people don't return this thoughtfulness to you. At the same time, you aren't the bartering type and rarely expect presents.

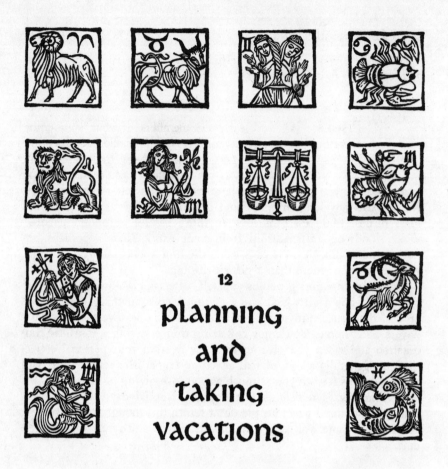

12

planning
and
taking
vacations

ARIES ♈ You're so gregarious that you don't mind
living in a densely populated area, although sometimes you
may feel frustrated by the slowness of traveling by car, subway, or bus
from your home or place of work. Yet given the chance to get away
from it all, even at vacation time, you're likely to choose a place where
you'll still be under pressure from people.

Logically, your best vacation place should be one which can provide a contrast to your normal way of life, with the idea of W. B. Yeats'
poem, "peace coming dropping slow." There's no real desire in you to
go to a romantic Isle of Innesfree, such as Yeats wrote about—you'd
fear boredom. You like to take a great deal of your own things along,
probably traveling by car. In no time at all, you'll discover best restaurants and night clubs.

132

At home, you cram as much into a day as possible—moving at frenetic haste from home to work to cocktail parties and back to your base—leaving little enough time to restore your Mars-driven energies with sleep.

Vacation time certainly doesn't mean extra rest. You try to pack in as many exciting things as possible, as if trying to make up for time you've spent at work. Generally, you succeed in doing this, but you shouldn't wonder that, after a vacation, you get a let-down feeling—nature's way of telling you to rest and relax. After vacationing, it's often too late, because there are so many things to catch up with. You're forever gathering momentum, re-energizing yourself, until a major illness forces you to be quiet.

You may find that a peaceful vacation need not be dull. You've never had a quiet vacation before and the newness of it will create its own interest. If you live in New York, it might be a daring adventure *not* to go to Miami in season this year. You can afford to give one vacation period to something different and may be very surprised to find that a remote mountain village can offer enough excitement to make you want to explore.

Planning expeditions for yourself and the family can also be challenging. And remember, a complete change of scene can benefit your health instead of constantly seeking masses of humanity. Your normal type of holiday can really be hard work. Let some of the Mars energy and curiosity take you to strange, remote places. Give yourself a chance to discover different ways of life. Think what a conversation piece you can make out of your new approach to a holiday, too!

TAURUS ♉   Many of you are fortunate enough to take two vacations during the year, even if one may be a combination of business and pleasure. You look forward to your official vacations as periods when you can be relieved of personal and business tensions.

Since water has a therapeutic value in releasing tensions, you often get the best out of a vacation taking you to a tropical island in the Pacific or the Caribbean. The same relief from tension comes from taking one of the many cruises offered by travel agencies, especially if you spend a lot of the year in a business.

A cruise can also be the answer to the housewife who, although devoted to family life, sometimes feels it would be wonderful to have meals cooked. Get free of planning. Let someone else worry about the washing up and don't feel guilty sitting around on deck, lazily enjoying the sunshine. This type of holiday leaves you pleasantly relaxed and you can cheerfully return home to tackle household chores or business ventures with renewed vigor.

Many of you like holidays with all the family along. This is fine when children are young. But when they become teenagers, there can be so many conflicts, that it's best to have at least one short vacation a year on your own. Try not to take worries with you, even though when you return you may have to face an untidy household. Youngsters will enjoy the experiment of keeping house for themselves. It's not too high a price to pay if you return from a vacation feeling rejuvenated.

There's also the temptation to vacation with business friends, believing that perhaps a business deal can be resolved better this way. This rarely happens, and should only be considered if you're able to take another vacation later on by yourselves.

You're rather conservative in so many ways that there's a likelihood that once you've found a satisfactory holiday place, you'll go back to the same place year after year. This again is fine if you can have two vacations. But try to be adventurous enough to explore at least one different place periodically.

As housewives, you're quite capable of saving thriftily for the family holiday. This is fine, too, but sometimes spending a little more than you've budgeted for can be advantageous if it takes you to new places. The length of holiday is not so important to you as the quality —you expect to feel better after being away from home, and that's your criteria of how good a holiday has been.

GEMINI II   You're one of the dreamers of the horoscope when it comes to taking vacations, imagining some very special holiday where everything's perfect. Perhaps the intangibility of this type of holiday has a charm of its own and sustains you throughout the year even if it doesn't truly materialize. However, when the time comes to have your special dream holiday, accept it without trying to find any imperfections, and make the best of every minute.

You're so apt to plan a vacation and then change plans at a moment's notice. Perhaps you've bypassed some perfect vacations just as you bypass some of the problems of life. Mercury induces you to be changeable, but remember that if you're taking a vacation with other people, your changeability can affect their lives also. You're more inclined to a touring vacation as this never gives you the chance to be bored. Frequently, however, it never gives you enough time to absorb either the country you're passing through or the people you meet. If the tour is under your own control—such as one in which you're driving—try to linger even half a day longer in any place which excites you. You may be surprised at the result. It could turn out to be a place which compels you to return at a later date and could even be part of your dream vacation.

Whenever possible you have a tendency to spend vacations in a country or state outside the one you were born in. Romantic places have a great appeal, but sometimes the advertising doesn't live up to your expectations, and so you move on. A Continental holiday has a compulsion about it at some period in your life. You can combine an exciting period of sight-seeing with some cultural interest. You're sure to like music, and so a visit to one of the great European music festivals can be an inspiring holiday. You're not likely to want to rest, but if you can link a holiday to any of the creative interests which appeal to you, there's a chance you may be able to rest physically—even though your mind can still go spinning along.

You're rarely happy vacationing on your own. But you're gregarious enough to find interesting companions all along the holiday route. Try not to get romantically involved, though this is difficult for you. If you indulge in a holiday romance, you're capable of forgetting it. But chance acquaintances have a habit of reappearing at inconvenient times in your life.

You have a tremendous capacity for enjoying leisure time even though you can spin like a top. Boredom is never likely to creep up on you because you like the idea that variety is the spice of life. For you, it is indeed. But have you ever considered that it could be a variation to deliberately take a vacation which doesn't simply offer you excitement? There can be fun in making your own excitement!

CANCER ♋ Although you like to travel, there are many years when you're quite happy to holiday at home, leaving the house each day but returning to sleep in your own familiar room. Providing you can do this without making it into a major operation, you can benefit as much as from a long vacation involving planes, and advance planning.

The greatest snag in your one-day vacations is that you're apt to take a lot of time to get the show on the road. You may find half the day gone before finally making a start and then wonder why you couldn't get in all the sight-seeing you'd planned. You like to be with people, and even your day excursions can include asking a neighbor to join you. But do try to choose someone who's compatible so there's harmony in the adventure. Plan a time for starting and stick to it, impressing it on your friend to do the same. Think about where you'll eat. If you're having a picnic lunch, make a list of essentials the night before, but don't try to take everything but the kitchen stove with you. It's one thing to remember the salt, but don't pack *everything* you think you might need but can actually manage without.

Most of your vacations—either from the house or involving a journey—can be spoiled by lack of planning. If you can't do it yourself, have other members of your family responsible for tickets, baggage, and so on. If you travel by car, remember to have it serviced before leaving and be sure that maps are in the car.

If you're staying at a hotel, remember it's, indeed, a hotel and not your home. Some things won't be quite as you like, but there's no point making a big issue about small irritations. Many of the members of your sign, while enjoying traveling, can only do so under near-perfect conditions. When there's a departure from normal procedure, due to your own carelessness or things beyond your control, you can become emotional. This can be trying on your companions, even members of your own family. Your most restful and beneficial holidays will always be somewhere near water or at least places with romantic backgrounds. You're not exactly the fearless, intrepid tourist, so avoid places where you're expected to be frightfully energetic. Relaxation is necessary to you and there's little need to prove that you're the safari type when you're under the feminine influence of the moon.

LEO ♌   As children of the sun, many of you try to extend the summer. If you live in climate that has a distinct contrast of seasons, you like to go to a warm sunny spot for a late fall or winter vacation. You're capable of planning this type of vacation, but you need to discipline yourself to save money for it. You feel that going on holiday gives you the chance to live as you'd truly like to live all the year round—in an aura of luxury with the good things of life within easy reach. You're one of the signs who can really feel like a millionaire even on a brief holiday and would rather have one week at an expensive hotel than four less expensive weeks.

A vacation has to offer contrast. The investment of time and money must give you a feeling of regal living because you feel this is exactly as life should be for a lion of the zodiac. You like to go where you can rub shoulders with celebrities and where there's bright activity when the sun goes down. But the real success of your vacation rests with the hours you can spend getting a good tanned body.

Once you've found a place that suits you with its warmth, bright lights, and sparkling people, you're conservative enough to return often to the same place. Although you enjoy traveling, you're very conscious of the difference between traveling on business and traveling for relaxation. In this way, you're one of the signs that benefits from at least a three week vacation in one place. There, you can absorb the atmosphere and retain memories of regal living long after the holiday is over.

Although you're sun-lovers, one of the strange things about members of your sign is that you're inclined to pack far more clothes than you'll ever need and forget that excess baggage has to be paid for at airports. Small things like this can give a bad start to a vacation and make you sullen and resentful the first day. A little thought about the clothes you'll actually want to wear can eliminate this—bikinis and bermudas should be plentiful, but if you're on the beach, you'll not need too many day clothes. So use the space for your most glamorous evening clothes. Plan your accessories so they're interchangeable with several dresses.

If you take a holiday with the family, try to be patient when they want to do things on their own. You can be very imperious, but a real vacation for everyone can't be organized with military precision. Allow time for everyone to do things they want to do when they want to.

VIRGO ♍   For several years now, you've not had the time or money for a real vacation. But once Jupiter brings better financial gains as part of its benevolence, you have the chance to plan one of the holidays you've dreamed about. As a reaction against past routine responsibilities, either of work or money or absorbing health problems, you're likely to want an unorthodox holiday. At several specific times in your life, when the planets make certain patterns in your horoscope, this reaction against the normal will send you flying off on holidays which surprise your friends. It's as if a sense of revolt crops up. You sit down and think of holidays you haven't been able to have for so many reasons and one of your rare extrovert moods creeps up on you.

This type of holiday can do you a lot of good and sustain you for several years. There's nothing like making up for lost time, and with the thoroughness that you do everything else, you apply the same care to the extraordinary times when you take a holiday.

While in the past you've made do with small, inexpensive vacations—perhaps even of the day-excursion type—when your extrovert periods come around it's quite possible that you could take off for a trek to Alaska, a safari with camera to Africa, an exotic flight to Hawaii. This is also a time when you're likely to take a fair proportion of your savings and spend more than you've spent in ten years on one single glorious holiday. Capture memories with your camera, for most of you are excellent photographers. Providing you can come back without guilt feelings, you'll have a holiday well worth the extravagance.

You're generally so content to live life on a placid plateau, not really envious of others who can take several vacations away from home, that when the time comes for you to spread your wings you go to extremes and really live it up.

Vacations spent on your own are no hardship to you. But, quite likely, when extravagant holidays come along, you're also ready to go with a few old friends or a single special companion. In fact, everything that's away from your usual characteristics of being reticent gets woven into the special holidays.

To the surprise of your friends, you show a new side of yourself. And even if you revert to the retiring personality which is more consistent with your character, your retentive memory will enjoy reminiscing about your holiday for many months afterwards.

LIBRA ♎   Although you firmly intend to take a vacation, your first plans often have to be cancelled, either by circumstances or because you're capable of changing your mind at the last minute. Studying travel brochures can build up your interest so that you're firmly convinced you must see one of the romantic spots of the world. Then you're likely to be influenced by someone just back from a place he raves about and you find yourself taking a vacation there instead. It's always helpful if you must take a vacation with your family or someone close to you, for in this way—with the wish that others enjoy themselves, too—you become more consistent and keep to your original plans.

There's no doubt that other people influence your vacation plans each year. But you're philosophical enough to enjoy whichever place you go to.

The best vacation for you is one which offers maximum possibilities for relaxation. Forget about tours which rush you through a dozen countries in ten days. Choose a place which is geographically romantic but has a good hotel known for personal service. You enjoy being waited on: it's necessary for your happy holiday. You rarely expect to put up with anything uncomfortable on vacation. It has to be an upgrading from your home status, and if anything goes wrong, you're very capable of firmly complaining until you get the room and service you expect.

For some people in the zodiac, a stimulating holiday in which one is constantly rushing around with little time to think, is an essential. For you, a fine holiday is the exact reverse. Venus makes you want luxurious surroundings, fine food and, if possible, enough companionship to be pleasant. But the last thing you need on a vacation is stimulation. It's a chance to renew your mental energy and physical strength, and you expect to return home feeling much better and less tired than when you went.

Most of you prefer to leave the car at home, fly to your vacation spot, and then hire a car. A long car journey before getting down to enjoying the vacation rarely enters your plans unless it's for reasons of extreme financial pressure. But a holiday with little money to spend would really be as bad as not having a holiday. In this, you're very wise and, with help from someone else to encourage you to save, you're much more likely to wait until you have enough money before even considering a vacation away from home.

SCORPIO ♏   One of your ruling planets, Mars, has an influence on travel plans, while your joint ruling planet of Pluto can lead you into holidays with an adventurous flair.

Generally, a vacation can be quite dramatic for you as you're quite capable of falling violently in love with a place or having a torrid holiday romance. Of the two, falling in love with a place is perhaps the safest, since a holiday romance which doesn't continue when you've returned home, can throw you into a dark mood. A vacation is generally intended to provide a beneficial change with results lasting through a whole year of work or household chores. A flamboyant love affair, in which only the memory lingers on, can defeat this and make you so touchy and emotionally upset that no one would know you'd had a vacation.

Try to choose your holiday companions with some discretion, or at least be aware that love affairs flourishing on a highly romantic level away from normal conditions are merely to be enjoyed for the moment. This is naturally difficult for you, but in the end it saves a lot of unnecessary traumas.

If you're unable to take a holiday in another country, you are more inclined to take one providing a romantic setting together with things like theatre and music festivals. You have great need for music and drama as a relief to the depressing moods which overcome you from time to time and are part of the secretive, smouldering nature characteristic of members of your sign. While your best holiday would be one in which relaxation plays a part, you rarely go with this intention but, rather, with the idea of escaping from normal routine. Sometimes you take a vacation to escape from a bad love affair, and that's when you're much more vulnerable to holiday romance. It's rather like jumping from the frying pan into the fire and is obviously fraught with dangers.

Living dangerously, however, is part of your code. It frequently takes many devastating experiences to bring you to a time when a holiday can be the uplifting, beneficial thing you start out hoping it will be. If you start on a holiday with problems, you either have to make up your mind to resolve them during the vacation, forget them, or move away from them. Changes of scenery and companions provide the means to do this, if you really try to help yourself and stop being masochistic.

Learn to relax, at least mentally, and be decisive enough to aim at making the best of your holiday, putting some meaningful effort into each single day. If you return home jaded and tired, as well as emotionally insecure, it can reflect on your health.

You have so much drive and energy created by Mars plus an ability to cope with the expected influences of Pluto. All you need is the willpower to enjoy life on whatever terms it presents itself.

SAGITTARIUS ♐   The majority of you will always be attracted to a holiday that's action-packed, and where you can participate in your favorite sport rather than loll in peace and lazy relaxation. The mountainous part of any country appeals to your love of rugged nature. So many mountain resorts have facilities for golf, skiing and riding, that you can enjoy these while the rest of the family is sightseeing. It seems that your vacation needs to be filled with challenges, and physical activity can often provide this.

Planning a vacation, if you have a family, can present some difficulties because of your own preference for action which may not coincide with theirs. So take time each year to discuss places and times for your vacation with your family, unless you're able to get away for a short extra holiday on your own.

A large number of people under your sign seem to go for several years without being able to get away for a long holiday because of family responsibilities—perhaps having to look after an aged companion. When this happens, you can get the best out of a long weekend, providing you're free to follow your own inclinations. The length of the holiday is not as important as how much you can pack into it.

When you manage to take a long vacation, you have enough stored up energy to lead an active life and still return home with energy to spare. The danger is that you may be impatient with less active companions and, because you look forward to the vacation so much, compromise isn't easy for you.

Under these circumstances, it's better for you to state quite plainly that you feel everyone would have a better vacation taken separately. At least, aim to get one week in the year entirely on your own or with an organized group with similar sporting interests.

You enjoy the rugged scenery without becoming too lyrical about it, and if necessary can be content with primitive accommodations and plain wholesome food. Companionship is preferable to you, but Jupiter gives you a hail-fellow-well-met attitude to life. Even if you travel on your own, you'll soon make friends without getting romantically involved.

CAPRICORN ♑ When you're forced to combine business with pleasure on vacations, you take pains to consult with your partners whenever possible. You're easily influenced by their decision as to the time and place. Because most of the year is involved with mundane problems, you can look longingly towards a yearly vacation as an escape. But it can only be beneficial if you leave your business affairs at home, and it's false economy to think that you'll save money and time by spending vacation time on projects.

Since Saturn influences your moods, causing periods of depression which can lead to poor health, no one needs a truly relaxing vacation more than you. Indications are that in the next few years, the ideal type of vacation will be more easy to attain. But you have to begin planning for it.

You're very much children of habit. If for the past twelve years you've packed a briefcase as well as a suitcase, intending to work while on holiday, you may find yourself still doing this. One of your major faults is that you frequently hear opportunity knocking, but rarely have the courage to open the door. Your mass of fears prevents any full, zesty enjoyment of life. A constant need to save money for the proverbial rainy day also impedes vacation enjoyment, for this is when most people want to feel free to spend a little more money than they normally would at home. You have a knack of surviving many rainy days without touching any nest egg, but there'll never be a better time than the next few years to take at least one memorable holiday. Going away feeling free can lead you to enjoying a new style of vacation in which you return able to face any worries which may have accumulated while you were away.

If you can aim at a holiday which gives you a complete change of food, environment, scenery and companionship, you'll benefit for many months after. Jupiter now encourages you to break new ground and do the exciting things which come from exploring unfamiliar places.

You're at your best sharing a holiday with the responsibility of looking after someone else, a child or a married partner. Let them try to please you as well. Don't always be the usual patient burden-bearer, willing to go along with whatever anyone else wants to do. It may well be that your partner will also get a new enjoyment just from seeing you enjoying a more relaxed vacation.

Staying within the practical limits dictated by your income, try not to count the cost of the vacation in money but, rather in terms of how much better you'll feel if you relax.

AQUARIUS ♒   Your ruling plane of Uranus has the remarkable quality of erupting suddenly in your life, so it's not surprising that you're one of the most spontaneous travelers of the zodiac. Unfortunately, this planet is not always concerned with making pleasant reasons for traveling. With so many humanitarian instincts, you're quite likely to be whisked away to visit a sick friend or look after a relation, and then be grateful if you can stay on for a few extra days as a vacation.

Pleasing your family is an important trait. You'll sincerely plan towards a single holiday each year, but often have to forego your original plans because of the unexpected forces of Uranus. Personally, you don't mind having a holiday at home, but if the family shows any resentment or indication that it's upsetting to them, you're the first to begin to wonder if the idea of a vacation is worth the effort. As you get older, you tend to stay more and more at home unless you're sent spinning on your way by Uranus.

If you're fortunate, on the better years when the planets are creating an harmonious pattern, your main goal should be to take a holiday in a place where you can unwind. Peace and quiet, plenty of fresh air, food you're used to, and interesting people will give you the most beneficial holiday.

So many of you develop a guilt complex if you're sitting around doing nothing. Get rid of this feeling when you're on vacation. Be philosophical enough to know that while you're resting, your nervous tension is being reduced so that you can return home full of energy and unafraid to tackle anything.

When you can take advantage of off-season rates, secluded resorts are more likely to appeal to you than changing from one large town to another. While you can never be completely rural-minded (inasmuch as you need to be involved with one of the mainstreams of life) you can find relaxation and enough to stimulate the mind if you can go where some specific event may be taking place. This could be a music or drama festival rather than a sporting event, although some male members of your sign enjoy a special game—baseball or tennis.

Desiring to be independent, you often take too much baggage with you, always fearful of running out of your favorite pills or toothpaste. Remember, most places have shops, and there's often adventure in visiting new shops.

PISCES ♓ There's literally no limit to the variations you can play around with when planning a vacation. The expansive character of your joint ruling planet of Jupiter encourages you to think of magnificent holidays. Neptune, your other ruling planet, inclines you to consider places with romantic appeal where there's a lake, river, or ocean. No matter where you go, how much or how little money you have to spend, you're gregarious enough to enjoy yourself in a hundred different ways and manage to find pleasant companions.

Living where you can extend the summer is helpful in counteracting any health problems. You enjoy vacations and very often like to get away someplace completely new and different to revitalize your physical and mental system. Small, cramped places rarely appeal—again, due to the infinite nature of Jupiter.

If you're born after the first ten days of your sign, you'll be more retiring, content to see less people, and generally prefer a vacation with lots of time for contemplation.

If money permits, you're likely to take more than one vacation each year—another indication of the dual character of your sign symbolized by the two fishes. The contrast in living which a good holiday gives helps you get into many creative moods and occupies your mind weeks after you've returned. It's essential for you to get the best out of a vacation. If you have a romantic, interesting holiday, the mood continues when you return. On the other hand, if you run into drastic and unhappy adventures, you feel the effects keenly even when they're over.

You're very impressionable. People and places make indelible prints on your mind, so it's important to show care choosing an important main vacation spot.

Loneliness rarely worries you. If you start out on your own, you'll always meet someone with whom you have rapport. If you deliberately choose seclusion, you can be very happy just enjoying the scenery without companionship.

All Pisceans should take regular vacations even if it causes an additional strain on the budget, for the change from normal routine has therapeutic effects which can influence your health for many months. It's wise to think that money spent on a vacation may save on visits to a doctor. You rarely have a guilt complex about spending money, but some of you may feel guilty about spending time away from your home —especially those of you with creative talent.

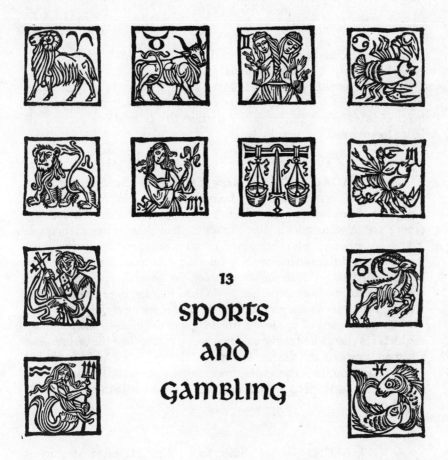

13

sports
and
gambling

ARIES ♈ You prefer individual activities like golf or
sailing to team sports and enjoy letting off energy in strenuous play. Unfortunately, you're also inclined to let off steam with verbal
remarks about the particular game you're playing. You're rarely content
to be a spectator, although if you have no choice, you'll follow your
favorite sport avidly on television and in magazines.

While you have an aptitude for most sports, you can excel in horseback riding, golf, and tennis. If you're forced to play in team events
(such as a friendly game of tennis doubles), realize that you're indeed,
playing with a partner and plan to work *with* him. Save your analysis of
the game for the postmortem conversation. Although you have the
vitality and ambition to become one of the best players, learning to lose

145

graciously becomes an emotional trial. Just try to profit by losses and never blame anyone else but yourself.

You're impulsive when gambling and not the type to spend long hours working out a system. You prefer to follow a hunch, but you can become an excellent bridge player because the calculations are a challenge to your active mind.

TAURUS ♉   Many of you enjoy gardening and walking so much that they become a form of exercise as well as a pleasure. Conventional sport doesn't attract you so much as it does the other signs. You're more inclined to watch than be an active participant. You enjoy swimming however, even if you often spend more time floating in the pool than trying to show off your style and speed. It's a form of relaxation rather than an actual sport. In general, you usually feel you've something more important to do than indulge in orthodox sports, although you may join a golf or country club for status sake.

Since so many of you lead a life dedicated to business, any gambling instincts are channelled to the stock exchange rather than the casinos. But when on vacations and the facilities are available, you can enjoy a modest bet as relaxation, or a concession towards your spendthrift companions. You're more inclined to be selling sports equipment than to be part of the game.

GEMINI Ⅱ   Since your ruling planet of Mercury is always making you restless and versatile, it's natural that you'll be interested in sports at some time of your life. Your age is unimportant: this interest may catch you when you're adolescent or middle-aged, but it will simply be a phase among many others.

When a sport has finally captured your interest, you're only happy when you're in the thick of it, and the faster the action, the better you like it. Badminton, which can be a very fast game, seems to appeal to members of your sign—also swimming, diving, skating and skiing. Because you're an avid buyer of equipment (and clothes) once your interest is aroused, many of you are ready for practically every known sporting activity. In all sports, remember that you're accident-prone and it'll generally be an accident that brings your interest to a swift end.

Although you may never become a professional racing car driver, your instincts for speed always provide some danger that you regard the family car as a form of everyday sport. You enjoy gambling, being quite happy to win and lose alternately just for the thrill of it.

CANCER ♋   You have little fear of the water. Your ultimate in sporting pleasure comes from any of the aqua sports—swimming and diving, scuba diving, water skiing, boats. Most of you can swim at an early age and grow up enjoying the relaxation energetic swimming gives. Always possessive and taking pride in ownership, you're unlikely to change your ideas or your equipment with changing fads. It isn't rare for you to point out proudly that you've had a favorite swim suit for years.

You're rarely competitive, sports being a social or relaxing pastime providing a happy balance when life's daily problems cause too many pressures.

Generally, you're very fortunate when gambling. You have an intuitive instinct for timing. This lucky aspect is consistent whether you buy a ticket for a lottery or play the tables.

LEO ♌   If there's a group dressed in the lastest sportswear or playing cards by a swimming pool, chances are that members of your sign are among them, firmly convinced they're having a sporting time. You love to relax in the sun, getting a deep tan, and generally enjoying all the sun can give you. If you swim, it's likely to be in a desultory manner—a quick dip and then back to the sun. Yet your sign can produce some spectacular professional sportsmen and women, especially if you're born with Mars in Leo at 19 degrees, which produces the drive to go into action and win. When you're involved in team sports, you can act as a catalyst, keeping the rest of the team on their toes, and always being a fine example yourself.

You can also become avid, almost compulsive, gamblers, working out systems and yet still gambling recklessly. Because you thrive on the dramatic, you're able to win high stakes as well as lose your shirt. In gambling there's rarely a happy medium for you.

VIRGO ♍   Because you're always health-conscious, you're generally interested in sports because you're convinced they'll do you good. Members of your sign have a general tendency to view organized sports as a tedious business. You don't want to get too involved with clothes and equipment, and you often limit your interest in sports to reading about them. Occasionally, there are planets strong enough to upset this cycle, and a few Virgos become fine sportsmen, using their intellect as much as their physical drive to achieve success.

As a sign associated with service, you can be an invaluable friend to sports-conscious acquaintances who need a reliable baby-sitter. You're also very good at administering first aid. You never see sports as an escape route or a relaxation. If your planetary problem compels you to go into sports, it's always on a thoroughly professional basis, and when you retire you'll become a judge or referee.

You gamble, after having prepared a system which can be successful. You aren't likely to play just for the fun of it, but out of a precise desire to win and make money. You can be quite content to have one good win and then leave from gambling for many months. In this decision you have a built-in sense of timing which is characteristic of your careful nature.

LIBRA ♎   To interest you, most sports have to have a social connotation—it's the occasion that matters, not the sport. You're likely to become members of country and yacht clubs, enjoying the amenities, mostly as a spectator, but sometimes participating. Conversation around the pool interests you just as much as wearing the right swimsuit or making a graceful dive. You can attain a reasonable proficiency in any sport that gains your interest, and when strongly influenced by Mars, you can become quite aggressive in team sports.

Golf, tennis, and swimming appeal more to you than boating, and you're better when playing with a partner than competing on your own.

Gambling is something you can take or leave. If you're on vacation and the facilities are available, you're inclined to make a few modest bets, but rarely feel a compulsion to gamble. Indeed, you expect to lose if you buy a lottery ticket and are rarely optimistic about your success in games of chance.

SCORPIO ♏   Most of you are determined to be successful in everything you undertake, so if you become interested in sports, you're never content until you're proficient. You'll take lessons before appearing in public. You're mostly interested in sports with a solitary aspect—such as mountain climbing, spelunking, or fishing.

Because you're determined to get the most out of everything, you're often able to combine two interests at the same time—if you enjoy mountain climbing, you're quite likely to write about it. You're especially good at water sports, and the advent of scuba diving and deep sea diving has opened many opportunities. Sometimes you can combine such activities with a pastime as exciting as treasure hunting. As a spectator, you avoid rough games of ice hockey or football and can be quite content watching graceful ice revues and aqua shows. You're likely to belong to very exclusive clubs or those catering for the specialist, rather than merely social ones. You don't have the competitive drive for team sports, but you have remarkable determination to achieve on an individual basis.

Your tastes are always highly individualistic, and when it comes to gambling you either play *chemin de fer* (and nothing else) or ignore gambling altogether.

SAGITTARIUS ♐ No one has a healthier, more robust attitude towards sports. You can appreciate sports on many levels—competitive, as a means of relaxing, and for keeping physically fit. You can become an excellent instructor. Your physique equips you to take part in any sport that appeals to you, but you have a versatile enough mentality to be proficient in many.

Under the sign of the Centaur, half man, half beast, you can become very spectacular horseback riders—although rarely professional jockeys because your bones are too large. In show jumping, members of your sign have received the highest honors, and female Sagittarians are fine riders, whether for pleasure or professionally. You like plenty of action and have tremendous stamina. You're also marvelous in team sports, always aware of the need to keep in peak condition. You can retire from professional sports, rest a few years, and then go back to another sport, still physically fit.

When gambling, you're not conservative by choice. If there's a game of chance going, you're quick to play. Unfortunately, members of your sign have gained a certain notoriety as compulsive gamblers, winning and losing fortunes at the turn of one card.

CAPRICORN ♑   Although few sports give you complete personal satisfaction, you consider exercise essential in keeping your body trim. You apply yourself best to any sport you feel will be good for you. You enjoy restrictive body exercises and can become very fine practitioners of Yoga, but you're most likely to excel in sports that have a link with dancing, such as skating. Once you begin to play tennis and golf, you're able to keep up a constant form, your style of play never varying much. You rarely play a spontaneous game, preferring to keep a set time each week for playing.

Buying expensive equipment or clothes doesn't appeal to you, since you aren't interested in putting yourself on show. But you're sensible enough to know that good golf clubs or a fine tennis racquet are good investments, and you're careful to maintain your equipment so that it lasts a long time.

Not very interested in gambling, you can enjoy watching others play. Or you may give yourself a fling at a few of the one armed bandits, setting yourself a maximum of a few dollars. You're able to take part in sports at an age when others have retired; at this point, you play more for relaxation than for keeping fit, which was your motivation when you were young.

AQUARIUS ♒   It's rare to find members of your sign enthusiastic about sports, either as participants or spectators. But if you have chilrren, you may try to keep one step ahead of them by reading about certain games. Sometimes your interest in clubs and humanitarian aspects will necessitate your organizing softball or basketball games, and you'll be excellent in this. Many members of your sign have a poor sense of balance, which may explain your general lack of enthusiasm, and moreover, you really don't like to try anything unless you can become proficient in it.

You're inclined to worry when children are engaged in sports, fearing they'll hurt or exhaust themselves. This is a tendency you'll have to curb if you're going to enjoy attending little league games or field day at Junior's school. Although you approve of exercise in theory, you're apt to limit your own activities to brisk walks.

Gambling doesn't appeal to you very much, although you'll enjoy visiting casinos on occasion, simply to watch, since your interest is mainly centered on studying the psychology involved.

PISCES ♓   You can achieve great proficiency in water
sports—swimming, diving, yachting, canoeing, skating and
sometimes ice hockey. It's not unusual for you to become a professional.
You're so adaptable that you can be interested in several sports at once
and may go through phases of enthusiasm for team playing. However,
you don't have the drive necessary for highly competitive sports.

You're so spontaneous that you need little urging to plunge into
any game at a minute's notice, and it's from these impulsive occasions,
rather than more organized ones, that you derive the most personal enjoyment. Often, it's the good luck spread over you by Jupiter, rather
than skill, which carries you through to success. Often you can bring off
some totally unexpected win after defying forces which would upset
anyone else.

You enjoy gambling, not really caring whether you win or lose,
because the fun of watching other people interests you as much a playing cards or dice. This happy-go-lucky attitude seems to relieve the tension of gambling.

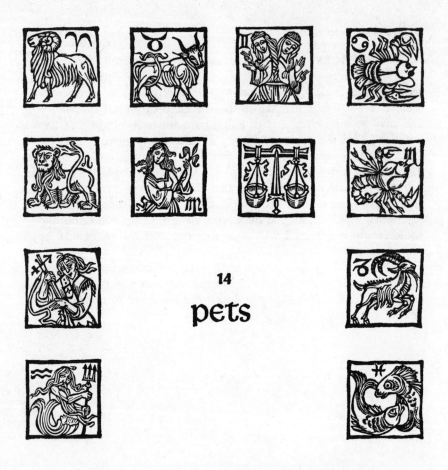

14

pets

ARIES ♈   Because you like movement, you generally enjoy a pet who's active as well as mentally alert. Although you can be quite happy with an orthodox pet, such as the domestic cat or dog, the influence of Pluto in your chart can make you unpredictable in your choice. Your friends need not be surprised if they find a cheetah or ocelot purring by your chair. You have an unsentimental approach to your pets and like them to realize from an early age that you are the boss but this doesn't mean you would be unconcerned if they became ill. You're inclined to seek professional advice at the slightest sign of illness rather than trying to cope with it yourself.

TAURUS ♉ Because you dislike fads as much as you
resist change, your type of pet is no exception to this basic
characteristic of members of your sign. You usually make pets feel like
members of the family and keep them a long time. Your affection for
your pets can be so great that they contribute significantly to your feeling
of domestic euphoria. Most animals appeal to you but you prefer handsome, well-bred dogs or cats.

Your pets always seem happy because you give careful attention to
their physical needs—feeding them regularly and seeing that they have
their own bed or special chair. In return for this attention, you expect
an affectionate response and get it from them. You also like to feel your
pet has a special rapport with you and it's not unsual for you to allow
other members of the family to keep their own pets rather than share
the affections of your special one.

GEMINI ♊ Always under the influence of changeable Mercury, you love to follow the latest fashion in anything. This can lead you to change your pets according to the newest
trend. But it's also important for your pet to be attractive as well as
fashionable. Generally, you like a pet that can be looked after pretty
easily. A lively, smooth coated dog such as a dachshund with high intelligence, or a pretty, colorful bird, appeal to you.

It's advisable to avoid highly strung animals who might aggravate
your own naturally nervous system. More because you're caught up in
a whirlwind of business rather than mere forgetfulness, you may have
to make special efforts to see that your pet is reguarly fed and exercised.
You're likely to be better with all pets when they're very young.

CANCER ♋ So many types of pets appeal to your
affectionate nature and you like to have more than one about
the house. It's not unusual to find members of your sign cheerfully taking in someone else's pet or one which has been abandoned.

Because of the influence of the moon on your watery sign, you
enjoy colorful fish. But your real favorites are large guard dogs which
give you a feeling of security, or plump comfortable cats. You have a
tendency to overload your pet with kindness and concern. Does he have
enough to eat? Is he feeling sick because he's not so lively as yesterday?

You allow him to share your bed and occupy most of the furniture. You don't bother training your pet to know his place in the household. Incurably sentimental over your pets, the death of one can cause grief. You'll always love having a pet who returns your affection generously.

LEO ♌   You enjoy so many aspects of exotic living that it's not surprising to find you attracted to any large colorful pet, especially one full of vitality. You'd prefer a handsome, showy St. Bernard to a toy poodle or a really BIG cat, and you'd rather have one brilliant carp than an aquarium filled with guppies. You demand a great deal from your pet. He must be good looking, well-bred and obedient, and you're prepared to give lots in return. You rarely begrudge the cost of keeping pets—even a St. Bernard—and love to give them the best of food and living quarters, as well as the latest pet toys. While you don't make an obvious show of fussing over your pet, you keep it in top physical condition and take pride when others admire your choice.

VIRGO ♍   Medium-sized dogs and cats who are not too demanding are most appropriate for your naturally conservative nature. Although it may tax your patience to house-train your pet, it's advisable to get one while young so that he learns to adjust to you rather than you to him. If you acquire an older pet, he may be house-trained but will probably have a pattern of living which will be hard to break.

With Mercury, the planet associated with intellect as your special planet, it's more important to you that your pet is intelligent rather than flamboyant or fashionable. Because you're a born worrier, it's best to have regular veterinarian check-ups for your pet. Members of your sign worry a great deal about health and hygiene and it's not unusual for both sexes, when children come along, to wonder if the household can sustain children and pets and, all too often, the pet is found a good home. You accept the responsibility of any pet you keep and perform all duties necessary for its well-being.

LIBRA ♎   A beautiful, fashionable pet with good manners and an illustrious pedigree suits the beauty-conscious members of your sign. Your need to have an exquisitely turned-out pet makes you unafraid of the expenses involved in keeping a dog (such as a poodle) which requires frequent trips to a canine beauty parlor. In choosing a pet, remember you're not likely to enjoy the kind that needs long, healthy walks in all weather. You may prefer an exotically plum-aged bird or a non-demanding, unusual type, such as an iguana—both of which need comparatively little attention and whose domestic habits can be kept well under control.

SCORPIO ♏   A one-person pet is most appropriate for you who are naturally possessive and like to have a constant companion. You can become so devoted to your pet that you'll even experience guilt if you have to leave it with someone else for any length of time.

Dogs of all kinds have a special appeal providing they're alert and are of an unusual breed that satisfies your love of the dramatic. Japanese dogs, West Highland Whites, or any of the Spitz family provide you with bright enough companionship and also make good conversation pieces. Many of you enjoy pets as unusual as monkeys. You like warm-blooded animals whose energy matches that of the driving force of your ruling planet of Mars. Generally, the influence of Pluto brings a pet into your life by some unusual circumstances rather than the usual one of planning to buy a pet.

SAGITTARIUS ♐   An inborn desire to be kind to animals is especially characteristic of members of your sign. You're nature's own gift to the lost dog fortunate enough to find his way to your house and you're literally a collector of lame ducks. This is noticed by friends who'll have confidence in your ability to look after pets. So you can expect to be an official foster parent to other people's pets during vacation periods. It won't bother you unduly if your friends are late in collecting their pets.

With Jupiter, the planet concerned with expansion, as your ruling planet, it's not unusual for you to find yourself taking a professional interest in breeding different types of animals on a semi-commercial basis. Although you find all types of pets appealing and can rarely re-strict yourself to one, you'll generally find your favorite is one who shares activities with you and is noticeably faithful.

CAPRICORN ♑   Being practical, you're likely to worry about the safety of your possessions and generally want a pet that supplies companionship and doubles as a guard. This will probably limit your choice to some well-trained protective dog, such as a Doberman.

Dark colored dogs appeal to you more than light ones. Your sense of duty makes you take a real interest in your pet's physical well-being but you may consider displays of affection secondary. You're not likely to be influenced by fashionable trends. You want good value for your pet money.

You'll probably be faithful to one breed of dog all your life. The ideal pet for you shows strength in his appearance, with angular lines and a close coat. You're naturally body-conscious yourself so a well-structured pet has instant appeal. Also, you need a pet who is active and intelligent, a companion who won't make too many demands when you feel moody.

AQUARIUS ♒   You're always so concerned about the welfare of humans and animals that you may wait many years before keeping a pet because you respect the responsibility it involves. Your humanitarian feelings often make you uncomfortable about any animal losing its natural freedom. For this reason, you'd never be completely happy with a bird in a cage but might keep a gentle little dog or cat.

Your ruling planet of Uranus, which is associated with sudden, unexpected increases, makes it likely that when you acquire a pet, it will be through someone else's influence. For instance, if your children bring home a stray dog or cat, you can accept it more easily than deliberately making up your mind to go out and buy a pet. Even if you don't find a pet truly pleasurable or necessary, once one is introduced to your home, you'll accept the responsibility with equanimity.

PISCES ♓   With your happy-go-lucky attitude towards animals, you're rarely bothered by the amount of time and money it may be necessary to spend on your pet. You're generally attracted to unusual pets of all shapes and sizes even though your household may become chaotic by the introduction of yet another one to what is probably already a strange assortment.

Because you're not naturally energetic, you'll show a preference for pets who need little exercise. Your sensitivity will attract you to pets with distinct personalities.

Since Neptune encourages you to travel, keep pets small enough to travel with you, rather than have the worry of leaving them with friends.

You have a great affection for any pet in your household and like to establish rapport with them. You often have an uncanny instinct in understanding them, probably because members of your sign have intuitive qualities and highly developed extrasensory perception.

15

cookⁱng
anⅾ
nutritioⁿ

ARIES ♈ Most of you eat too quickly, as if you hate
to waste valuable time on anything so prosaic as food when
you could be out looking for adventure. You seem to see food as a
means of replenishing the energy which your Mars-oriented nature uses
up so quickly.

But Mars gives you an insatiable curiosity, and this enables you to
try new styles of cooking which aren't motivated strictly by gourmet
appreciation. You can't be accused of having conservative tastes in food,
since the novelty of a new dish provides the variety you need and enjoy.
You like colorful food with eye appeal, and prefer anything that's
highly flavored. If the flavor isn't in the dish itself, you'll always use
condiments, spices, and relishes profusely. This willingness to over-
season, combined with a devil-may-care attitude and a natural inclina-

tion to experiment, makes it likely you'll become painfully aware of your digestive system quite early in life. Unwise food habits lead you to keep generous supplies of indigestion remedies in the medicine cabinet.

Meat is essential to you, and should be the major part of your diet. You need this source of high-protein to keep up your strength. Carbohydrates, on the other hand, produce only quick spurts of energy. Instead of taking the time for a proper meal, you may often be tempted to grab a snack in which there are too many carbohydrates to be truly good for you. As the head and brain are the most vulnerable parts of your body, your desire for quick-energy food makes you neglect the nourishment you need for quick, active thinking. Astrologically, each sign has its own related cell salt, and for you this is potassium phosphate, found in lettuce, cauliflower, onions, pumpkins, lima beans, lentils, walnuts, and apples. Nervous disorders can ensue unless you regularly replenish your own cell salt to meet the demands of an active body and mind.

You can delight in cocktail snacks, but should be careful not to indulge in too much liquor. Herbs associated with Aries are hops, nettles, gentian, cayenne, broom, garlic, and honeysuckle. Your taste buds are specially active, and many of these herbs are piquant. Aloes, ginger mustard, cress and mints also have a tangy flavor that you'll enjoy.

Remember though, when catering for an Arian, the cook should be careful not to extol the herbs as being "good for what ails you." This is a sure way to make Arians feel defensive. It's better to introduce herbs into the food without saying anything about them.

Lamb shish-kebab, marinated roast lamb, cranberry glazed ham, barbecued chicken, love-kebabs and Chinese beef will almost always appeal to you.

TAURUS ♉   You enjoy gourmet meals and love rich foods. Many of the world's finest chefs have been born under your sign, and practically all Taurean women excel in cooking. If Taureans are fortunate enough not to have financial difficulties, their good taste and desire to find satisfaction in food can make them true gourmets who'll have eaten always in the best restaurants of the world.

As a Taurean, you have the potential for a great knowledge of wines. You generally always expect your favorite dish to be prepared at the same high standard. Meat is very important to you, and, fortunately, most menus are planned around meat as the main dish. You like to dine in elegant surroundings and take plenty of time for the main meal of the day. The male Taurean is generally a strict three-meals-a-day advocate, although interest in slimming sometimes makes Taurean woman skip lunch. Both sexes can go through the day and give their best, providing they've had a substantial breakfast and can look forward to a good dinner in the evening.

Your particular astrological cell salt is sulphate of soda, which is abundant in many uncooked foods. Unfortunately, you're not too fond of uncooked food unless it's steak tartare, so it is important to plan a fresh salad at least once a day. Thyme and sage are very good herbs to use frequently, and of course, they blend well with many meat dishes.

Given the opportunity, you can develop the most discriminating palate at an early age, and a love for all kinds of delicacies. Not only do you tend to eat substantial meals: for you food can become a recreation and a social asset. Very often you'll be given the opportunity to be professionally involved in culinary matters. No one is quicker to express an opinion of a meal, especially if it's not to your taste or if a dish is prepared without proper attention to detail. You're meticulous in serving dishes correctly, and any well-planned, formal dinner you give can be a topic of conversation long afterwards.

Although meat is a must for you, you can enjoy anything as simple as a potato, if it's dressed up. Desserts have to be exotic: you'll seldom settle for a constant stream of pies when banana soufflé or a rich plum pudding is available.

GEMINI II   You're always complicated in your ways of life, and your food habits are no exception. Your menus display your characteristic seeming fickleness as you change your mind from one day to another. You have not set eating habits, liking whatever's available at the moment—good conversation and companionship being as important as the food itself. Culinary pursuits appeal to you through their variety, and you're always eager to try new recipes and new drinks.

You love to live in a constant whirl which can upset your metabolism, and the hyperactivity can best be maintained by attention to how you're eating. If left on your own, your meals become more and more abbreviated, and many times you'll settle for just a cigarette and coffee. When you reach the quick-snack stage, it's time to sit down and realize that food may have something to do with the tricks your delicate nervous system is playing on you.

More than any other in the zodiac, your body needs nourishment very frequently, and Mercury, always sparking off your alert mind, also needs to have its refreshment. To keep well, eat well-prepared meals regularly. If you're unable to prepare them yourself, some member of the family should concentrate on seeing to it that you eat properly. A diet need not take every calorie into account, but a diet properly balanced out for your special needs is essential to your mental as well as your physical health. You can best help yourself by deliberately allowing so many minutes per day to sitting down quietly and eating; this schedule definitely excludes stand-up lunches or quickly thrown together dinners.

Your specific cell salt is potassium chloride, which builds up the fibrin in the blood. An insufficient supply results in circulatory problems. Essential foods for you are asparagus, green beans, beets, celery, oranges, peaches, plums, apricots, pineapples, and pears. It's not unusual for you to choose a vegetarian diet, often simply because it's easier to pick up some raw fruit or vegetable than to spend time cooking. The sensitivity which is a characteristic of your sign directs you instinctively to some of the right foods. Astrologically, your best herbs meet all the requirements of a well-adjusted nervous system. Parsley, for example, is more than a mere garnish—it's a great purifier of the blood stream. Skullcap is good as a soothing tea and can help you sleep. Caraway seeds will also benefit you, and can be used in many ways besides being sprinkled on bread.

It may be easiest to nibble your way through life, but for you it's also the quickest way to ill health, and nervous and physical disorder. With care or help from a friend, you can find dishes which don't take long to cook, provide a variety of flavors, and still contribute to your well-being; burgundy lamb with cranberry sauce, veal marsala, vegetable and seafood stew, spiced meat balls, asparagus, shortcake are all good and good for you. Try gala grasshopper pie—even the name will appeal to your love of the different.

CANCER ♋   You're always impressionable, but can sometimes be hard to live with when it comes to food. Yesterday's dishes, which appeared to delight you, can raise no enthusiasm whatever when they're served today. To enjoy food, you need a constant variety. You have a capricious appetite, yet beyond this distinctly erratic

behavior, you display a great interest in gourmet food as an exciting part
of life.

You're always delighted when a meal is well-prepared, the dining
room table well-set with crystal and a pleasant floral arrangement.
You're gregarious and prefer to eat in company. In your own household,
devoted as you are to home and family, you don't find it easy to get into
the routine of preparing meals. Left to your own resources, you're not
conscious of time, even if you have a cookbook to tell you how long a
dish should be cooked.

In the last twenty-six years, the biggest problem many of you have
had to face is the conflict between your vanity and your normal desire
to eat exotic food. The advent of weight-watching has made you diet-
conscious, trying to maintain a girlish figure at the expense of your
health and temper—for you actually need a well-varied diet, not a restricted one.

Your astrological cell salt is fluoride of lime. A lack manifests
itself in such things as varicose veins, relaxed tissues, dental decay, back-
aches and poor eyesight. Fluoride of lime is found in most animal and
vegetable foods, but two easy sources are the yolk of eggs and rye bread.
Also, it's essential that you eat in a congenial atmosphere, since moon
children are so emotional that their digestion is easily upset. All types of
seafood are excellent; also cress, watercress, pumpkins, eggs, meats and
a lot of liquids. Practically all culinary herbs appeal to you, and parsley
is especially beneficial, since it helps nervous stomachs. Dill and fennel
help counteract the gaseous condition which many of you suffer.

You change your eating habits frequently, but again, this is motivated more by the dieting urge than by any conscious effort to find the
well-balanced diet which can help keep you healthy. Many dishes with
unusual names, such as spiced Japanese fruit cake, appeal to your imaginative mind as much as to your gastronomic juices. Because you like to
travel, you're generally able to keep a private cookbook of recipes you
found in distant corners of the world. The romantic connotations, again,
lend much of the flavor.

LEO ♌   Attractive, eye-catching, colorful food appeals to you, and no one appreciates a well-set table of regal
status more than you for you do love to eat in great style. You will frequent the classic, well-known restaurants if you can afford them, but
even at home, you'd like to sit down to at least a three course meal.

When dining out, you enjoy having your hostess remember you prefer Irish coffee to any other. Unfortunately, you also have a certain defiance in your food habits. Even when you know that over-stimulating foods are detrimental to your cholesterol count, you'll rarely give up your favorite fatty dishes until you are forced to do so by something drastic like a heart tremor.

It's not unusual for you to suffer from some strange eye complaint. Any of the herbs of the sun, such as marigold and nasturtium seeds and young dandelion leaves, are helpful if used in salads. The main herbs associated with members of your sign are dill, fennel, comfrey, comoile, and all types of garden mints.

Your astrological cell salt is phosphate of magnesia, but this is harmful if taken in its commercial form, which the body cannot assimilate correctly. Therefore, it's important to arrange menus in which this cell salt is present naturally. Barley, rye, wheat, almonds, lettuce, apples, eggs, asparagus, figs, coconuts, cabbage, cucumber, onions and blueberries should offer enough variety to make a feast fit for a regal Leo. Walnuts are especially good for Leos, and remember that pickled walnuts can lend a piquant flavor to home-cooked fare.

Correct amounts of phosphate of magnesia restore muscular vigor and help form albumen in the blood—and a poor bloodstream can be a problem to many of you. Meat is essential but in limited quantities, and should always be eaten along with adequate supplies of salad and vegetables. You enjoy crêpe suzettes, in fact any dishes which are flambéed. This is to be expected from the major fire sign of the zodiac. Moreover, your constant love of the ritualistic approach makes you appreciate anything served with a flourish, be it champagne or flaming shish-kebab.

Although a meal without wine may seem like a day without sunshine, the wise members of your sign limit their intake of vintages and hard liquor, no matter how hard it is to restrain themselves.

Barbecued foods of all kinds appeal to your palate, and turkey roasted on a spit pleases you. There's something equally succulent and exotic about a roast suckling pig with herbed apple cider stuffing. Even reading a menu can excite your sense of the spectacular, and no bland, ordinary-sounding dish will ever catch your attention.

VIRGO ♍ The sixth house of the zodiac is called the house of service. You want so much to give the best of yourself that even if you have to dictate terms in a cut and dried manner, any imbalance can cause illness. Nervous disorders crop up but the seat of your trouble is generally the liver. For this reason, you may be forced to pay attention to all the food you eat, and many of you may turn out to be "faddist" eaters.

You're excellent as dieticians, but can carry it to the point where you no longer have the freedom to relish a good, honest, hearty meal. You generally establish an eating pattern based on habits formed early in youth, and rarely can you be tempted to deviate from that pattern. You often regard eating as a necessity, not as a social function.

The cell salt you need is potassium sulphate, which works on the albumenoids and the oils of the body. A deficiency of this salt results in a malfunction of the liver and subsequent digestive troubles, not to mention certain forms of skin trouble. The best sources for the cell salt are found in chicory, endive, lettuce, carrots, figs, apples, strawberries, and whole rye and whole wheat bread. Potassium sulphate has a laxative effect and helps unload impurities. It also induces the sleep you need to relax tense nerves and tone up body muscles.

Your best astrological herbs also help to tone up the liver and soothe the intestinal tract and nervous system. Skullcap, taken over lengthy periods, is most helpful, as are fennel and dill. You're not very fond of vegetables but can generally take salads. Neither do you favor fish, or most rich sauces. A plain, bland diet seems to suit you best. Since you're noticeably fastidious about food, it's essential that all your meals be prepared under completely hygienic conditions. The monotony of a limited menu does not upset you. Although you seek culinary simplicity, you can appreciate well-served meals and like to eat in a tranquil atmosphere. Macaroni and cheese is likely to be one of your favorite standbys, as well as simple chopped steak.

LIBRA ♎   With your natural love of beauty in all its forms, it follows that fine food served with elegance should interest you. You can enjoy dining in famous restaurants or in a pleasant dining room at home, but in either case, you must have harmonious companionship and a well-planned menu. You're not likely to enjoy a snack except under starvation conditions, and aren't completely happy dining alfresco or at a picnic.

Members of your sign are considered arbiters of good taste. This is reflected when you entertain, but your basic requirements are always the same: a good menu, a finely set table, and intellectual companions.

While you show great originality in a variety of creative forms, not too many of you are good cooks. The male Libran is generally better than the female, who sometimes has a snobbish approach to the idea of food in general.

Your astrological cell salt is sodium phosphate, which helps to dispel carbolic acid and other carbon wastes. It's absolutely necessary for you to maintain a balance in your body chemistry, especially between acids and alkalis; otherwise your nerves, stomach, liver and brain react in a way which can set up lengthy periods of illness. Your cell salt is contained in unpolished rice, oatmeal, blueberries, fresh coconuts, raisins, strawberries, apples, figs, corn, asparagus, and celery. To get it, you'll have to eat freshly prepared food, not warmed-up leftovers.

Because your back is a vulnerable part of your body, your kidneys can give difficulties. The astrological herbs you need are ones that can induce you to eliminate waste in all ways—even through the pores. Thyme is an excellent culinary herb. Burdock, an age-old country ingredient for making an excellent homemade wine, has a therapeutic effect on the kidneys. Skullcap, fennel, dill, marshmallow and chicory are also good for you. You enjoy salads, especially more unusual ones made perhaps with watercress or cress instead of lettuce.

So many of you are subject to quick changes of moods that there are days when you won't exert yourself about food at all. After a period of depression, you can cheer yourself up with imported delicacies or out-of-season foods which you love. Dishes cooked in wine—such as scallopini à la Marsala, duckling with a rich sauce, and Florida orange bread —can generally tempt you to enjoy eating and help you bolster your reputation of being a fastidious host or hostess.

SCORPIO ♏ Your digestion is generally so good that you can eat a rich Lobster Newburg as a midnight snack and go right to sleep without discomfort. But you must eat the lobster because you want to and not because someone tells you to. You're so highly individualistic in everything that you demonstrate particular likes and dislikes along with an unconventional attitude to food.

It's as if your symbolic animal, the Scorpion, must always defy the world. You have to give the appearance of being in control of everything you do, thanks to the strong Martian influence and the added dash of Pluto that eggs you on to be unpredictable. You enjoy spicy dishes such as curry and Mexican recipes, as long as they have more to commend them than merely being hot. Your taste buds demands exotic spices and sauces. You can enjoy meat, fish, and seafood dishes with equal abandon if they're well prepared and not bland. Creole beef roulades, steaming bouillabaisse, all types of curry; stuffed, rich, hot peppers; and rich sauces and desserts should all appeal to you.

Sulphate of lime, your cell salt, has a cleansing, antiseptic power which encourages the body's elimination of waste matter. But you need to take this cell salt directly from food, not in its commercial forms. Onions, garlic, mustard, cress, turnips, radishes, leeks, cauliflower, asparagus, kale, figs, prunes, blueberries, fresh coconut, and gooseberries should be part of your diet.

All herbs associated with your sign also force impurities to leave the body through the natural channels of bladder, intestines, or pores. Horseradish, horehound, wormwood and blackberries help in therapeutic purification.

You enjoy flouting conventions and have little use for diets, often deliberately choosing to ignore the relation between your health and your eating habits. You're attracted to foreign foods, dishes with plentiful amounts of meat and seafood served in a highly flamboyant manner. You eat with pleasure, enjoy robust company and full-blooded wines, and generally love to exaggerate about foods you've eaten.

SAGITTARIUS ♐   Nearly all Sagittarians enjoy outdoor life. If you live in a region like Florida or California where much of your time is spent out of doors, you're happy to have patio and pool parties or old-fashioned picnics. The barbecue appeals to your fire sign as do flambéed dishes, but since you love to be actively involved with food, you'd rather arrange a barbecue yourself than sit in a restaurant and be served. Male Sagittarians are better at impromptu meals than the female, who are more inclined to be down-to-earth, honest-to-goodness cooks, providing meals more substantial than creative.

You're gregarious, enjoy preparing foods for others, and generally over-cater just in case you have unexpected visitors or provide a midnight snack for yourself. Certainly there's little wasted food in your household, and you're adept at making leftovers into tasty second-round meals.

Your cell salt is silica, or common quartz. A deficiency causes thin, lacklustre hair and poor nails. This unusual cell salt is found in vegetable matter such as the edible skins of fruits and vegetables, figs, apples, prunes, and strawberries. Many herbs used for seasoning have silica within them. Burdock, chicory, sage and all the pot herbs are excellent. You enjoy well-seasoned food but can generally use pepper and salt heartily once the food has been served. The herbs suitable for you also help counteract the over-heated blood condition which you can be prone to—especially if you're a male who's spent a good part of his life in sports.

A good breakfast is as important to you as a hearty dinner, and you rarely take a light lunch. In fact, you like to feel that you've had a real meal, not just a snack. Thick soups, hefty club sandwiches, plenty of cheese appeal to you, and you often show a partiality towards German cooking with plenty of sausage and meat.

In common with the other fire signs of Aries and Leo, you're inclined to eat too quickly and excessively as you grow older. Baked picnic ham with apple raisin stuffing, Austrian beef goulash, sauerkraut, beef balls, and spare ribs generally show up on your menu.

CAPRICORN ♑   Throughout your life you tend to like foods that are easy to eat and assimilate. Vegetables are better for you when mashed, and desserts should have a milk base. You have a highly intuitive approach of eating, choosing mostly foods which are right for your particular sign, but you can cause an imbalance by too much liquid or an excess of hard liquor.

The influence of your ruling planet Saturn causes your appetite to become capricious. It reflects your moods, particularly when you're depressed. At such times, you often rationalize that food's an expensive item, and that you must give up meals appearing to be extravagant. This trait becomes more obvious after you pass middle age, although female Capricorns are excellent at making an appetizing meal out of very little. The male of this sign is more likely to reduce the number of meals he eats than try to cook for himself. His general feeling is that food is intended for nutrition and not to be a plaything. Capricorns prefer to read menus written in English and like straightforward meals such as meat and two vegetables without too many frills.

Your cell salt is phosphate of calcium, found in fresh whole milk which is a necessary part of your diet all through life. Strawberries, figs, plums, blueberries, spinach, asparagus, lettuce, cucumber, lentils, beans, whole wheat, rye, barley, and salt water fish are necessary for your well-being. You expect—and demand—that your body should function almost like a machine and intuitively know that the right food is needed to keep it running. When your diet suffers a shortage of phosphate of calcium, aggravated by the Saturnine predisposition to worry, you tend to have digestive troubles, duodenal ulcers, thinning hair, skin blemishes and general depression.

Your best astrological herbs are thyme and slippery elm (which can be used in soups) sage and skullcap. You often have a general aversion to any strong distinctive flavor such as onions and garlic, for your palate and nose are two very sensitive organs. While never particularly inclined to any sort of fancy cooking, you can be quite happy with a broad variety of vegetables, especially root crops, even if you precede them with one or more cocktails. Oven pot roast with parsnips, vegetable pot roast, baked apple, noodle pudding, cumin spice cake and many dishes with a milk base appear frequently on your regular menu.

AQUARIUS ≈   Generally a pacifist, you're prepared to fight for principles or the betterment of mankind, but never want to fight just for the heck of it. There must always be a good cause.

You approach food with much the same explosive enthusiasm so that within your sign we find many food faddists, cracked wheat dieters, and vegetarians. You can carry on your personal diet even to the point where you'd rather starve than change it. The male of your sign is more inclined to be a food faddist than the female, although she may well take up an exclusive rice diet if she feels she's saving nourishment for her children. Both sexes are happy to philosophize over a cup of coffee, preferring intellectual conversation to gourmet fare.

Your cell salt is sodium chloride, or common table salt, used as a seasoning and a preservative. Careful chemical balance of your body liquids is important to your well-being, and salt helps by creating a thirst and clearing the irrigation system. Too much salt can leave your body through the kidneys, leaving an imbalance between the intake and output of liquid, but you're quite able to decide what's good for you as an individual. Although I have a personal distaste for salt myself, it never upsets me to see an Aquarian adding large quantities of salt to lettuce. For members of your sign, salt is a necessity which you take intuitively. Trouble can begin if your food fetish takes you into a salt-free diet. It's a popular idea that may be excellent for some people, but not for you.

Natural sodium chloride is found in coconuts, spinach, cabbage, asparagus, carrots, chestnuts and radishes, but you should pay particular attention to your cooking methods. Quickly boiled vegetables, for instance, retain minerals better than those simmered too long.

Your best astrological herbs also carry sodium chloride in a concentrated form and these include all the well-known culinary herbs—sage, thyme, mint, and rosemary as well as oatstraw, which is excellent for tea. You like to eat at regular times and have a preponderance of fresh fruits, vegetables, salad crops and desserts. Sometimes, as you get older, it's important to see mealtimes as something to be enjoyed and not just as an interruption in the flow of your energetic life.

PISCES ♓   The more extroverted females of this sign can become very proficient cooks who take a delight in preparing and eating food. However, Pisces is a most complex sign, containing the sum total of all the other signs within it. It's hard to be sure which will manifest itself. Jupiter emits a certain predictable quality and a desire to be generous, so the extroverted Piscean is a good hostess. But the diffuse quality of Neptune is unpredictable: you can prepare and enjoy a fine meal one day and be content with the plainest of sandwiches the next. Many of you, however, take pleasure in all forms of food and drink, even to the point of over-indulging in both. You seldom worry about having "favorite" dishes, however. Seafood of any kind is probably the closest thing you'll have to a definite preference, fish being more palatable to you than meat.

Your astrological cell salt is phosphate of iron, which attracts oxygen and redistributes it to strengthen the blood vessels and arteries. If you suffer from circulatory troubles, an increase of fresh air is as important as food, but be sure to take in the fullest amount of your cell salt.

Kelp and seaweed are very good—quantities or iron are found in lettuce, radishes, horseradish, strawberries, spinach, kale, lentils, barley, apples, and pumpkins. Fresh fruit and salads are helpful, and can be prepared in many ways to provide the variety you like in food. You can become very interested in herbs and use them extensively in your cooking. There's literally no limit to the herbs which are good for you. Irish Moss, little known in the United States, is invaluable for you as a valuable source of iron. It can be made into a palatable drink by adding fruit juices, or used as a soup stock.

Ginger pepper and hops also add variety to cooking. You don't have much interest in milk—even disguised as ice cream. This, no doubt, is your intuition telling you that milk isn't good for water signs, predisposed as they are to pulmonary complaints.

You're a good judge of food and drink and absorb exceptionally large amounts of liquids—often in the form of soups—especially fish chowder and seafood bisques. A warm, friendly atmosphere helps you get the most enjoyment from meals, because you're either completely extroverted and gregarious or absolutely the reverse, quite content to eat alone. An attractive table pleases you and often becomes the framework for romantic, exotic meals reminding you of the days when you traveled. Simply the smell and taste of a certain dish can evoke nostalgic memories.

16

GARDENING

ARIES ♈   You enjoy all that nature offers in flowers
and shrubs but the actual work of serious gardening doesn't
truly appeal to you. Gardening requires an orderly rhythm to pursue it
to its highest potential and this conflicts with the demands Mars makes
on your life. You can work in energetic spurts but can rarely sustain the
enthusiasm needed by a really dedicated gardener round the year. Many
members of your sign prefer living in urban communities without a
garden. You're content with an easy-to-care-for house and patio plants,
such as cacti. Since your sign signifies the first push of life in the spring,
all the early flowers—daffodils, tulips—appeal to you as well as the first
early flowering shrubs, such as jasmine. You don't expect praise for
your rare gardening efforts and certainly won't spend sleepness nights
if a few plants wilt and die.

TAURUS ♉   As the first of the earth signs, you have
        a real emotional need for a garden and if this isn't available,
you'll always have a full supply of potted plants in your house. The
male members of this sign are among the finest gardeners when given
the opportunity and can become very frustrated without some means of
using their green thumbs. Female members can also do wonderful things
with their Venus-inspired sense of beauty. Many love raising specialized
plants, such as roses, and your gardens are usually well organized. If
you're restricted to an indoor garden and have enough money, orchids
also appeal to you. If you're fortunate enough to have a large enough
garden you can expect to produce fine vegetables and colorful displays
of rich red and orange flower beds. If you're unable to raise flowers,
you're likely to be a good client of the local florist. You rarely see this
as an extravagance. The need for beauty is as necessary to your happiness
as making money.

GEMINI ♊   You always see gardening in terms of
        work rather than pleasure and contact with green growing
things is not as necessary for you as it is for your preceding sign of
Taurus. If you have a garden, it's often to please others more than yourself. You can be quite happy with a very casual look rather than any
formal landscaping. Vines of all types appeal to you—particularly any
climbing plant such as clematis and morning glory, whose flowers are
delicately suspended in air, so that the slightest breeze gives the illusion
of flowers floating freely in space. Blue and silver or white flowers have
a special appeal to you but you're quite happy to buy your vegetables
rather than raise them yourself.

CANCER ♋   You're at your best when attending a
        garden and are one of the signs having a green thumb. A
careful saver of seeds, pips, stones from fruit, and plant cuttings, you
can casually put them in water or earth and shortly afterwards trium-
phantly show your friends a strong little plant. Liking variety in everything you do, you're very much a year-round gardener, although you
generally have to rely on someone else for heavy spading. As the first
of the water signs, if you have enough land you're sure to want a pond
for aquatic plants. Your garden always shows an abundance of colorful

vegetation but you can't resist the temptation to add more. If you don't have land, you're likely to create a garden room within your house. If you have any fault in gardening, it's not knowing when enough is enough and your window boxes and house plants can be as profuse as the bric-a-brac you love to collect.

LEO ♌   If there's a plant to be grown that can win a prize for the biggest and best, chances are a Leo will have grown it. You're willing to spend time, money and energy if you can be sure of getting the best results. But the end product must justify the effort; it must be truly outstanding. As children of the sun, massive flaming yellow and orange sunflowers appeal to you as do hollyhocks and gladiola—tall, straight sentinels greeting the sun. You prefer displays on a grand level to small delicate flowers which have little interest for you except as a contrast. Very much a seasonal gardener, it seems impossible for you to do long term planning. You also like enough garden space to walk around and enjoy the fruits of your labors.

VIRGO ♍   Although you're the second of the earth signs, you don't approach gardening with the same happy enthusiasm as your fellow earth sign, Taurus. A garden can often be just another problem in life and you're prepared to deal with it dutifully. You enjoy some armchair planning and many of you like organized gardens with formal arrangements of plant types in geometric arrangements. It's not unusual for members of your sign to cement small patches of land, leaving just enough room for a few easy-to-care-for plants, such as ornamental grasses. This relieves you of too much worry. Indoors, you enjoy cut flowers that last for a long time. You want lawns that are well-kept, well-watered and conform to a geometric pattern. Although you may not be a keen gardener, any unkempt land will arouse your characteristic need to tidy it up.

LIBRA ♎   Although you're rarely eager to start the hard part of gardening, Venus encourages you to want to do the best and you can create a spare patch of land into something beautiful. A garden, indoors or outdoors, must first of all be a thing of beauty for you and then you truly enjoy it, forgetting the backbreaking hours it took to achieve it. Because you have a need for balance, your garden generally expresses your sense of symmetry. Many members of your sign like the formal Italian garden style with rows of elegant cypress framing formal flower beds.

Collecting garden furniture can be important to you. So can pretty pots and vases to display your plants and flowers, especially hydrangeas, begonias and camellias. You also like the idea of a room devoted to plants. This can be a showpiece for your decorating skill as well as a means of escaping the hard work associated with outdoor gardening. Indoor gardens can be charming when arranged by your Venus-inspired touch which can use such decorative things as Victorian wire plant holders and tiered tables.

SCORPIO ♏

For you, there's no middle-of-the-road approach to gardening. Either you love it or you hate it. If the latter emotion dominates, you won't mind letting your land grow into a mass of tangled undergrowth. If you've discovered a love for gardening, Mars will give you enough enthusiasm to work long hours for spectacular results. You always capitalize on your sense of the dramatic. A reluctance to prune or throw out old plants may be a problem and you may have to force yourself to realize that this is part of successful gardening. As the second of the water signs, succulent and fleshy plants, such as begonias, houseleeks, and ice plants appeal, as do ponds for aquatic plants. Magnolias and tulip trees also seem to satisfy the part of your nature that demands dramatic, eye-filling beauty.

SAGITTARIUS ♐

You're one of the signs of the zodiac with a compulsion to possess your own piece of land to be completely contented. Since your love of sport is greater than your love of gardening, it's more likely that you'll use your land as a tennis court, croquet lawn, or swimming pool than as a well-planned garden. However, when you're involved in creating a garden, you're a willing worker whose help is often sought by friends. You need to be careful if you have garden machinery to maintain. You're apt to use the lawn mower and forget to clean it. You like flowering shrubs and evergreens and can make good use of these as a framework for your sports area. Indoors, you can be very happy with branches giving you the feeling of being in the country, especially if you're restricted to living in town.

CAPRICORN ♑   Saturn gives its children so many restrictions that it's natural to find these restrictions even in gardening. This trait can make you a compulsive pruner with many of you literally cutting a valuable plant away to death. A sense of order is necessary for you and you have a wonderful ability to landscape difficult areas. Your garden generally presents a neat, well-cared-for look. Seasons are clearly shown with bulbs for spring, herbaceous borders for summer and chrysanthemums for fall and winter.

You can excel at the art of bonsai gardening—for here, pruning and restriction are important. If you have space for it, many of you like a glass hothouse for raising plants from cuttings and adding salads to the family table.

AQUARIUS ♒   When we understand that, astrologically, the mission of your sign is to water the parched earth until it blooms, it's surprising how few active gardeners appear under your sign. For you're the armchair gardeners of the zodiac with a humanitarian interest in producing more food for the world. You take a technical interest, wondering how to make two blades of grass grow without actually trying to do it yourself. You can be a great help to others in planning their gardens, advising them as to the best fertilizers and the most efficient tools to use, but you'll generally limit yourself to very simple forms of indoor gardening. A window box of herbs can be just as important and inspiring to you as a great bowl of cut flowers. In the last 26 years, most members of your sign haven't been free from financial pressures. But those who've had land available have made it pay dividends with vegetable gardens—sometimes using hired help or the aid of family members. As advisors, you're invaluable.

PISCES ♓   No one appreciates nature as much as you, a trait that makes you able to cope with gardening at almost any level, indoors or out. You're not particularly good at planning and can be quite illogical in your approach and then confound more experienced friends by producing results. It seems you have a special type of tender loving care with plants—irrespective of value—and if anyone can bring a sickly-looking plant back to life, it's you. You abhor monotony and this means your garden can be full of surprises. Indoors, you'll like to have cacti and succulents, while outdoors you'll enjoy great bursts of riotous color such as bougainvillia. As a water sign under Neptune, pools of water lilies and iris have great appeal for you. If you have enough space, it's certain that you'll devote part of it to herbs and vegetables. While you may seem to be a slap-dash gardener, you'll always get results—whether it's with flowers, shrubs, fruits or vegetables. A garden which seems only one step removed from nature can have special appeal to you and your family.

17

SPRING
CLEANING
AND
DECORATING

ARIES ♈   You generally can face the idea of spring
cleaning with enthusiasm. But you like to get it over and done
with in record time. Perhaps planning your time more effectively would
produce a more lasting effect than usual. Surface cleaning is just not
enough, and often you forget the small repair jobs, always thinking
you'll get around to them but never quite managing to do so.

For you the secret is planning well. Make a time schedule for
actual cleaning, a list of repair jobs, and a check list of tools and materials needed. With your love of organizing, cut down on your own work
by encouraging responsible members of your family to take care for
particular rooms. Since 1967, you've wanted to avoid gloominess in the
household and this desire to bring more color into your surroundings
will continue for several years. You're not conservative and the newest

shades of yellow and orange attract you. If you're intent in doing a major decorating job throughout the house, discuss color schemes with other members of your family and above all, let them have the shade they prefer in their own bedrooms. It isn't easy for an entire family to live with striking yellows and oranges.

Most of all, before you start decorating, take time to consider your financial situation: you can often be in the mood for an extravagant decor without budgeting for it. It's always disappointing to start decorating an entire home only to find that you've spent too much on one room. You may have done extremely well with that one room, but in the end, it will only serve to emphasize the drabness of the rest of the house. If you find your bank account doesn't give you enough leeway for extensive changes—such as new drapes, cushions, and lampshades—settle for a thorough cleaning and rearrangement of furniture. You may even discover unexpected talent in your family for *making* drapes instead of buying them.

TAURUS ♉   Many of you consider yourselves gourmets and your interest in food often effects your plans for spring cleaning—starting with a change in decor in the kitchen. You'll certainly insist upon having your own way in this area, and your taste will probably run to sets of new dishes and pans in the latest orange, red, or avocado green—with perhaps a few interesting copper items. When it comes to rearranging the rest of the house, your latent resistance to change often crops up and you may prefer simply to rearrange the furniture. If you have a family, talk things over with them and let them choose colors for their own rooms. While you'll have a preference for reds and greens, don't try to dissuade a Gemini from blue or primrose yellow.

Try to start any major housework when you're feeling your best, and don't become discouraged if the work takes longer than you've estimated. You're rarely impulsive about decorating or spring cleaning, but in an effort to present a very charming house, you can often exert yourself just before some special visitor is due to arrive. Not being the quickest of workers, you'll usually be frustrated when the guest arrives, having fallen hopelessly behind with your schedule and having to apologize for the smell of a half-painted room. Being painstaking and really turning rooms upside down, you can become very involved in checking small repair jobs which can turn up a few surprises. Then you have to take time to check further in case something else is wrong.

New furniture polishes can intrigue you, and you'll always pay particular attention to old scratched furniture, taking pride in bringing out old patina. All in all, cleaning and decorating fill you with enthusiasm, but you often think you can do the whole job in about a week. Remember that you're a slow worker, organize the family to help, and attempt to achieve a look which will last for many months.

GEMINI II   You aren't likely to be very organized when it comes to spring cleaning. Quite likely you'll start a major job on an impulse and then be appalled that the work is taking longer than you anticipated. Try not to start in a great burst of enthusiasm with gallons of paint. Your drive may dwindle when you've only completed two walls instead of four. A half-done job can be very upsetting to others in the family.

Sometimes you find cleaning and decorating a form of therapy and you'll tackle it like a demon. But you know—or should know from past experience—that such work needs planning if it's to be effective. A chance glance through a magazine can inspire you and start you on a spurt of creative activity, but more thought may help you realize that a changeover from Early American to Danish Modern can be extremely expensive. Better plan one room at a time if you want to make a complete change. If you're truly intent on a new, more modern look, try and redo some of your old furnishings. Move them into another room. Most of all, window or catalogue-shop before you actually start the job.

Also, try not to wreck the rooms of other members of your family before consulting them. It's fine to start on your bedroom or the living room as they'll understand that you are an impulsive worker. But it's not so good if Junior comes home from school to find his favorite desk, lamps and books rearranged with lemon and blue bedspreads and drapes when he has a passion for his old ones.

CANCER ♋   You enjoy your home so much that any opportunity to rearrange, redecorate, or improve it is almost a compulsion. Unfortunately, you're inclined to be carried away with every new idea, and finally wind up worn out from attempting too much.

Spring cleaning can be hard work in your household, for each year sees you adding more and more bric-a-brac to rooms which are already overstocked by normal standards. Plenty of closets and cabinets are a necessity for you, but you also consider it a challenge to fill them quickly. You cannot bear to throw anything away. When you decide on new furnishings, you simply add an extra chair or sofa to the existing furniture. The more clutter you have, the longer it takes to clean, especially if you insist on dusting valuable pieces yourself. Remember that you have a natural tendency to gild the lily if left on your own.

At spring cleaning time your best friend is likely to be a member of the family who's blunt enough to tell you that the household simply cannot take any more furniture and that the place to start is your own clothes closets and chests. If that same advisor can stand by and help you, there's a chance that the entire task will be done efficiently, since it's difficult for you to make decisions on your own.

You like making all bathrooms pretty and feminine. But remember that the men in the family may get tired of the pinks and pastel greens you enjoy so much. Give everyone a chance to express their opinion. Don't interfere or tell them how to do their own rooms, for there's nothing a man hates more than a woman who thinks she knows all about decorating. Even if you're in the interior decorating business, remember that men like to *think* they're experts in home decoration. You'll invariably get the best cooperation by fostering this illusion!

Try to work out a time schedule for starting and finishing, since you often work in fits and starts. Long, drawn out cleaning and decorating, with chaos ruling the household, can fray nerves. Make jobs as painless as possible by firmly tackling one room at a time, clearing up all mess by the end of the day, and remembering that the family still wants to eat.

LEO ♌   You're all such busy people that when it comes to cleaning and decorating you're inclined to procrastinate, always waiting for the free moment which rarely comes unless you create it. You may even have to define your own season for "spring cleaning" according to where you live.

As sun children, you're not likely to be happy working indoors when the sun is calling you outside. If you're financially able, it's better to have your house thoroughly cleaned or decorated professionally. If you have to face these matters as personal chores, make a date to start, and abide by it firmly. Decorating and decor will always appeal to you more strongly than cleaning, but there's no point in putting new drapes against grimy walls and worn paint. So start at the beginning: clean well and *then* enjoy the more exciting moments of adding flashes of color to a room. As a child of the sun, many of your schemes will be dominated by various shades of gold. If you're tempted to experiment with the latest psychedelic yellows, you may have to consider an entirely new plan of decor for a specific room, since the new yellows and oranges can be fatal to the more conventional colors.

When collecting, most people are inclined to go overboard, and the chances are that you'll be interested in models of lions, your symbolic zodiacal animal. Because you like everything to be large, see that your lions have plenty of space around them; otherwise, you'll get a cluttered look which will ultimately upset your own love of freedom. Strong colors, strong figures, and strong furnishings need space to look their best. You love light and rarely like to sit in a subtly lit room, so, undoubtedly, one of your most noticeable items of decor will be extravagant lighting fixtures and lamps. Try to give some thought to careful placement of lights as much as to buying ornate lampshades. Not everyone enjoys being subjected to a glare. Dimming devices are a fine investment, and can take the strain off friends and members of the family who may not enjoy bright lights.

Don't skip cleaning chores. Do repairs in each room as you find the need, then rearrange and add to your furnishings. If doing the job properly takes more time than you anticipated, cheer yourself by remembering that the effect will last longer.

VIRGO ♍   An annual spring cleaning isn't as much of an upheaval for you as for others, since you have a natural inclination to be tidy all through the year. You're meticulous about keeping closets neat with everything at hand. The male Virgo is especially good at keeping his own clothes in careful piles, providing he's supplied with enough closets and chests.

You're not often inclined to change rooms completely, generally liking to add another piece of furniture only when it's absolutely necessary and functional. The demands of a growing family or the need for more bureau space will be the reason you buy more furniture. You'll always see neatness and practicality as more important than creating expressive splurges of color to keep up with the contemporary scene.

However, harmony in decor *is* important to you; choose pale yellows, grays, or off-white walls with a few dashes of turquoise or clear blues. You can create a tasteful and elegant household without any distinctly dramatic effects simply by underplaying any particular room. You're likely to achieve good lighting effects with a minimum number of fixtures and be very practical about special lighting for reading or on desks.

You tend to redecorate bathrooms and kitchens more frequently than other rooms, always allowing plenty of open space to exhibit bottles and dishes. Most Virgos have an interest in health and diet, and this expresses itself in remarkably efficient kitchens and well-appointed bathrooms. Such rooms may seem rather clinical in the eyes of other member-before of the zodiac, but they will indeed be functional. You're thorough when you spring clean and pay attention throughout the year to the dry cleaning of drapes, slipcovers, and clothes. Accordingly, when the spring cleaning season comes round, you have time to go around serenely, wondering why your friends look hot and tired. Your effort to spread the spring cleaning workload through the year has a great deal to recommend it, but remember, this technique appeals to you because you're born with the sun in Virgo. It isn't possible for everyone—particularly other members of your family—to approach cleaning in the same manner.

LIBRA ♎   You'll rarely find yourself feeling fine when the thought of spring cleaning comes around, since the idea of any upheaval in your household produces an emotional reaction which in turn can influence your health. Though you're wise enough to know that such things have to be done, you'll work better if someone else can help you with the heavy work. If you can hire a cleaning woman at this critical period, you can concentrate on such lighter, personal things as clothes, silver, porcelain, and any changes in rooms.

The male Libran has a greater problem in facing spring cleaning than the female. He'll fight to put it off as long as possible, coming up with some remarkably rational ideas as to why things are better left as they are. It takes a very determined wife to involve him in spring cleaning, and often it's better just to send him away while the job gets done. A few Libran men are very efficient in making repairs (once they're gently encouraged), but it's fatal to make a big scene by insisting they attend to doors that don't close easily or bureaus that need new handles. A Libran's wife needs as much tact as she does enthusiasm.

Libra women are always interested in interior decoration, and a few magazine articles can prompt them to change a room's entire decor. This is generally expensive, and it's fatal for you Librans to let your enthusiasm override financial considerations. Try the greater challenge of introducing a few new items into a specific room while retaining the more expensive pieces of furniture. You'll find you can be remarkably inventive once you realize you may not have enough money to buy all you want. It's possible to make beautiful drapes yourself, if you spend time choosing exactly the right fabric. A practical Libran male can make cornices to cover the top of the curtains, and this always gives an elegant look to a room. Light walls appeal to you, since these provide a foil to good furnishings which you can highlight with turquoise.

You love a beautiful bedroom, and it's likely that this room will be a constant expense to you when spring cleaning comes around. You'll want to change the color scheme, buy new lamps, or even new pieces of furniture. This is fine if there's someone else in the family to whom you can pass on some of the hand-me-downs. Many of you like antiques, and it's sometimes possible to exchange one antique for another if you have a shop where you're a well-known customer.

If you can finish spring cleaning feeling better than when you started, you'll have been justified in your work. But generally you'll want a few days rest after it's all done. Be bold! Take a long weekend away from home, if possible, and come back with all your beauty-loving senses alerted to the fresh look you've created.

SCORPIO ♏   Once you've made up your mind to clean or redecorate, your co-ruling planet of Mars will give you enough energy to do it in record time. Pluto, however, will encourage you to do it at some remarkably odd times of the year, generally when the rest of the family least expects it. Try to warn them ahead of time that you've been bitten by the change-bug, for it's disconcerting to arrive home and find it impossible to get in the front door because Pluto-inspired Scorpio has decided to do some impulse decorating.

Again, although you can enjoy expending energy on spring cleaning, try to plan before you upset the whole household. Decide which room is the worst and work your way through to the easier ones. This way, your maximum Mars energy is right there to cope with the more drastic tasks. You're always thorough and careful to clean well before decorating. Someone should be ready to pinch-hit at mealtimes, since you lose sense of time, forgetting to eat yourself, and certainly neglecting to have meals ready for the rest of the family. Although you have enormous energy when Mars is traveling through your sign, remember that energy has to be replaced. So keep some easy-to-nibble, high protein food available, and literally chew your way through spring cleaning with nuts, cheese, and plenty of liquids.

If your energy keeps up, you can clean in record time, have a marathon of furniture rearranging, and once done, be ready to start all over again.

You like dramatic gestures—rich heavy covers and drapes for example. But if you have an impulse to cover an entire wall with large yellow Texan roses on black wallpaper, try to ask yourself if you really want to live with anything that dramatic all year round.

Your tastes are likely to be expensive in carpets and soft fabrics, and this is where you may have to reconcile your desire to be distinctive with your need to live with your tastes for several years. Zingy, startling highlights in a room are often the secret of good interior decorating, but there should be a difference between a room used by all the members of the family and a rumpus or guest room. A heightened sense of impact can be maintained in a room you don't use frequently, but the same effect can rarely be sustained if seen every day. It becomes rather like seeing *Hamlet* every night for a month—the novelty wears off.

SAGITTARIUS ♐   The last two years have seen a change in the attitude of Sagittarians towards redecorating, although they've always been aware of the need for an annual spring cleaning. Because Jupiter is now in a better position to encourage Sagittarians, you want to expand in all ways. This includes giving your old furnishings a long, hard look—often followed by a shudder and a determination to start literally from scratch.

Suddenly you'll be feeling less reluctant to discard furnishings which have been around for a long time; to clear out closets and throw away accumulations of papers, magazines, and junk. You weren't able to do this while Saturn was influencing you. Pluto and Uranus can also show you the way to new household activities, and this trend will go on for seven more years. You may be tempted to mix various types of furniture until you finally get your ideas sorted out. It's also a little early for your conservative ideas of color—browns and autumnal greens—to give way to lighter, more modern ones, but this will change every year. You'll no longer feel that you have to be so intensely practical and that dark paint, for instance, will last longer than lighter shades. You'll strive to create a new aura within your household that will surprise friends and family and will definitely make you feel more harmonious within yourself.

Spring cleaning that has been performed in the past as just another burden for the hard-working members of your sign will seem much better in the future. An increase in income is always a help, and is part of Jupiter's bonus to you. Many of you will want to spend it to make the household more pleasant and convenient for all. In future cleaning, let everyone help. Have family discussions, and don't be shocked if younger members of your family want to decorate in what you personally think an impractical manner. Enjoy Jupiter and the cloak of expansiveness which it is spreading around you.

CAPRICORN ♑   You generally like to follow an annual routine of spring cleaning, working on specific dates established years ago. You can be quite rigid about this, as you hate being put off. Of course there are years when ill health has hampered you at the crucial time, so the whole operation has been a dreary chore. There's no point in being a martyr, but unfortunately the children of Saturn, your ruling planet, usually make spring cleaning yet another notch in a pattern of martyrdom.

The influence of Saturan attracts you to dark, utilitarian colors and cleanliness seems more important than new creative ideas. Your approach to spring cleaning is thorough, but it would be more pleasant for your family if in the future, when Jupiter transits your sign, you could pay some attention to decor and give it some enthusiastic treatment too.

Try to allow others in the family freedom of expression with their own rooms, even if you continue to keep the living room conservative. Saturn causes so much restriction that the idea of spending money on anything except necessities becomes abhorrent. You may have to let Jupiter encourage you into a few small extravagances in the future. A colorful cushion or new side lamps here, perhaps a new throw rug there, can work wonders and be the first step in achieving a brighter look about the house.

The male Capricorn is excellent at home repair jobs, taking pride in saving money this way. But it's a good idea to use good tools so that jobs can be done more promptly. Male Capricorns can be dedicated borrowers of other people's tools, always returning them conscientiously, but you might as well spend some money on basics.

So many of you can put up a very brave show, making the best of a little money, and you're most apt to spend money on the living room where others can see its effects. Now's the time to concentrate more on bedrooms so that members of your household are comfortable and satisfied that a Capricorn house can indeed be a home.

AQUARIUS ♒   Planning is excellent and meritorious, but you're more apt to spend time *intending* to clean or *planning* decoration than you are in actually getting down to business. If there was ever an "armchair decorator," it's you. Your house is likely to be strewn with catalogues, fabric samples and so on, long before you get down to any positive action. You can find many excuses *not* to do annual spring cleaning—such as good charitable work which takes you away from your own untidy hearth.

Try to be decisive about a starting date; throw yourself into the work with the enthusiasm you feel for social work; give yourself a deadline to meet. "Talk less and do more" should be the motto for all would-be Aquarian spring cleaners. You're a little more enthusiastic when it comes to decorating, but the female Aquarian is usually much better at small home repair jobs than the male. In fact, the males are deliberate philosophical procrastinators, hating to have papers or chairs moved.

An Aquarian husband needs to be treated with care when spring cleaning is in the air, and it should be made as painless as possible for him. Explain that such things have to be done, don't fuss around his private living area, and literally work around him. Personal discomfort can lead to two actions: he'll either accept cleaning as a reasonable procedure in a household or he'll escape from the house, maybe go to a meeting. Make the best of the times when he's away.

Aquarian women aren't the best housekeepers unless there are special planetary patterns such as Mars in Cancer to channel enthusiasm towards keeping house. But you're conscientious about your family and you'll get at fresh furnishings and decoration if they show you it's necessary.

You're naturally inclined towards fresh, clear, airy colors—white, silver, pastel blues, and lemons—and you desire an uncluttered look which you can rarely maintain as tidiness is not your thing. But you do have enough conscience to want to *try* to do a valiant job of cleaning, even if it's for Christmas Day. Appropriateness of the cleaning season is the last thing you'll think of. But obey the impulse when it comes, and you'll do better in the comfortable family atmosphere which is essential to your harmonious well-being.

PISCES ♓   Once you're aware that it's time for spring cleaning, you enter it with a spurt of activity, and can become carried away with a great spirit of adventure—especially if you can go in for some interior decorating at the same time. The danger is that you may become so intrigued with where to hang a new series of paintings or in making drapes and covers that you forget to clean as much as you should. Be firm with yourself—start your cleaning routine decisively before you become creative. It's easier to work artistically in an uncluttered mess than trying to sew drapes with paint cans all around.

Window and catalogue-shopping is a great temptation, even though it's time consuming. If you want a new decor, look through the shops or catalogues, buy the materials you need, and then put them away until everything is spic and span. While your heart is willing to do small repairs, you haven't much ability in such things, so if you have no one in the family to help, consult a neighborhood handyman. It'll be cheaper, more efficient, and less time consuming, than trying to do everything yourself.

Piscean men are not good at cleaning up, but are remarkably adept at achieving unusual effects in decor. Often they achieve dramatic results with handmade lampshades or unusual art forms. Most Piscean males are not great spenders, preferring to do-it-themselves, but a Piscean's wife owes it to him to do a thorough job of spring cleaning before he starts decorating.

All members of your sign can achieve comfortable, if unusual, effects that commend the admiration of family and friends, but you sometimes get so carried away that you don't know when to stop. You're quite likely to feel that burlap wall coverings are just what you need, but try not to burlap the whole house—concentrate on one room. Bathrooms are a great challenge to Pisceans who enjoy decorating them in strange ways, often using collections of shells and other products of the ocean to make collages.

Your most harmonious colors are sea green, revealing your Neptunian planetary rulership, and many shades of lavendar. The latter is a hard color to live with unless used discreetly, and some of you will really go overboard. Restraint is something alien to your nature due to the expansive patronage of Jupiter. Splashing about with paint in the house, either artistically or in a practical manner, seems to be a form of therapy to many of you. It's not unusual for you to change the design and paint in your house practically every year, and the main thing ever holding you back is lack of time—never lack of enthusiasm.

18

chilDREN
of the
zoDiac

ARIES ♈   If you have an Aries child, he may not be
easy to deal with in his early years unless you understand that
his life literally depends on being active. Although a child who wants
to dominate his parents can develop into a small monster, an Aries child
reacts beautifully when love is the guiding factor. Discipline may be
necessary, but should never be administered in anger or defiance and
a vicious circle of rage may become the result.

Always praise an Aries child when he's been good. He thrives on
pats on the head and demonstrations of affection. Understand that this
type of child's energies must be allowed full rein. He may not easily be
put to bed early or kept quiet, but will respond to natural fatigue.
Aries children are at their best in the mornings and should be allowed
to use up their energies before mid-afternoon. Many of them can man-

189

age quite well without a mid-afternoon nap and will then be glad to go to bed in the evening, being naturally worn out.

Such children develop a sense of individuality and responsibility at an early age and like to fix things for themselves. They also like to give orders to younger brothers, sisters, or companions and may need some careful guidance which a sensible parent will effect without breaking the child's spirit. The Aries nature is highly strung and, although they appear to want independence, they need a parent to shield them in the early days of their youth. Too rigid parental control seems to bring out the worst in them, and this becomes noticeable when they reach their teens. Maintaining interest in everything they start isn't easy, and the parent has to expect this child to be naturally experimental. Only if they can be encouraged to retain an enthusiastic interest in the many things they want to do, can they enter their teens posing a minimum of problems to themselves and their parents. They can show signs of tantrums at an early age, and a parent may need to be around to deal with them tactfully and reasonably.

TAURUS ♉   At an early age, the youthful Taurean shows sign of being quick-tempered and unusually stubborn. Boys are much more likely to be a headache than girls, since the Taurean son can become very aggressive with his schoolmates. From time to time his parents may find themselves faced by his playmates' irate parents.

It's never wise to punish while the child is still having a tantrum. Wait and try to approach him later in a reasonable manner, pointing out that as he gets older, he has to learn to live with people who may not see life in the same terms he does. The secret is never to break the spirit of the child—the very traits which can be upsetting in youth may be the very virtures he needs as he grows up.

Taurean girls are much more clever at avoiding the consequences of their acts, especially when they can use their charm on their fathers. At an early age they should be taught to tell the truth. When impressing a child to be honest, the responsibility of being a good example also falls on the parents, who should never promise a Taurean child anything they won't be able to fulfill.

Being born under an earth sign, the Taurean child is always aware of physical needs and he'll be distinctly stubborn in trying to get a second helping of some favorite food or persuading his parents to buy more toys. Charm becomes a Taurean child's stock in trade at an early age, and the child always has the desire to be affectionate as well as to be shown affection.

It's essential that a Taurean child learn to use his hands as soon as possible. Chanelling his attention into creativity, whether in the form of modeling clay or making crude drawings, is a helpful means of keeping him happy and less inclined to be irritable. He'll soon begin to appreciate his home and generally react badly to changes unless they're explained to him. When moving, give him the reasons he has to leave the house where he's lived for several years. He needs to feel very secure, and wants certain things around him which he understands to be his own. Even a favorite toy can provide this emotional security when a Taurean child is too young to respond to reason. However, he can mature very much more quickly than his parents may realize, and this is especially evident in Taurean daughters.

GEMINI II   Your Gemini child should always be kept busy. He'll show signs of wanting to be occupied almost as soon as he can walk. As soon as he can experience sensation by touch, there's literally no holding him and nothing can truly be kept out of his reach. He certainly won't want to break your favorite vase, but he may not be able to resist shoving it to see if it's really as smooth as it looks. The remedy is to put anything valuable out of his reach until he's old enough to discriminate between a kitchen drinking glass and a Tiffany lamp.

Gemini children love to talk and have a fertile imagination. A parent who doesn't understand this may wonder if his child is living in a world of fantasy. Allow for this imagination, but try to channel it. Encourage the child to learn to draw or write early in life so that he can express himself.

Above all, never let a Gemini child hear any domestic quarrels. He needs a quiet, harmonious world to grow up in, without being a buffer or confidant to adults' emotional disturbances. Nearly all Gemini children are highly strung, even when young, but future psychiatric counseling can be avoided if parents don't subject their child to problems which can only bewilder him.

As he grows older, his mind becomes capable of logic. If you don't give him the answers he wants, he'll make up his own and go off once again into the realms of fantasy. A Gemini child after the age of ten is constantly asking questions, for such children have an insatiable curiosity. They hate being put off and can become quite nagging in their insistence to find out. Once they begin to read, a great deal of the pressure is relieved, and the parents can begin to relax—providing a constant supply of books on a variety of subjects is left within the child's reach.

It's often necessary to begin a deliberate policy of teaching a Gemini responsibility at an early age—such as the need to empty a waste paper basket. Some discipline and training is always necessary on simple things like this, for the child's agile Mercurial mind can quickly produce excuses for not having done the job allocated to him.

The parents of a Gemini child share a great deal of responsibility, inasmuch as whether he'll lead a happy life as a young adult largely depends on how they're treated in early youth. Getting into mischief is very easy for the Gemini child, but his parents should always remember that curiosity is linked with experimentation, even if it starts on a very childish level.

CANCER ♋ When young, all Cancer children are intensely affected by people and environments. Their ability to absorb vibrations remains with them all their lives, but is not always understood in childhood. If a Cancer child is left in the care of anyone he expresses a positive dislike for, the situation is likely to lead to drastic results. He may not be able to tell you why, and you may not understand it, but such a person can induce very real fears in him. Attention is therefore especially necessary for a Cancerian child, so that he is conscious of the love around him and can feel emotionally secure. As a moon child, his disposition varies according to the phases of the moon. To a parent who is not herself imaginative, it may seem that the child is too moody or even discontented. Yesterday's beloved toys may be discarded and forgotten a few days later. But you should leave them for the child to return to when his "rejection" mood has passed, as it always will.

It may be difficult to encourage a gregarious Cancer child to sleep alone. Be firm but kind, making bedtime into a game and giving the child a possessive feeling about his own room. He may not respond well to the idea of going to school in the early days, and a wise parent will prepare the child before actually sending him to school, encouraging him to mix with older children and casually discussing areas of school life so that it doesn't come as a shock the first few days. Sometimes it's possible to take a small child to school before he's enrolled as a pupil so that he can see what it's all about. Then his curiosity becomes aroused and he'll begin to look forward to it, unconsciously accepting it.

Cancer children develop an early love for home life. You should put a great deal of thought into sending such a child away on his own, even to visit relations or for his own good. Family holidays are generally a better idea until the child's in his teens. He'll become obviously affected by changes in residence whether it's on a temporary or permanent basis. If parents try hard not to let him grow up insecure he'll develop much more confidence and be able to face the eventual responsibilities of making a life for himself.

LEO ♌   One of the first lessons you have to teach a Leo child is self-control. The best way is to keep him mentally and physically occupied, for Leo children are the most self-willed of the zodiac, who can wreck a parent showing signs of weakness.

Very early in life, the shrewd Leo child discovers that adults have an Achilles heel and that he has a special power of his own to attract attention and obtain whatever he wants. Like his symbolic animal, the lion, he learns that roaring and noise can upset and frighten others. Still, a youthful lion can be most affectionate, impulsive and imitative.

Allow your child to show off his talents if he has worked hard at drawing, playing the piano, or perhaps even sewing. Your child doesn't take easily to any type of work when young until he's helped by tactful parental pressure. There's no need to worry about inattention to studies, since the Leo child can race ahead when he suddenly discovers that it's advantageous to do so.

Although parents need to control their baby Leos, they should never do so with anger and impatience, for a Leo's nature is basically sensitive. Like the domestic cat, his outcries can be reduced to purring if he's assured of love and security. Discipline without harassment will be a parent's best tactic as the child matures; and the reward is that Leo children are close to their families even when they've grown up.

VIRGO ♍   Being born in a sign associated with dedicated service, the Virgo child has a tendency to be almost *too* good, *too* constructive, and *too* noble. He's almost wise beyond his years, but like all children, he can be influenced by his environment and the people in his immediate domestic sphere. Being alert to criticism, he's also conscious when he's being criticized, and parents should not be aggressively sharp with a Virgo youngster. He may respond to criticism with a genuine effort to do better next time, or he may develop a guilt complex, fearing that whatever he does may be wrong. It's very difficult for him to realize that criticism should not be unkind and as he grows older, he can become a dictatorial protagonist himself, with a tendency to nag and pick at people.

A Virgo child is often intellectually precocious and naturally studious. The prototype of the bookworm is generally a Virgo. A wise parent will allow access to plenty of reading material, but won't forget that social attributes—such as being able to meet people graciously—is also important. There's little point worrying if your Virgo son doesn't wan to be on the school baseball team and isn't interested in sports like the boy next door.

A Virgo child is able to express strong likes and dislikes early in life, and generally carries these prejudices right into adulthood. He'll always need encouragement to do anything different. He can be a defiantly fussy eater, and it's little use telling him that spinach is good for him when he's quite sure it isn't. A sensible parent will tactfully encourage a young Virgo to at least sample a variety of food.

LIBRA ♎ Children born under this sign thrive and do their best when praised and encouraged. Any harsh criticism or exposure to domestic quarrels can upset their delicate attitude towards life. They're easily frightened if family security is threatened and will respond to reason better than to any stricter form of obvious discipline. They're very demonstrative, liking to kiss and cuddle, and unlike so many other children of the zodiac, they don't show any great desire to have their own way. They throw fewer childish tantrums and instead display an obvious desire to please their parents.

This can make for a very happy family relationship when the children are young, but it may worry the parents when the children reach their teens and still don't show any great ambitions. Once the Libran child has discovered what he wants to do, he'll become much more enthusiastic, but this enthusiasm is generally produced only by an involvement with a creativity or a form of art. Attempts to make a Libran teenager take a menial job just for the sake of making pocket money can bring out his worst. The parent of a Libran should always realize that beneath the sign's gentle surface, there are characteristics which can suddenly turn aggressive and that the child will react drastically if forced into a job he doesn't want.

Libra children are inclined to exaggeration, but never of a vicious nature. It's merely a manifestation of their imaginative nature. Much more serious is their ability to take great interest in material possessions when young. This can lead to a need for self-gratification and over indulgence.

SCORPIO ♏ The Scorpio child shows early signs of wanting to dominate, and needs to be carefully instructed in all functions of the body. Otherwise his curiosity can lead him into difficult sexual situations as a teenager. He's not an easy child to manage because his basic obstinacy and willfullness can take him into dangerous areas for a child. It's necessary to impress upon him at an early age the ideas of right and wrong, good manners, ways to treat other children, correct speech, and just about everything else.

He'll always question an adult's every instruction because the Scorpio nature is always a probing one. A Scorpio child can take criticism, but he's also adept at being critical of parents or companions, and can achieve an early reputation for being preciously fresh. Sometimes he gets a reputation as the local *enfant terrible* and is likely to be blamed for things he may not have done. This represents a real problem, for a Scorpio child will never forgive a false accuser. He has a prodigious memory for injustices, but will remember kindnesses equally.

He is fearless and, because of this, can be exposed to all sorts of risks that most children don't get into. To forbid a Scorpio child to do anything without explaining why is generally a good way of challenging him to do it. Commands should be followed by reasons that he can understand and respond to.

Scorpio children can be very healthy, but are likely to fall sick during epidemics, such as influenza. Mainly, however, they can thrive in much rougher circumstances than are usually expected for a more average, less extroverted child.

SAGITTARIUS ♐ The young Sagittarian is affectionate, truthful, sensitive, and wants to be helpful to his parents. Daughters can aid mother early in their lives by clearing away tables and doing simple household chores. But parents should realize that a willing horse shouldn't carry all the burdens. If there are other children in the house, they should do as much work as the Sagittarian child. A Sagittarian thrives on love and affection, and his desire to help others is often a manifestation of the personal drive to receive the praise his subdued ego needs.

Although appearing to be a good mixer, amiable enough when playing with other children, and sharing toys, the Sagittarian is very sensitive. This may not be apparent to parents who are happy to go along with the idea of having a good, obedient child. Some dangers can therefore occur when the Sagittarian becomes a teenager, since he may resent the idea that he's always the one doing the extra work. Only praise can make it possible for him to want to continue doing so. In short, his good intentions shouldn't be taken for granted as he gets older.

A Sagittarian child loves the companionship of brothers, sisters or pets. He has to build up his self-confidence and know that people like him for himself, and never should be told lies. Don't promise him something for his birthday and then forget about it—no explanation will be reasonable enough for him. Although he may not make a scene, every disappointment will make a dent on his sensitive nature. Neither should you voice tactless remarks or make comparisons between your other children in front of a Sagittarian. He'll like the thought of going to school, but should be encouraged to mix his love of sports and physical activity with more intellectual pursuits once he's old enough to do so.

CAPRICORN ♑

This is another sign which puts old heads on young shoulders. A Capricorn child can accept responsibility from an early age and takes life much more seriously than other youngsters. A Capricorn, though, seems to be able to become young again after he's passed middle age—as if he wanted to catch up with some of the pleasures he missed as a child.

The Capricorn infant is always conscious of his environment. He never forgets his early background—good or bad. He may not always be bright when young, so if your child is a slow reader or doesn't dress easily, don't compare him with a sister who reads at five and dresses herself neatly to boot. This can cause irreparable damage. He needs help and understanding from the beginning, and patience when he makes mistakes.

It's good to realize that a Capricorn child is born under the influence of his ruling planet of Saturn. This can produce obstacles to just about all the child wishes to do unless there are some especially stimulating planetary patterns—and, unfortunately, such patterns are rare.

The Capricorn child will eventually exert himself to catch up with his more enterprising companions. But criticism and impatience will hinder rather than help him. It may be necessary to supervise and gently advise him, extending praise when he responds favorably.

Parents should accept the times he seems remote and detached—this will occur when Saturnine moods influence him. He'll soon be his cheerful self again, but at these times let him go off on his own without too many questions. The truth is that when he's young, the Capricorn child rarely understands himself, but feels the need for periods of withdrawal.

Capricorn children are generally loyal to their families as they grow up, often taking on responsibilities far in excess of their years.

AQUARIUS ≈   One of the Aquarian children's big faults is a tendency to procrastinate. This shouldn't be construed as naughtiness or even forgetfulness—daydreaming is essential to the Aquarian child. He wants to please and will promise to do anything to help—and then fail to do so because his mind goes into orbit about some project he's dreaming about.

Most Aquarians are restless. A regular, orderly life is necessary for them—and parents should set an example by living orderly lives themselves. Parents should note their child's potentials and encourage him to develop them. For instance, an Aquarian often shows interest in music at a very early age. This should be developed.

Restrictions are always abhorrent to an Aquarian child. From the start, he knows freedom is important. Punishing him by confinement—sending him to his room for example—can result in a trauma which may stay with him all his life. Freedom is going to be the key that unlocks many doors for him. He'll have a natural inventiveness which should be encouraged, even if it first displays itself when he takes his father's favorite watch apart. He has to know why it ticks; why such an intricate mechanism is necessary; for how else is he to learn how to make a better one? This seemingly destructive quality always acts as a prelude to the child's progressing into constructive areas. He understands, but often throws his parents into turmoil.

If your Aquarian child asks numerous questions, bear with him even if you have to teach him that interrupting conversations is bad manners. When he's old enough to read, your best investment will be a good encyclopedia. Aquarians are about to go into an especially beneficial age right now, allowing full rein for their curiosity to conquer the unknown. You may have a future Edison or an astronaut in your family, but his genius potential sometimes makes him hard to live with as a child.

PISCES ♓   Ideally, a young Piscean should be born into a loving atmosphere. The Piscean tendency to self-censure results in a lack of self-confidence which can be eased by understanding parents. When very young, a Piscean child can be shy and reserved, not wanting to be left with people he isn't used to. A baby-sitter should be a kindly, motherly soul rather than a young person who may be impatient.

If your child shows generosity as he reaches the age of six, don't curb it, since this is one of the natural Piscean traits manifesting itself. Your child seems to know instinctively that it's better to give than to receive.

After the age of seven, a shy Piscean may suddenly become more extroverted if home conditions have been congenial. With this new trait, comes precociousness. Music, dancing, speaking and singing emerge. If a Piscean can have lessons in these arts at an early age, he can become so surprisingly extroverted that he may seem a show-off. Obviously this trait can earn him praise from the adults he wants to impress, but the wise parent will be firm and see that hard work is applied to dancing and music lessons. Impress on the child that he did very well, but that he can always improve.

Piscean children are often sick. They can be good patients, but should always be encouraged to believe they're less sick than they may really be. Most of all, they should be hurried back into the flow of family life as soon as the worst part of the illness is over. Sickness can sometimes develop into a means of getting attention which, in itself, is an unhelathy state of mind if carried on into adult life.

Your Piscean child may prove to be a bewildering mixture of angel and imp, with changes of pace in tastes and behavior very apparent. Consistency simply isn't one of the many attributes which the joint ruling planets of Jupiter and Neptune bestow. To understand the vagaries of a Piscean, you'll have to be a resilient parent, able to maintain discipline without coming over as the aggressive, fearsome enemy which could easily happen in the mind of any Piscean child.

19

parents

ARIES ♈   An Aries mother or father is fascinated
by anything new. And the arrival of a new baby can have
such an impact that the other children feel neglected. Fortunately, this
phase soon passes, and the Aries parent can get back to normal. If you're
an Aries, it's wise to explain to your older children that they, too, created
just as much interest when they were born, and that babies need more
attention simply because they're tiny and helpless.

Both sexes find it easy to understand their teenagers and can become much more affectionate as the children reach their teens. The Aries
mother is more interested in her sons, while the Aries father often relates much better to his daughters. It's best to try to balance this out so
that each feels he is getting a fair share of parental interest. Often an

Aries father feels like a brother to his children, while an Aries mother thinks of herself as an elder sister.

Although Aries parents feel compelled to organize family activities, they're always quick to cooperate with any new ideas their children offer. Being rebellious themselves, they're sympathetic to the problems of adolescents today, though rarely able to offer solutions. Most Aries parents are popular with younger friends of the family and again, the attempt to be a big brother or sister is apparent.

The worst problem of an Aries parent is an explosive temper. Younger children don't understand it, although older members of the family will retaliate. The fit of temper rarely lasts, but it may leave damaging effects on more sensitive members of the family, especially if they're born with the sun in any of the water signs. Aries parents relate very well to a child who's constantly active and interested in sports, but they don't have enough patience with one who is happy simply to stay at home and read.

TAURUS ♉ Taureans of both sexes need to have children around them. If unable to have children of their own, they'll often be fine, conscientious foster parents with a tremendous concern for a child's basic needs. Only when they deal with an ultra-sensitive child does conflict come and the relationship become strained.

Actually, there are few children in the world who couldn't benefit from a Taurean parent's influence in the early years of life. The Taurean mother has such great depths of maternal sympathy and kindness that her children are generally devoted to her throughout her life. A Taurean father, however, can run into trouble with his children, even though he provides them with such material things as education, a good home, and plenty to eat. His stubborn nature and conservative inclination often keeps him from understanding teenage children; he may earn the reputation of being a hard, overbearing father from whom children plan to escape as soon as possible.

Taureans need to remember that children will grow up and often grow away from them—not through lack of affection but because youth needs to express itself in its own way. For this reason, many Taureans find great solace in their grandchildren, conscientiously making sure they're well fed, clean, and taught good hygiene early in life. Because of their dislike of change, Taureans fight to retain control of their children. Rarely are the apron strings broken without an emotional scene on the domestic front, complete with such phrases as "It's all for your own good." Ironically, the Taurean parent is so entirely concerned with children that any deviation from their own standards becomes a major concern.

If a Taurean parent can adjust to children growing up and being entitled to express their own views on life without losing any of their parental affection, a happy family life can result.

GEMINI II   Gemini mothers and fathers need a great deal of evidence that their children love them. Their success as parents depends on how much affection they receive. Sometimes the Gemini mother in particular forgets that she must show a great deal of affection. She's not the easiest mother to have, being inclined to make demands which her children aren't always able to fulfill. For instance, many Gemini mothers take pride in their children's scholastic achievements, and express disappointment if the child doesn't come up with straight A's.

The Gemini father also wants to be proud of his children, but sometimes thinks that high grades and a good sports record come naturally. If you're a Gemini, it's better to relax these high standards and concentrate on being an industrious homemaker without making too much fuss when report cards aren't outstanding. Try to understand and be able to discuss school grades without showing anger or hurt.

Both sexes are great when real emergencies arise. You can put everything else away in order to help your children. No obstacle is too great, and a Gemini mother can become a tigress when it's necessary to defend her young. The Gemini father isn't so aggressive, but he'll take the time to probe the reasons *why* such an emergency occurred and spend more time, money, and energy to correct any trouble. With Mercury as your ruling planet, being reasonable is often your best response to the generation gap.

Most Gemini parents relate well to their teenagers, but more in a sisterly or brotherly manner. This is fine. But if the offspring are born with their sun in any of the fire signs, they'll prefer the security of a mother or father only as a parent and not in a sibling relationship.

CANCER ♋ A love for children is natural with both sexes of those born with the sun in Cancer. Strain can enter the family, however, if a Cancerian father interferes too much in the realms of home life. He's inclined to fuss over his children, always checking the baby's formula and wondering where his older children have gone off to. There's a real danger that he'll infringe on his wife's prerogative of being a mother.

In the case of motherless children, the Cancerian father is well-equipped to fulfill the role of both parents. He can, however, be too indulgent as a parent and lose some of the respect he's entitled to as man of the house. It's great for a man to rise to an emergency and cook the meals, wash the dishes, and clean the house, but it's not good policy to make this a habit. Children generally like to catagorize their parents in a clear-cut arrangement, where Father goes out to work and Mother attends to household duties.

A Cancerian mother is much better with her children when they're young than when they're adolescent, for she herself is a complex character. She may demand that the children look after *her* as they grow up, and this is always evident if she's left a widow. Boys of the family may be told that "if your father were alive he'd do this for me," and many sons have become slaves to Cancerian mothers.

Ultra-feminine herself, the Cancerian mother encourages her daughters to enjoy being female. She's not always so successful with her sons unless she can resist making demands on them as they grow older.

Both sexes enjoy providing a good home, but may not let their children find their own identity until they're able to leave the family. The departure of any offspring is generally accompanied by tears, even when the occasion is a wedding. Both parents need to be assured constantly that they are the pivot around which the household revolves.

LEO ♌ No sign of the zodiac produces women with a more deep-rooted and passionate devotion to their children. Both sexes love children—often, unfortunately, seeing them as an extension of their own personalities. Leos also have the problems restraining a tendency to domineer. Although the Leo mother will be indulgent, the Leo father can be pompous and overbearing. It's difficult for him to know that filial freedom is necessary and that discipline has to be tempered with love and trust rather than with "I know best." As children of Leo parents reach adolescence, they're inclined to rebel violently, causing hurt and disappointment. More than anything else, Leo parents want to be proud of their children. If a child's behavior makes them lose face among their friends, even the slightest misdemeanor can be exaggerated into a major and almost unforgivable offense.

Although well-meaning and motivated only by her children's welfare, the Leo mother can develop into the type of woman who becomes the target for mother-in-law jokes. She can become matriarchal, just as the Leo father can become the archetype of the overbearing father. It's very important that the undoubted love these parents feel should continue to show itself as their children grow older. The children need to realize that behind the disciplinarian there's a sensitive person who can be hurt, as well as a sympathetic, staunch parent who can be trusted in times of need. Leo parents seem to run their families more by instilling fear than by revealing their deep love. As a result, a teenager who runs into trouble may try to alienate himself from the family circle rather than face stern criticism.

It's particularly hard to be a Leo parent today, since modern values are abandoning the rigid dogmas on which conscientious, proud Leos like to build their lives. But adjustment is possible when the Leo parent realizes and accepts that it takes all kinds to make a world. Leo parents need to practice the art of giving and taking. And their children should make every effort to understand their parents.

VIRGO ♍   A Virgo mother's natural devotion for her children is often hidden behind a facade of coolness, as she's seldom moved by emotion alone. She may feel that homemaking isn't too pleasant a duty, but the Virgo father will provide for his family with a great sense of dedication and duty.

Both sexes like a well-run house, and their children don't always remember to be neat and careful. The Virgo mother is excellent with childhood sickness, while the Virgo father will always see to it that the right doctor is called and he rarely grumbles about paying medical bills.

Both sexes are at their best with other people's children and can develop into favorite aunts or uncles—and remarkably good grandparents. They often relate better to a nephew or niece than to their own children.

Virgo parents like a well-regulated, prompt family. If a Virgo mother decides that her son can watch television for an hour, he might as well accept the fact that he won't get a minute extra. Virgos like their offspring to fit into their organized schedules and adult ways of life. This is easy when the children are young, but problems arise when the young people want to spread their wings.

But when in difficulty, children of Virgo parents have one vital weapon at hand if they're wise enough to use it. Ruled by Mercury, Virgo parents will always listen to teenage problems and painstakingly try to offer a solution, rarely condemning anything they don't understand. On the other hand, they expect their offspring to make mistakes but to profit by them, and will never condone one who makes the same mistake twice.

Both sexes instill a sense of law and order into their children at an early age, paying special attention to virtues such as truthfulness and respect for other people's belongings. And despite a seeming lack of emotion, a Virgo mother or father consciously strives to be an example of good taste and conduct, and can have a very stable influence on a child's life.

A Virgo parent is probably the best preventive antidote to the spoiled child who has been over-indulged and is a disciplinary problem as he grows up. The Virgo father may not thoroughly understand the problems of adolescence, but he'll take painstaking efforts to try. With children who cooperate and try to relate to an example of such fairness, there's little real conflict to worry either part.

LIBRA ♎   The Libra mother is not fond of routine, and often can't enjoy her children's early years. The regime of fixing formulas, attending to diapers, scolding and training, often makes the early stages of child-raising a great burden to her and she is a much better mother if she has help. A good mother-in-law or aunt can be an asset to a Libra mother. She wants to be a good parent and is always concerned about the welfare of her children but often lacks confidence in dealing with them. This is particularly evident if any of her children is a Leo: she can become quite overwhelmed by the child's energies even when it's very young. The Libra mother vitally needs a strong mate who isn't afraid to accept his responsibilities as a father. He must be the ideal provider for his children—never forgetting to pay attention to their mother, too.

Libran men are fond of children and will take great interest in their education though leaving the day-to-day responsibility of raising them to their mother. They're much better with teenagers than with babies, for very young children seem to make Libran fathers very nervous.

When faced with domestic situations which others take in their stride, any Libra parent will flounder and need someone called in for advice. There's always a danger that Libras will spoil the children by lack in basic dicipline, or a "peace at any price" attitude. Children can generally cajole and charm just about anything out of a Libran father or mother. Usually, however, Libra parents maintain a good relationship with their children long after they've left the family circle. They'll become inordinately proud of their first grandchildren, and it often happens that the second generation can relate very well to Libra grandparents.

SCORPIO ♏   A woman born with her sun in this sign can be either a completely devoted mother or a very self-centered one. There are also many Scorpio women who don't want a family, preferring to tackle a career rather than raising children.

Although they realize the need for harmony within the home, many Scorpio mothers have some compulsion to highlight every domestic incident until it reaches a pitch of a drama. Their tendency to express the Scorpion's sting through displays of temper is never hampered by the presence of children. Such mothers can be very critical, expecting their children to live up to impossibly high standards at an early age, as well as being obedient and well mannered.

Yet despite these seeming drawbacks, a Scorpio mother can be a delightful companion to her children, amusing them with delightfully imaginative stories when they're young or regaling them with appropriately instructive episodes from real life as they get older. The driving force and dynamic quality of a Scorpio mother generally rubs off to produce fearless children who may seem reckless by other standards.

Certainly a child with a Scorpio mother is rarely dull. Although fiery and dynamic, the unpredictable quality of her joint ruling planet of Pluto can make a Scorpio mother unexpectedly tender with a sensitive child. She'll take more pains with him than with one who's merely precocious. Children of Scorpio parents have every opportunity to become individuals at an early age, if only because it's expected of them.

The Scorpio father is easier to understand than the Scorpio mother. He'll be interested in his children in an indulgent way, but expect them

to understand his moods and not bother him. This can become an exact-
ing way of life for a child, who never quite knows whether to expect
a pat on the head, a rebuff, or to be ignored.

All Scorpios tend to offer their children an unorthodox education,
always remembering how important it is for the children to identify
themselves as individuals and to express themselves creatively or physically. When forced to send their children to an ordinary school, Scorpios
are likely to be rebellious parents, allying themselves with the children
against the teachers. A far happier situation occurs when a Scorpio parent has enough money to choose a school that suits his children's needs
and doesn't violate their personal standards. When this happens family
life can progress fairly harmoniously.

Scorpio parents are rarely upset or resentful if a child wants to
leave home at an early age, but they like their offspring to keep in touch
by telephone or letters. Puppy love and teenage romances are dealt with
in quite a down-to-earth manner. Scorpio parents make few judgments
and definitely assume that romance is a necessary part of growing up
that need not be painful. They have little time for languid children who
moan and complain about too much homework or dates going wrong.

If a Scorpio's child shows any signs of being gifted in a specific
way, he'll do all he can to encourage the child. Scorpio parents generally
have many unusual traits of their own and nature seems to allow for
this by seeing to it that the children thrive as much on the unusual as
others do on the orthodox—providing love is in the household.

SAGITTARIUS ♐   A Sagittarian mother is conscious
of her family's every need. Always helpful and devoted during bouts of childhood ailments, she's equally ready to listen to a teenager's problems. She may not be good at supplying the answer to emotional problems, but she'll at least be sympathetic, especially if her
children are honest. She can be a most discreet confidante as well as a
go-between for family quarrels.

While not particularly tactful in dealing with arguments, she can
offer a practical approach and doesn't mind giving a slap to a child
who's getting out of hand. This is rarely done with malice or anger, but
the Sagittarian holds no pious maxims such as "spare the rod and spoil
the child." Although in the past twenty-six years, many Sagittarian
mothers have been overburdened by family responsibilities (such as
aging relatives) they rarely let any personal unhappiness or fatigue affect

the lives of the children. When children grow up and leave home, the Sagittarian's responsibilities don't end. She can still remain faithful and ready to help any who need her, and hasn't any desire to intrude deliberately in the lives of her grown-up children.

The Sagittarian father isn't so inclined to carry the burden of family responsibility in a practical manner, although he'll philosophize about it and give the impression that the strength of the family rests with him. True, he'll do whatever he can. If his wife is unable to cope with the family, he'll be available, but he'll take advantage of any chance to look the other way when things need to be done. Deliberately bring matters to his attention—such as the need to discipline his son—and he'll respond. But left to himself he'd be lenient and give the boy plenty of freedom because this is something he values himself. He adopts a friendly rather than a paternal attitude as his children get older, especially if they're active in sports. He'll enjoy taking the children off for a day's camping, fishing, or to watch a ball game—in fact, his influence is twice as important outside the home as it is indoors. He'll make swings for them in the garden and encourage them to exercise, but prefers to hand authority over to his wife once he enters the living room. The Sagittarian mother is always especially good to any child who's afflicted physically or mentally, but a Sagittarian father prefers to be with healthy children and is far better with an active child than a hypersensitive one.

CAPRICORN ♑   A Capricorn is naturally reserved when it comes to displaying affection towards members of his family, since so much of his time is taken up in dutiful providing. Young, sensitive children may find it a problem when mother or father don't have time to play with them because of business or household chores. There's often a noticeable generation gap between Capricorn parents of either sex and their teenage children, since vital areas of communication had fallen into disuse when the children were young. Many Capricorns seem to discover their children only after the youngsters have actually left home and made a nest for themselves.

This relationship can be very sound and friendly, rather than loving. Many Capricorn fathers show devotion simply by supplying their children with a good home and the means for education. A Capricorn mother sometimes has fastidious standards which her children can upset, and she may despair at their apparent indifference to what she holds sacred. These personality traits can be very strong and foster rebellion in late teenage children, and so a vicious circle is completed: the children are hurt by the parents' coldness, and then the parents are offended by the children. Although neither the Capricorn mother nor father can be called an ideal parent as far as understanding their own offspring is concerned, they have tremendous strength, resilience against adversity, and never shirk their duty in any way.

It isn't unusual for Capricorn parents and their children not to see each other for many years. Then, a great reunion takes place, after which all participants enjoy the traditional happy ending of living happily ever after.

AQUARIUS ♒︎   Both sexes derive a great deal of pleasure from activities outside the home, but no matter how busy they are with social or sociological activities, they find time to be capable, conscientious parents. They are conscious of the physical needs of young children, and as the children grow older, the Aquarian father can become a very good counsellor. The Aquarian mother isn't always aware of her growing children's emotional needs, but if they're brought to her attention, she'll respond magnificiently and do all she can.

Rarely does either parent allow child-raising to interfere with their own basic interest in humanitarian pursuits. Generally the offspring of such parents are brought up to appreciate that there are people in the world who lead lives different from their own.

Finding the correct school for their children seems to come naturally to Aquarian parents, and in the last 26 years, they have tended to select the more avant-garde types of educational establishments. Both sexes try to help their children intellectually throughout their lives. They rarely sit in judgment on juvenile mistakes and are remarkably tolerant—though not necessarily indulgent—to their children. They try to raise their offspring on an idea of harmony, but may expect a child to grow up too quickly. Aquarian fathers in particular often expect too much intellect from their children too early.

Both sexes like to be busy and can forget that a good romp with young children need not have any specific purpose beyond everyone's having a good time. Often they buy educational toys and games without recognizing that a child's quite capable of enjoying an old-fashioned doll or toy truck. Aquarian parents, unfortunately, often adopt fads, especially in food, and can become rigid disciplinarians at mealtime, urging a child to eat spinach because it's good for him. They often are reluctant to allow children to have pets. This is because Aquarian parents are particularly worried about their children getting hurt and fail to remember that most youngsters are pretty resilient to falls, cuts and bruises. Should the child injure himself, the Aquarian parent suffers more than the child does. Aquarians should try to reassure themselves, after having taken the obvious precautions to make sure their children aren't exposed to unnecessary dangers.

Aquarians maintain good relationships when their children grow up and leave home. Such parents always show a desire to be close to their offspring, even though Aquarians often have their children later in life, producing more of an age gap. Since Aquarian men tend to marry late, to far younger women, they sometimes adopt a more grandfatherly than paternal manner to their children, always striving to be kindly and understanding.

PISCES ♓ The Pisces mother needs love from her children more than any other sign in the zodiac, but she'll always return signs of affection in a dozen different ways. Forget to send a card on Mother's Day or overlook her birthday and she'll be hurt: she always remembers her children's natal days even when they've left the family circle. She can be completely faithful and devoted to her children or go to the extremes of being slovenly and allowing her dilatory attitude to rub off on them. The positive Piscean mother is overanxious about her children's welfare and particularly intuitive about their emotional needs—always aware when they're under some strain. She relates well to her children as they grow up and prefers to maintain her mother-image rather than any egalitarian role such as that of a big sister.

Piscean males—especially those born in the March decanate of the sign—aren't so concerned with their offspring's emotional needs and are apt to place a great deal of responsibility on their wives. They enjoy their children as babies when they're defenseless against the world, and again later as teenagers when they have a definite point of view. But the in-between period is difficult for a Piscean father to cope with, although the more conscientious ones will deliberately try to keep in touch. Piscean fathers who don't personally enjoy sports will nevertheless try valiantly to share their son's interest in baseball. But they fight a losing battle. The child soon realizes that his Piscean father is not truly interested, and hates to feel that he's intruding when Pop would rather be doing something else.

Pisceans of both sexes make excellent in-laws and grandparents, renewing their own youth vicariously through the second generation. Both sexes are inclined to be unorthodox when it comes to education and have been known to defy local laws about sending children to school. They can put up a strong fight for their children's paths of interest.

While neither the Piscean mother nor father are experts at household management, it's amazing how happy a family can be under the leadership of one Piscean parent. This is probably because the intuitive Piscean trait usually comes out and leads to very effective spiritual guidance of the children. Pisceans never seem to be domineering. They're also very careful not to set up impossibly high standards for the children and to make allowances for differences of age.

A Piscean father will generally do just about anything to keep his family happy and then be content to remain in the background while they enjoy the fruits of his labor and the suggestions he's made for their enjoyment. If his family appreciates this he'll be very happy and contented and will always struggle to keep the family together, even when finances are low and the planets seem to be playing tricks upon him.

20

health

ARIES ♈   Your ruling planet of Mars endows you with remarkable energy, but this same driving force can also make you feel that life is a battlefield. At times you begin to feel worn out and nervous tension begins to affect your health. Your most vulnerable areas are your head and brain, so you're likely to suffer from such nervous disorders as irritability, frequent headaches, and migraines. Problems of the ears, nose, and teeth can also ravage you. You'll rarely immobilize yourself voluntarily because of illness, always trying to keep in the mainstream of things until something drastic—like a nervous breakdown—prevents you from destroying yourself. Mars' energy is remarkable, but it can run down at certain periods of the year when only rest will bring it back. In the meantime come those periods when you're most susceptible to illness. It's important for you to try to rest before this happens but, so great is Mars' driving force that it's impossible to ask you to take rest periods willingly.

TAURUS ♉   You need be very careful when there are virus epidemics around. Although you have a strong constitution, a virus can immobilize you more quickly than anything else. Your vulnerable area is in the throat, and if you get through any year with only a few minor problems there, you'll be very lucky. Strep throats can be dangerous; laryngitis inconvenient; and even a slight irritation of the throat can upset your usually robust constitution.

Uranus is now moving into the sixth house for the next seven years and you may suffer hard-to-diagnose illnesses—such as allergies. One of your worst tendencies is brooding over minor illnesses before consulting a doctor. But once you've established faith—preferably in an old-fashioned, conservative doctor—you can become a most cooperative patient. You're very resilient after an illness and realize a convalescent period may be necessary. But it's good to remember that the proverbial ounce of prevention is worth a pound of cure. Guard against throat infections by avoiding crowded places when there's an epidemic. Use a mouthwash or gargle as frequently as you brush your teeth.

GEMINI ♊   With lots of energy emanating from your ruling planet of Mercury, you're very active. But Mercurian energy is more intellectual than physical and at times you become accident-prone, especially in the throes of emotional conflict. You need lots more sleep than many of the other signs, but you don't get enough because you tend to lie in bed thinking, often having insomnia as you magnify fears of the day.

Erratic hours and neglect of regular habits, such as eating, frequently disrupt the harmonious state necessary for your body, mind and spirit to remain balanced. Most of your illnesses are brought about by this neglect. There's rarely anything organically wrong with you, but psychosomatic pains can afflict you so that you can feel as sick as one in need of real surgery.

Domestic conditions also effect your health pattern. When upset, you're so accident-prone that a simple thing like pinching your finger in a door can immobilize you. Always take care to keep your circulation stimulated; this can be erratic in members of your sign.

CANCER ♋ Many of you suffer very much from psychosomatic ills. If you're near a sick person, you tend to be so sympathetic that you begin to take on his symptoms. Therefore, it's important to surround yourself with healthy people. This isn't always possible for you, however, because often you like to be solicitous and your friends think of you when they feel ill. Unfortunately, there are times when many of you appear to enjoy bad health, simply because it arouses attention or provides an excuse from something distasteful. Those of you who use a mythical headache as an excuse not to visit someone may be surprised how many times a real headache takes over a few hours after you've used that little white lie.

Few of you go through life without surgery—often in the stomach —but you're remarkably resilient to such things. When illness truly catches up with you, you can be very brave and come through operations that would terrify persons seeming much stronger. Sometimes the planetary patterns involve Mars, pushing you along at a pace which isn't really your own, and, at these times, you become ill from fatigue. This often occurs when you're in the midst of social activities and can probably cause you more misery than an operation. Learn when the cycles of Mars are at their worst and get lots of rest.

LEO ♌ Your sign of the zodiac is noted for its longevity and recuperative powers. You can survive the ravages of many illnesses, endure surgery, take short convalescent periods, and still live to a ripe old age. But this is possible only if you can reduce your emotional involvement in the lives of others who are sick. You can literally worry yourself into the grave if you have an ailing dependent whom you love.

Sensitive to others' physical welfare, you expect others to feel the same about you. You'll enjoy the practical help of someone near to you if you feel symptoms of a cold or headache—although many of your illnesses start with muscular pains across the back and chest. Because you consider illness a sign of weakness, you recover as quickly as possible—following the doctor's directions.

You're always conscious of any dependents and like to keep well to take care of them. You should have regular checkups. Be on the alert for any peculiarities of the bloodstream or the heart, which can be your most vulnerable organ.

VIRGO ♍︎   You're most likely to suffer from disorders triggered by upset emotions. Although you give the appearance of being cold and unemotional, this very reserve can generate unhealthy conditions and affect the nerves, the solar plexus, the digestive system, intestines, and cause general malaise.

Although you may suffer inwardly from devastating fears, once you're ill, you're quite resilient. When the emotions settle, so do the fears, and with that many of the sicknesses disappear. You can be very difficult as a patient, not responding easily to loving attention and alternating between being resigned and non-communicative to being outrageously hostile to the very person looking after you. You neither need or ask for sympathy and have little grace in accepting well-meaning offers of help when ill.

You tire very easily and rest is your greatest need when feeling ill. If something is organically wrong, naturally more than rest is needed for recovery.

LIBRA ♎︎   It's not unusual for you to suffer hard-to-diagnose ailments—chiefly in the vulnerable region of your back and kidneys. You rarely exaggerate your symptoms after adopting a grin-and-bear-it attitude until illness immobilizes you or examination shows something's wrong. While a brave face is meritorious, especially when you don't want to worry your family, it also delays getting medical care and finding the cause of the trouble.

When you're sick, you still need to be surrounded by the things you love and which your beauty-loving spirit demands, due to the influence of your ruling planet, Venus. You appreciate flowers, get-well cards, loving messages and frequent inquires about your health. When you have these attentions, you can be an excellent patient. But it takes a great deal to immobilize you. Many of you rarely look sick, even when you may be in pain, so it's likely that there's little sympathy when you need it. Take an interest in your own welfare and be willing to seek sound medical advice when you feel the first twinges of pain.

SCORPIO ♏︎   Ruled by Mars with the drastic overtones of the co-planet Pluto, you're subject to extremes in all areas of life. Illness is no exception. Add to that, some masochistic quality which makes you burn the candle at both ends when you know you should slow down and rest. Also, your private nature often makes you delay going to a doctor until your symptoms become too aggravated for you to handle.

You have a tremendous threshold of pain, can bear discomfort bravely. But once you're forced to go to bed, you're one of the worst patients in the zodiac. You hate lengthy periods of convalescence and, once on your feet, you try to get back into the mainstream of life as if nothing happened.

Your vulnerable area is connected with the reproductive organs. Because this is a delicate matter, you're apt to put off seeing a doctor.

SAGITTARIUS ♐

You're likely to get through life with a minimum of sickness or the discomfort which comes from sickness, because you don't give in easily, accepting things like headaches or a few aches and pains as part of life.

You have great concern for the health and welfare of others and you often carry the burden of other people's sickness. This also prevents you from giving in to illness unless forced to. If you're the breadwinner for a family having periods of bad health, you think that sickness is a luxury you, personally, can't afford. When you're sick, you're apt to be independent—battling solidly away at colds, wisely taking rest, warmth, and a few home remedies—rather than making your illness into a big production.

Your natural liking for fresh air and an active life help you resist sickness. But, as you become older, it's important to guard against such things as rheumatism which can progress by neglecting things such as keeping your feet dry. Those of you who live in large cities generally join health clubs or try to spend weekends in the country. All these things help maintain a sensible pattern of health. Strained muscles and accidents are more likely to immobilize you than anything else, so care in sporting activities is advised.

CAPRICORN ♑

Although members of your sign are associated with longevity, few of you get through childhood without illness. Many of you can suffer for long periods from illnesses which are not particularly dangerous but do cause discomfort. Bone fractures are common to you because you have a specially brittle bone structure, making your bones your most vulnerable part.

Because of the influence of Saturn, illness may take the form of general discomfort spread over long periods. You accept illness with fortitude but a constant amount of minor ailments can cause periods of depression. Try to avoid a martyr-like attitude toward illness. Man's normal inclination is to be healthy and there's no need to suffer from headaches and aching bones without trying to do something about it. When sick, remember that families are sympathetic to those who aren't well and the patient should allow such sympathies as well as practical attention.

AQUARIUS ♒   Ruled by the restless impulsive Uranus which has unpredictable qualities, most of your ailments have unusual characteristics which defy the medical profession. You can worry yourself about them and only add to the aggravation. You also fear being an inconvenience to your family and see illness as a form of weakness which is abhorrent to you as well as a means of restricting your freedom.

Sometimes, you defeat your need to keep well, even getting to the verge of a nervous breakdown, by worrying about others, working too hard, and generally taking on more than the accepted pressures of life. One of your biggest dangers is never giving yourself time to convalesce. Once you have both feet out of bed, you expect to function as if nothing's happened. Once you learn to respect your body as the remarkable piece of engineering it is, you're a much more tractable patient. Migraines are not uncommon to members of your sign and some discomfort can occur from middle ear trouble upsetting your delicate sense of balance.

PISCES ♓   You tend to become over-anxious about many things, particularly when illness is about, and there are times when you can exaggerate a simple cold into pneumonia. Your sign is so complex, however, that you may cry wolf many times and have nothing really serious wrong with you, and then be caught, unexpectedly, with the cold that really does turn into pneumonia!

Once you're faced with anything serious, you accept it very well, facing illness without much fear—helped, undoubtedly, by the better aspects of Neptune which gives you a philosophical and spiritual outlook on life. It's probably when sickness is around that you can rise to some of your best traits, helped by Neptune, and making the best of everything. As a patient, you can be cooperative. If you have a sympathetic and understanding medical adviser, you gain confidence in him if he doesn't try to deceive you. Nothing irritates you so much as half-truths when you're sick. Pulmonary diseases are likely to beset you through your life but many of you can combat this by living in an area beneficial to your pulmonary conditions.

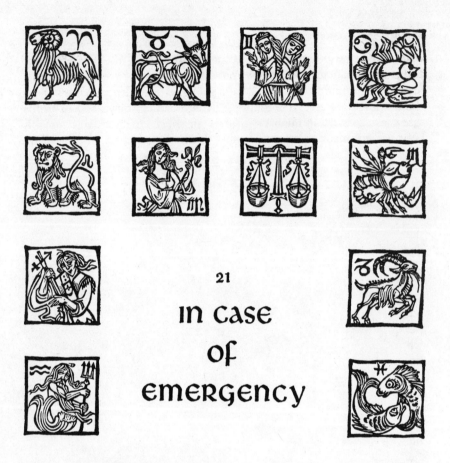

21

in case
of
emergency

ARIES ♈   Mentally and physically you're very well
equipped to deal with personal emergencies, and when someone else calls on you for help you really rise to the occasion, showing
some of your best traits. Faced with an accident or an attempted burglary
you're likely to act first by reflex and think later, with little regard for
your own safety. Indeed, at the time of spontaneous emergency you're
fine. But if there's time to think about it, you can become very garrulous
and start theorizing—especially if someone's listening. This can sometimes confuse the issue as well as the person asking for help. But sometimes those second thoughts give you ingenious solutions to problems,
encouraging your companions to be as fearless as you.

    You have the qualities that make you a potential hero or heroine
in situations involving holding off an invader or preventing assault,

218

enabling someone to escape. Unfortunately, with the instinct to act first and think later, you should be the last person to keep a gun around the house. Your makeup is such that while you can theorize that you'd only use the gun to frighten, there's no doubt that you'd actually shoot in case of emergency. In all emergencies, your Mars-sparked temper should be watched.

TAURUS ♉   When you have time to use common-sense tactics in an emergency, you're great to have around. But in spontaneous emergencies such as street accidents, fears and emotions keep you from being helpful. You have the strength not to panic, and once you've fought back initial fear and emotion, you're able to take charge and organize others.

You're not a fast mover at any time, but always able to contribute something in an emergency. You're the friend who'll always take an acquaintance to the hospital and wait around patiently while the patient's being attended to. You're also good at taking charge of children whose parents have been called away in an emergency. Providing you have time to think and plan, no one can have a more calming influence on distraught people. You're able to listen and lend a sympathetic ear in a kind manner.

In sudden accidents, try to conquer those initial fears—and under *no* circumstances identify with the victims. *They*—not you—need the help.

GEMINI Ⅱ   If there's a controversial emergency, you're so mentally alert that you enjoy finding yourself in the middle of chaos. It's this personal enjoyment which can hold up settling the emergency. You have to be careful not to make a mountain out of a molehill. In your desire to support the underdog or victim, you can let your imagination run riot and often elaborate on facts. If you're ever called as a witness, your imagination can confuse others. Your well-meaning attempts to help can be defeated by talking too much. You're so quick that you see more than others. But you can get bogged down by details and wander from the important facts concerning the emergency.

Once the first excitement of an emergency dies down—especially if it's an accident—your second thoughts begin to muster, and you're able to present a true and factual account of what happened. If you're questioned by authorities, there may be some discrepancy between the first and second telling of your story which could put some doubt in the minds of the authorities. So in an emergency of this type, keep your eyes and ears open. But don't talk until you've had time to get over the first excitement of being involved.

Emergencies really must have a dramatic impact to interest you. The "conversation" type of emergency over the telephone where someone wants your sympathy or advice, rarely gets any interest from you. But you can be great in breaking all speed limits if someone needs to get to the hospital.

You're rarely likely to suffer from postponed shock or horror after an emergency. Your quick mind will begin to rationalize, telling you it all belongs to the past. For you, tomorrow always holds interest, never past happenings.

Being one of the most accident-prone signs, perhaps this ability to throw off the impact of other people's emergencies is a blessing. It would be most harmful to you to identify with the victim and think "there but for the grace of God, go I."

CANCER ♋   Once the first shock of the emergency has died away, you come through beautifully—especially when long-term or post-hospital care is needed. Then you can rise to the occasion magnificiently. At the time of an emergency, however, you're inclined to let personal impressions override judgment; sometimes fear can immobolize you. You have a capacity for sympathy and though there's a time for this (and it can be invaluable) at the time of impact, action is what's needed.

Someone usually has to call an ambulance, doctor, or the police and it's rarely you—though while waiting for help to arrive, you can play a valuable part in soothing the victim. Concentrate on this, but don't allow your imagination to run riot at the time. If you're called on to be a witness, you tend to elaborate and throw out red herrings impeding the inquiry. You don't do this deliberately, but your imagination is so great that it has difficulty sticking to pertinent details. You're inclined to see things as much worse than they really are.

Your major role in any emergency is that of a ministering angel rather than as a dramatic heroine. Recognize this, and you'll be known as one of the best friends to have around after the first blow of an emergency. You're very necessary to carry on where others have left off. Many other signs can be involved and very helpful in an emergency yet fail to realize that a mother rushed off to the hospital may come home debilitated and helpless for days. You can play a great part in all convalescences requiring tender loving care.

Your main problem will always be not exaggerating. Most of all, try not to identify yourself with the victim. It's also helpful if you don't dwell on the past emergency and do your best helping the victim to forget.

LEO ♌   You can be most helpful in all emergencies, especially if physical courage is needed. You forget personal danger and can plunge right in without thinking of yourself. Because of this personal courage—often aided by physical strength and quick reflexes of mind and body—you often emerge as a hero or heroine. The greater the danger (and when you're left alone to be the sole rescuer), the more likely you are to be successful in rescuing the victim.

A different pattern emerges if you're an eyewitness or arrive at the scene after others have taken the initiative. As an eyewitness you can be valuable because the same reflexes needed for physical action are transferred to powers of observance. Also, besides being capable of authoritative action yourself, you present a stable figure to authority and rarely allow emotion to cloud the facts. Your biggest danger comes well after the emergency is over. Given time to think, imagination runs riot and you begin to elaborate.

Always conscious of dramatic effects and having a need for the limelight, you need be careful not to tell the same story too often and become a bore. Even if you've been the hero or heroine in an emergency, it's better to let someone else tell the story. When you haven't been involved in action, you're more likely to embroider your own part, making it more dynamical than it was. This is because you're quite certain of how you would have handled the affair and can rarely sacrifice a chance to give a coloroful, wordy description of fires, traffic accidents, or other catastrophies.

These qualities of observation and lack of fear make many of you excellent newspaper reporters, as you're prepared to constantly face the kind of violence and horror that would upset less strong-minded persons.

Although you have strong humanitarian instincts, you don't often go in for hand-holding or soothing the victim of an accident. You're much more concerned with getting some action in the shortest possible time, feeling that sympathetic attention can be left to others. This is excellent, and, in many cases, can save a life when prompt medical attention is needed.

You're the one at home who has the phone numbers of the local doctor, hospital, fire brigade, and ambulance pinned up near your telephone. Again, this is fine—forethought can prevent minor emergencies developing into major disasters. But once you've fulfilled your role, try to step back from the scene and don't talk about it to family members who may also be emotionally upset.

VIRGO ♍   You're at your best after an emergency has calmed down. Often while an emergency calls for action, you will be more concerned with analyzing why the emergency occurred than getting down to extricating the victim or exerting physical effort.

As professional accident investigators, assessing insurance claims, you can play an important part in giving impartial judgments. You'll always weigh the facts, refusing to be drawn into family arguments. Perhaps you could mellow a certain coldness and detachment you have when dealing with relations or victims who are naturally emotional about the emergency. While efficiency is splendid and very necessary, a lack of warmth can earn you a reputation that does nothing to mark you as a humanitarian.

Use your quick mind to collect important data. But if this has to be done at the scene of the emergency, try to be tactful. Allow for the fact that the victim has already suffered and may not be able to give you clear facts. You can often temper your natural impatience to get on with things by appearing very painstaking and precise, but it'll always show as coldness. The victim, conscious only of personal needs at the time, will definitely not understand that you, too, may have a peculiar feeling in your solar plexus due to fear, and that the coldness is nothing more than a defense mechanism.

Sometimes the victim of an emergency is better left alone—conversation can come later. Don't hinder the work of others in providing physical comfort to ease pain. There's nothing to stop you from being observant and this will be valuable later. Your retentive mind enables you to remember everything, and you may be called upon to give a precise account of what happened. It's at this time you'll be at your best— reliable, unprejudiced, and stable. Such witnesses to emergencies can be the utmost help indirectly to both the victim and any authorities involved.

Few of you are good at witnessing scenes of horror, but your ability to control your feelings at the time is admirable. That you suffer personally afterwards is inevitable. Be careful to look after yourself—delayed shock can immobilize you.

Don't be afraid to leave the scene of an emergency if you really feel you can't contribute anything. If you can get others organized, you'll always do it efficiently. If you're sure everything's well taken care of, there's no need to stand by waiting to see what happens next. This way you can give that delicate solar plexus of yours time to settle down and keep your reputation for being cool.

LIBRA ♎   Providing you have moral support from others, you're able to react well in most types of emergency, although 60 percent of the members of your sign don't desire to linger at the scene of accidents. You can, however, be most kind and helpful in offering solace to victims, administering to creature comforts, supplying pillows or extra clothes—even holding the patient's hand or head or making tea or coffee. Your great forté is in offering enough support to raise morale, either in the victim or others around you. After the emergency is over, you may have a guilty conscience, wondering if you could have done more. You can help offset this by being decisive during the emergency, even if you have to leave physical actions to others. Gather your wits in case you have to make phone calls and be sure to get the correct number the first time.

As a witness after the event—providing you've kept your own emotions well in hand—you can be precise and detailed in reporting the scene. But try not to be verbose. Often when authorities are called, they need to interview many people. You could delay their work by being too flamboyantly descriptive or offering opinions, even though you're full of good intentions. Take a few moments before being interviewed to clarify your own mind and put facts in sequential order. If you're overly emotional, the indecisive quality will spoil the validity of your statement —especially if you refer to such things as "someone told me this." Keeping to the point is not one of your greatest attributes.

You can be very helpful tidying up after an emergency—something often forgotten after the more dramatic scene is over. Because you have tremendous sensitivity and sympathy for upset persons, it's often your lot to be the bearer of bad news after an emergency. In this, you manage to do this unpleasant task with dignity and diplomacy. While everyone can't be a hero, you have enough good sense to realize this and can be quite content filling the messenger's role.

You can be relied upon to share the burdens in an emergency and obey the instructions of those in charge. Not everyone is suited to take the initiative; there's a need for people like you to carry out important and minor duties.

Scorpio ♏

Your love of the dramatic can be both a plus and a minus when you're faced with an emergency. There's always an inclination to exaggerate a small emergency into a major one and you're likely to get everyone else upset when you do this. It's not unusual when members of your sign having a family member with a cold make it into pleurisy, pneumonia, or consumption.

You get a kick out of shock tactics even when you're relaying a message. It's important not to overemphasize the possible dire results of any emergency. Try to be objective in your efforts to help and don't allow selfish interests to take over.

In cases of real emergency, even those of an unpleasant nature, your strong will and quick mind react positively. If you have to play the doctor's assistant or give first aid, you can be one of the most valuable people to have around. It's only when your highly fertile imagination has time to run riot that you upset the scene, although you're always filled with good intentions.

You should allow your fine, deep insight into human nature to play its part even if a great deal of your ego has to be subdued. As witness to an accident, you're not one of the most reliable for you adore coloring a situation, making everyone feel involved in a big drama. Try to curb this instinct. Think first. Assemble the facts in your mind even though it will be difficult.

When an emergency is over, you can let some of your verbosity loose, but overemphasizing any gory details won't make you popular if relations or close friends of the victim are nearby. No one can describe exciting scenes better than you. You can hold an audience in captivity while you describe scenes. But this talent is best used in writing, not talking. You're never likely to be a bore, but you can be a nuisance in an emergency unless you take a firm grip on yourself and really struggle to help in a practical manner.

SAGITTARIUS ♐   You're always able to take the initiative—physically and mentally—in emergencies, and have
little patience with anyone who gets in your way or who's not prepared
to make himself useful. Your authoriative manner inspires courage in
others and generally manages to get things done in the shortest possible
time.

The one thing likely to defeat your effectiveness is having someone
as capable as you around. Then your competitive spirit is aroused, and
a personal desire to dominate may defeat the real business of attending
to the victim.

You're not at your best in hospitals and institutions. As a visitor
to a post-operative case, you can become restless and irritable. This, of
course, is not conducive to the recovery of the patient so it's better to skip
the visit and restrict yourself to sending get-well notes or gifts. You can
also contribute a great deal by remaining at home with relations who
are emotionally upset or bereaved, offering words of sympathy and administering creature comforts.

In cases of extreme crisis, you're a great booster of morale to the
victims as well as to those trying to help. You generally manage to do
this with very good taste so that no one thinks you're underestimating
the seriousness of the occasion.

If called upon to show great physical courage, you'll never consider any danger to yourself. Many famous firefighters have been born
in your sign. You generally keep yourself in top physical shape; even
after exertion you rarely know you're tired. In the horrible London Blitz
in World War II, Sagittarians were indefatigable workers, rescuing
victims from the debris, staying around to clear up the mess, and rarely
showing signs of fatigue even after 24 hours on duty.

Your emotions become less stable if the emergency involves an
injury to children or animals than it does when dealing with adults.
You're able to calm down frightened, injured animals. Your ability to
plan means of rescue is phenomenal, and you can apply great ingenuity
in this particular sphere if you're allowed your own way. You can be
ruthless with crowds who hinder you.

As a witness, you're sound and factual although you may express
your personal opinions very vehemently if you feel there's an injustice.
This can be a double-edged sword which may not always be helpful to
the victim—especially when there are professionals involved in handing
down a verdict. Restrain your emotions and indignation and stick to the

facts. Present them with decisiveness and dignity; this will add to their validity when a final assessment is made.

CAPRICORN ♑   While able to handle emergencies, there's always a danger you'll move too slowly in an effort to be thorough. This isn't due to fear or lack of initiative so much as a need for time to think out what's best. You're unlikely to run away from anything gruesome and can be depended upon to see an emergency through to the bitter end, whether it's a minor or major accident. If the victim is someone close to you, you have the advantage of not showing emotion and can call for help with cool, almost detached, efficiency.

This ability to detach yourself emotionally from an unpleasant situation is excellent—to a point. However, after the emergency's over and the victim perhaps hospitalized, you should try to develop a much warmer attitude. Remember to send flowers, write little notes and inquire about the well-being of the patient. It's not enough to calmly discuss matters with the doctor—and never try to do this when the patient's present or outside the door of the sickroom. This can make patients very suspicious and create inner fears which won't help them recover.

You're at your best in the most depressing of cases, probably due to your own grim relationship with your ruling planet of Saturn. In many emergencies, memory of a personal experience may help you foresee the way things may go. You rarely relate emotionally to the victim. When crisp decisions are necessary, you're more inclined to carry on with your work than to spend time murmuring words of sympathy. This is fine if there's someone else who can give emotional care to the victim, but it's not truly helpful if you're in sole charge. Try to be very patient and understanding during any post-hospital periods. Remember the patient has suffered a great deal and needs to be regarded as a human being.

As a witness you're reliable, factual, and completely detached and your evidence is usually highly respected. You'll often draw attention to a tiny detail which may have escaped notice. You should try to concentrate on the major facts, however, rather than the details—unless you feel they're truly relevant to the case.

It's also poor taste to inject sarcasm into your testimony. Most people want to be helpful after an accident, and it's wrong to consider officials as enemies of justice or mankind. It's their job to sift the facts to the best of their ability.

AQUARIUS ≈ Many of you are so idealistic that in emergencies it may take time for you to really relate to the scene and realize that something beyond the norm has happened. While you're always concerned with humanity as a whole, the individual needs of a human being may escape your attention.

It's important for you to find some way to relate to the victim. This isn't because you don't feel compassion, but because the emotion welling up in you literally stops you in your tracks. This compassion extends itself well beyond the time of the emergency for you don't forget anything easily. You can be relied upon to offer solace and practical help when the emergency's over, and others have gone about their own business.

Normally, you're a most active person physically, tremendously alert, but you like to plan your life, with little leeway for the inconveniences caused by other people. When there's an emergency, your first reaction is that it's highly inconvenient. This is followed by a desire to escape from the scene and to go about your own business. If, however, you're forced into staying and acting, you can rise to the emergency and perform simple duties efficiently and calmly.

You'd never desert anyone and yet it's probably good sense on your part to leave emergency work to others once you are sure they're able to deal with the situation. So many people want to be helpful but just linger around without contributing much. Sometimes they even hinder those better equipped to deal with the emergency. You don't have this fault.

Should you be called upon to give testimony or an opinion, you're very good at giving clear-cut, decisive answers with no elaboration on the theme. You'll never try to impede the law or anyone in authority, but neither will you go out of your way to help unless specifically called upon. Being in the limelight at the time of a disaster is alien to your nature.

When friends and relations are hospitalized, you'll always dutifully visit but you must guard against being too critical of both the patient and those attending him. In an effort to make the patient forget his illness or the emergency, you avoid referring to it. For some people, this is excellent, as it's never good to dwell on past unhappy events. But this can be carried to extremes. The one thing the patient can't ignore is that he's the one who has suffered, and a kindly, sympathetic, warm inquiry about his welfare doesn't do any harm.

PISCES ♓   Although you're very capable in some
spheres, including emergencies, speed isn't your forté. You
can daydream, wondering what to do. Sometime in your life you should
sit down and think ahead of how you'd react to various forms of emergency. This is particularly necessary if you have children who can sometimes have minor and major disasters from an early age. Learn the
antidotes for common cases of poisoning; keep a constant supply of
bandages, plasters, burn and antiseptic lotions on hand. Above all, make
a list of doctors, ambulance services, fire brigade, and keep it near the
phone. Once faced with an emergency itself, the less thinking you have
to do about details like telephone numbers and contacting help, the
better.

Fear of making a mistake can immobilize you, and you could literally worry yourself into being an emergency case yourself. Better call
in someone else promptly than waste time worrying or doing the wrong
thing. All members of your sign should take a short course in first aid.
Apart from being highly practical, psychologically this can help you
face an emergency should it happen. You're inclined to daydream and
see life through rose-tinted glasses, pushing away the idea that anything
horrible might happen. When it does, you're likely to go into a state of
shock unless you take simple precautions beforehand.

As a nurse you can be kindly, sympathetic and attentive to post-
emergency victims of any age, particularly with young children. The
authoritative executive side of an emergency leaves you bewildered and
frustrated because you can't cope—but you more than make up for this
once the shock has worn off.

Your protective instincts easly surface so that the post-emergency
victim not only gets adequate attention from you but also gains a
guardian against too many visitors. The welfare of the patient becomes
your prime concern but you should be careful of your own health during
nursing periods. You're willing to work long hours for others and sometimes this is far beyond your normal physical strength.

Many members of your sign are highly psychic and spiritually
evolved. This can help in soothing a fretful patient or one who has gone
into a traumatic state following an emergency.

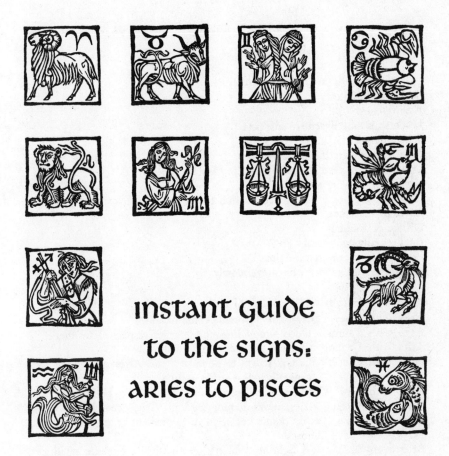

ınstant guıde
to the sıgns:
arıes to pısces

ARIES ♈   The Arian body is lean and firm with a
long head set on a strong neck. A broad, slightly rounded
forehead draws attention to the upper part of the face and the penetrat-
ing gaze of deep-set eyes—usually brown or gray. In contrast to the
broad forehead, the lowers cheeks taper off to a sharp chin. The nose is
fully arched, of heavy bone structure, with well-shaped nostrils. The
mouth is large, but thin, and the teeth are long, a bit irregular, with the
front teeth protruding slightly. The complexion is very fresh—becoming ruddy in later years. The hair is sandy to reddish-brown color.

Natural Element—Fire—Cardinal Sign

Ruling Planet—Mars

Gender—Masculine

General Characteristics

Dominant intellect
Assertiveness
Leadership and Executive instincts
Self-centeredness
Need for self-gratification
Dynamic—the need to lead an exciting life
Keen in mind and perception
Great driving force with determination to act
Lover of extremes
Dislike of routine
Intellectually egotistical
Proud, daring, often capricious
Impatient with others who move slowly

Action and Reaction to Other Signs

Aries with Aries   Successful, favorable combination
Aries with Taurus   Good—providing both parties respect each other
Aries with Gemini   Aries dominates whenever possible
Aries with Cancer   Cancer strives to dominate, and Aries resents this with generally unfavorable results
Aries with Leo   Can be an equal partnership, favorable to both
Aries with Virgo   Aries enjoys dominating and Virgo generally withdraws
Aries with Libra   Aries dominates often to the benefit of Libra more than himself
Aries with Scorpio   A fighting combination giving life a seesaw quality
Aries with Sagittarius   Aries dominates but better in business than romantically
Aries with Capricorn   By persistence, Capricorn can dominate, and Aries gives in—if mutual respect is there
Aries with Aquarius   Aries dominates physically, but intellectually there's a catalystic quality beneficial to both parties
Aries with Pisces   The domination by Aries is softened by the sympathy and understanding of Pisces

Your Most Favorable Climate

Although you can stand cold weather, it's better if it's the type found in Switzerland where the climate is mostly dry though cold with sparkling champagne-like air. A dry, warm climate suits you better than a humid or exaggerated tropical atmosphere.

You thrive in densely populated places where there is an element of excitement and constant "happenings." As a contrast you find pleasure, in arid, desert-like areas.

Sports
Energetic and adventurous sports appeal to you and you prefer being involved rather than watching.

Hunting   Rugby
Shooting   Wrestling
Riding   Tennis
Boxing

Flowers
Red roses; strong, brightly-colored gladioli

Perfumes and Incenses
Your nose is highly alerted to smell. Such things as cedar-wood chests and odoriferous woods such as pine and cypress, appeal to you. Flower perfumes—attar of roses.

Best Day of the Week
The French word for Tuesday is "mardi" and has an association with your ruling planet of Mars. The best day to begin to plan new enterprises and to expect good results is Tuesday. You're at your best in the mornings, being a day rather than a night person. Many of you may work on the "night shift," from 2 A.M. to 8 A.M. The early morning hours inspire you, while the afternoon is generally used for routine work, leaving time for plenty of rest in the early part of the evening.

Favorable Metal
Iron, although in the modern age steel is also favorable. You have a tendency to collect iron relics or amass quantities of stainless steel.

Favorable Precious Stone
Bloodstone—because of its affinity to Mars, your ruling planet.

Favorable Colors
Scarlet, cerise, magenta, claret, all "angry" shades.

Your Musical Keynote
You vibrate best to the note of "C," which is associated with Mars.

Your Best Numbers
The number assigned to the planet Mars is 3. This should not be confused

with Scorpio, who also has 3 as its planetary number. But Scorpio also has the influence of its joint planet of Pluto, which adds more mysterious influences on its subject than the more straightforward single influence of Mars on Aries subjects.

If your birthday numbers when added together add to three, it emphasizes that this number will always mean good fortune for you. It also means that the basic characteristics of your sign, both favorable and detrimental, will be exaggerated.

Vocations

All phases of science
Surgery in preference to general medicine; especially ear, nose and throat specialists
Dentistry
Foundry work engineering
All dangerous, adventurous occupations, including exploration
Reporting, if adventurous, such as crime or war work
The Army
Many areas of music
Barbering
Fire-fighting services
Professional sports
Jewelry making
Electronics
Cashiering
Stenography
Revolution
Anarchy
Acting

Your Body

The vulnerable areas are: eyes, nose and ears; the cranium; carotid arteries; the upper jaw; the face in general.

Too much alcoholic beverage can influence reflex actions of other areas of the body such as the liver. Heart, circulation, and blood deficiencies can occur because of the influence of the ruling planet of Mars. The placement of your corresponding fire signs, Leo and Sagittarius, as well as the Mars-influenced Scorpio, will also show the competent astrologer which areas of your body, beside the head, may be affected.

You have such an excellent dominant mind that there's scarcely any ailment which can't be dominated, even conquered, when the mind is master of the body.

Most Favorable Periods of the Year

March 21 to April 19   October 2 to November 21
July 23 to August 22   November 22 to December 21

Herbs Necessary for You

Aloe (as an antidote to burns)	Ginger
Capers	Hops
Cinnamon	Mustard
Coriander	Pepper
	Sage

As a fire sign, you're attracted to spicy herbs, anything with a distinct taste rather than a subtle one.

Your Most Favorable Trees and Shrubs

Cactus	Chestnut
Ironwood	Broom
Hemlock	Rosemary
Pepperwort	All thorny, prickly trees
Pine	

Wines and Liquors

All strong, high proofed spirits such as rum
Rhine and Moselle wines
Champagne

Famous Personalities Born With Their Sun in Aries

Actors   Charles Chaplin, Joan Crawford, Bette Davis, Marlon Brando, Peter Ustinov

Musicians   Aturó Toscanini, Sergei Rachmaninoff, Oscar Strauss, Béla Bartók, Johann Sebastian Bach, Leopold Stokowski

Explorers   Charles Wilkes, astronaut James Lovell

Military Leaders   Otto von Bismark, Charlemagne

Politicians   Thomas Jefferson, James Madison, Vladimir Lenin

Writers   Walter Winchell, Anatole France, Washington Irving, Henry James, Clare Booth Luce, J. P. F. Richter, Emile Zola, Tennessee Williams

How to Deal With an Aries

Be prepared to make first overtures to friendship. If he's arrogant, meet it with courtesy and good manners. Don't take offense easily. If you're forced into militant situations, state your own case fearlessly, but don't be provoked into mental and verbal fights just to satisfy his ego.

TAURUS ♉   The classic Taurean look is one of graceful charm, body strength combined with facial kindness. The large-boned body is pear-shaped, the chest being narrower than the hips, and it tends to thicken after the first flush of youth without losing its grace. The short head rests on a short neck. The eyes are dark and round, with a soft expression. The nose is full. The lips, too, are full and curved; the teeth are squared and placed close together. The ears are long and protrude slightly from the head. Many Taureans have quite beautiful hair that grows profusely—usually brunette in color. The legs are solid, and the Taurean is the epitome of dignified movement.

Natural Element—Earth—Fixed

Ruling Planet—Venus

Gender—*Feminine Sign*

General Characteristics
Physical and mental strength dominates all other characteristics
Tenacity
Inflexibility, sometimes to a point of blindness
Stubborn in a warlike manner
Responsive to duty, expecting others to observe their duties as well
Self-determined
Mentally conservative and traditionally conventional
Powerful executive
Reserved; cautious
Practical and careful
Long memory for wrongs
Resentful of contradiction
Faithful

Action and Reaction to Other Signs

Taurus with Taurus	This can be a most favorable partnership based on mutual dislikes and likes
Taurus with Gemini	Taurus dominates to the point where Gemini decides to move away. Short term relationships
Taurus with Cancer	Cancer softens any hardness in Taurus, using the iron-hand-in-the-velvet-glove technique. Better for romantic rather than business ventures

Taurus with Leo   Taurus dominates after building up confidence from Leo,
who'll always respect a strong person

Taurus with Virgo   Taurus dominates and is especially beneficial to Virgos
in their youth. After thirty, Virgo breaks away

Taurus with Libra   If Libra respects Taurus, then domination is allowed,
but relationships last longer when based on financial
consideration

Taurus with Scorpio   Scorpio dominates after proving himself and earns
the respect of Taurus

Taurus with Sagittarius   Taurus dominates so that all too often Sagittarius
carries many burdens

Taurus with Capricorn   Although dominated by Capricorn, Taurus is wise
enough to use the hard working Capricorn for the
mutual improvement of business. Capricorn is also
eager to please Taurus

Taurus with Aquarius   Taurus dominates, but this can be a good combination for business

Taurus with Pisces   Pisces mitigates some of the hardness of Taurus, and
this can be a tender romantic relationship not devoid
of business overtones.

Taurus with Aries   Equal paths

Your Most Favorable Climate

Business generally attracts and takes you into urban life with probably a second residence or vacations in mountains or green valleys. The latter would
pall as a permanent home, although a garden of some type is essential to you.

Sports

Walking	Mountaineering
Riding	Shooting
Rugby	Boxing

Flowers

Lily of the valley, jasmine. Most red flowers such as carnations and roses

Perfumes and Incenses

Musk, rose, carnation, honeysuckle, violet, saffron and satinwood

Best Day of the Week

Friday, which gets its name from the Norse goddess of love, "Frigg," is your
most fortunate day. Many people regard Friday as a day of bad luck because
of the association with the Crucifixion, but Scandinavian people regard it as
the most fortunate day of the week. With the planet Venus ruling Taurus,

it's natural that the day set aside for the love goddess should be fortunate to Taureans.

Favorable Metals
Copper is lucky either in jewelry or around the house

Favorable Precious Stone
Diamonds

Favorable Colors
Reds, oranges, and startling derivations of these

Your Musical Keynote
You vibrate well to the note of "A" or "la."

Your Best Numbers
The number associated with your planet of Venus is 6. If your birth date adds up to six, all the best and the worst of your characteristics will be accentuated.

Vocations
Agriculture, horticulture, stock raising
Mining (engineering)
Real Estate
Music
Writing
Theatrical agenting
Business executive
Cooking
Housekeeping
Investing
Military
Entertaining
Natural science and physics
Sculpting
Many derivations from agriculture take the Taurean into the distillery trade, the wine industry, and the sugar and flour industries.

Your Body
The vulnerable areas are: throat, neck; palate, tonsils and larynx; jugular vein; thyroid; ears; the seven cervical vertebrae.
By reflex actions, the placement of the other earth signs will influence

health. According to the placement of Virgo and Capricorn, you may suffer from intestinal and bowel disorders.

Most Favorable Periods of the Year

April 20 to May 20	September 23 to October 23
August 23 to September 22	December 22 to January 19

Herbs Necessary for You

Chickweed	Saffron
Coriander	Irish Moss
Fennel	Hoarhound
Mint	Sage
Peppermint	Thyme

Your Most Favorable Trees and Plants

Grapes	Elderberry
Chestnut	Alder

Wines and Liquors

Red wines
Brandies

Famous Personalities Born With Their Sun in Taurus

Actors   Gary Cooper, Harold Lloyd, Rudolph Valentino, Margaret Rutherford, Audrey Hepburn

Musicians   Johannes Brahms, Franz Lehár, Serge Prokofiev, Peter Tschaikovsky, Yehudi Menuhin, Nellie Melba, Ezio Pinza

Entertainers   Jack Paar, Mike Wallace, Fred Astaire, Edward R. Murrow

Military Leaders   Adolph Hitler, Nicolo Machivelli, Oliver Cromwell, Ulysses Grant

Physicists   Gabriel Fahrenheit, Marchese Marconi, Max Planck

Sportsmen   Willie Mays, Joe Louis

Inventors   S. F. Morse, Edward Jenner

Writers   Anita Loos, William Shakespeare, Rabindranath Tagore, Henry Fielding, Alphonse Daudet

How to Deal With a Taurean

Remember that they're susceptible to beauty in all forms. Appreciate their material acquisitions and their comfortable living conditions. Don't encroach on their liking for conventionalities and formalities. Listen to their advice and be prepared to take it—for if they're on friendly terms with you, it'll be offered after thoughtful consideration. Beware, however, if the friendship terminates—for then the mild and placid bull can turn into an infuriated animal.

GEMINI II   Geminis have very straight, small-boned, model-like bodies, with a tendency toward tallness. The face is thin, the forehead square. There is a variation of color in the eyes, but most typically, they're hazel. There is the first hint of a retroussé nose in the Gemini: the nose is full, the nostrils fine and sensitive. The cheekbones are high and bony, ending in a prominent dimpled chin. The small mouth has thin, pale lips and the teeth are fairly large and have an uneven appearance. The Gemini's hair grows quickly and is usually fair to light brown in color. An interesting point is that the left and right profiles have marked differences—almost as if it were two different pepole.

Natural Element—Air

Ruling Planet—Mercury

Gender—Masculine Sign

General Characteristics
Eloquence
Mental versatility
Fickleness
Thirst for knowledge
Charming manners and ways
Restlessness
Imaginative
Sensual when necessary
Capricious
Generous

Action and Reaction to Other Signs

Gemini with Gemini   Can be favorable and definitely never dull, but relationships may not be of long duration
Gemini with Cancer   Cancer dominates, but Gemini often becomes bored.
Gemini with Leo   Leo dominates, sometimes to a point where Gemini sulks, revolts, or just moves away. Where romantic attachments are formed, Gemini can also like the domination, especially if Leo shoulders responsibilities

Gemini with Virgo	Virgo dominates, and the intellectual combination engineered by both sharing the same ruling planet of Mercury can make this a lively relationship
Gemini with Libra	Libra dominates, enjoying, however, the generosity and quick-witted charm of Gemini
Geminin with Scorpio	Scorpio dominates and can outcharm Gemini who'll generally yield to strong magnetism of the contrasting nature that Scorpio offers
Gemini with Sagittarius	Sagittarius is excellent for a business relationship as he helps to stabilize the more flighty inclinations of Gemini, although appreciating the versatile mind
Gemini with Capricorn	Capricorn dominates, but rarely lingers long with Gemini who's rarely impressed by the Saturnine moods of Capricorn
Gemini with Aquarius	Aquarius dominates, and, in romantic or business relationships, takes on most of the responsibilities which Gemini refuses to see
Gemini with Pisces	Pisces dominates and supplies a contrast to Gemini which both parties can appreciate and exploit. Good for business and romantic relationships
Gemini with Aries	Aries dominates
Gemini with Taurus	Taurus dominates

Your Most Favorable Climate

Any cool, temperate one. You rarely thrive in tropical heat. Live in cities, but preferably within easy access of the seashore, and places where there's social life.

Sports

Tennis	Golf
Fencing	Badminton
Track racing	Calisthenics

You generally excel in any sport which appeals to you and, like your vocations, there are limitless sporting activities which appeal to you for varying degrees of time.

Flowers

Jasmine, honeysuckle, yellow roses

Perfumes and Incenses

Fresh sparkling colognes from a fresh flower base, in preference to heady perfume essences. Bayberry, mastic resin, sandalwood

Best Day of the Week

Your best day is Wednesday, associated with Raphael who aids the inspiration of the written and spoken word.

Favorable Metals

Both silver and quicksilver are favorable. Many Geminis are health-conscious and carry a thermometer.

Favorable Precious Stone

Aquamarine, crystal and diamonds are generally favored.

Favorable Colors

Yellow and blues. Always clear, clean shades with a tendency to blend colors into plaids and checks.

Your Musical Keynote

You vibrate to "E" or "mi."

Your Best Number

Your planetary number is 4.

Vocations

Practically limitless, but very dependent on the placement of other planets for particular success. Gemini is rarely the master of only one vocation and can happily thrive in two or more with equal ability and success.

Writing in all its many forms
Politicians and statesmen
Linguists
The motor industry
Electrical engineering
All forms of communication media—advertising, radio, television, etc.
Dancing
Public relations and hostess work
Aviation
Electronics
Most types of office work
Sports

Just as the air is limitless, so versatility can take Gemini into any vocational sphere—if only for a short time.

Your Body

The vulnerable areas are: shoulders, arms, hands and lungs. Fractures generally occur in the clavicle, scapula and upper ribs. The trachia, bronchi and radial artery may also be vulnerable.

Reflex ailments are derived from Mercury-ruled signs such as Virgo and the third air sign of Aquarius. These affect nervous afflictions and kidney ailments.

Most Favorable Periods of the Year

May 21 to June 21	September 23 to October 22
August 23 to September 22	January 20 to February 18

Herbs Necessary for You

Bay leaves	Parsley
Caraway seeds	Dill
Hoarhound	Clover
Licorice	Sorrel
Endive	

Your Most Favorable Trees and Plants

Juniper
Most nuts
Tropical trees

Wines and Liquors

Champagne
Tokay
Sauternes
Rich golden wines and liqueurs

Famous Personalities Born With Their Sun in Gemini

Actors Douglas Fairbanks, Judy Garland, Bob Hope, Al Jolson, Sir Laurence Olivier, Marilyn Monroe, Rosalind Russell, Beatrice Lillie

Musicians Igor Stravinsky, Charles Gounod, Edvard Grieg, Robert Schumann, Richard Strauss, Richard Wagner, Cole Porter, Burl Ives

Politicians and Statesmen Jean Paul Marat, William Pitt, Queen Victoria, Peter the Great of Russia, John Quincy Adams, John F. Kennedy

Sportsmen The Duke of Edinburgh, Rocky Graziano, Gene Tunney

Painters John Constable, Paul Gauguin, Sir John Millar, Diego Velasquez

Writers Honoré de Balzac, Sir Arthur Conan Doyle, Thomas Mann, Walt Whitman, Ralph Waldo Emerson, Cornelia Otis Skinner, Harriett Beecher Stowe, Pushkin, Garcia Lorca, Elsa Maxwell

Gemini is the sign producing the largest number of multiple births. The most notable was the famous Dionne Quintuplets—Cecile, Annette, Emilie, Marie, Yvonne—born in Canada, May 28, 1934.

How to Deal With a Gemini

Appeal to their reason in all difficult matters even if they start off on a highly emotional pitch. Go along with them on some of their seemingly mad schemes. Never underestimate their intelligence. Remember that although they may use a butterfly technique, flying hither and thither through life, they're one of the most sensitive signs of the zodiac.

CANCER ♋   In stature the Cancerian is of medium
height. The bone structure is small and the figure is inclined to be rounded with short arms and legs. The head is large and round with well-proportioned features. The expressive eyes are huge and round in soft gray or blue colors. The upper part of the face is full, dropping away to a sweet rosebud mouth and a small chin—the teeth are small and evenly spaced. The skin is soft and pink and is easily bruised. The ears are shell-like—excellent in shape, neatly fitting close to the head. The hair is one of the many brown shades and has a fine frondlike quality to it.

Natural Element—Water—Cardinal sign

Ruling Planet—the moon

Gender—Feminine

General Characteristics

Unconscious egotism
Intuition
Persistency
Self-centeredness
Super-sensitive
Full of good intentions
Fond of wealth
Home-lover
Susceptible and capricious
Sensitive to personal criticism
Friendly and sociable

Action and Reaction to Other Signs

Cancer with Cancer   A very favorable combination
Cancer with Leo   Cancer dominates in an affectionate manner which covers
latent determination to have your own way

Cancer with Virgo   Cancer dominates, especially when Virgo is younger. The domination lessens as the ages become nearer

Cancer with Libra   Cancer dominates and Libra enjoys it with financial and personal comforts assured

Cancer with Scorpio   Cancer dominates but only in short periods. Friendships can always be revived

Cancer with Sagittarius   Cancer dominates, but there's always the danger that Sagittarius will revolt

Cancer with Capricorn   Cancer dominates, especially with an elderly Capricorn. The influence is not so strong with people of equal age

Cancer with Aquarius   Cancer dominates when intellect is even

Cancer with Pisces   Cancer dominates and this can be one of the most lasting of romantic relationships. It's also good on a professional basis

Cancer with Aries   Cancer dominates, but not for long

Cancer with Taurus   Cancer dominates, and in youth this can be a good personal relationship

Cancer with Gemini   Cancer dominates, but it's an uneasy relationship, given to fits and starts

Cancer always relies on charm to get its own way and can adapt—if only for a time—to any of the other signs. Sometimes it's so obviously a contrived effort that the other sign withdraws. Such is the charm of Cancer that there are few complete breaks in relationships. Friendships can always be renewed, with little animosity on the part of either parties.

Your Most Favorable Climate

Because of the extremes in the Cancerian temperament, you can thrive in almost any climate—cold, temperate or tropically humid. However, you don't feel quite as well in a very dry, desert-like climate.

Being gregarious, you thrive best in populated places; seashores and lakes; social resorts

Sports

Swimming   Calisthenics
Sailing   Tennis
Dancing

Flowers

Water lilies; all water plants; all nocturnal flowers; larkspur

Perfumes and Incenses

You enjoy all fragrant leaves, all odorous vegetables, and most forms of tree and plant life, such as: aloe; bay leaves; camphor; cedar; myrtle; cinnamon; sandalwood; poppy

Best Day of the Week

Monday, the day traditionally associated with the moon.

Favorable Metal

Silver, as the metal associated with your ruling moon; aluminum; antimony

Favorite Precious Stones

Pearl, whose translucent quality is related to the moon influences; crystal; diamond; emerald; onyx

Favorable Colors

The clear fresh tones of green—such as those of early spring; iridescent hues; pink; silver

Your Musical Keynote

You vibrate best to "B."

Your Best Number

The planetary number of the moon is 2.

Vocations

There are few vocations which are not open to you because of the fluidity of your nature.
Real estate
All art forms
Naval work
Gynecology
The perfume industry
Civil law
Banking and finance
Wine and liquor dealers
Nursing
Consulting for home matters on personal or national level
Import and export business
The theater
Theology and reform

Your Body

The vulnerable areas are: the breast, chest, stomach and digestive organs.

By reflex action, you may also suffer from rheumatism, circulation troubles, as well as trouble in the sex organs, foot pains, tumors. Reflex ailments are derived from the water triplicity as well as from the moon, so the afflictions of the other two water signs, Scorpio and Pisces, often have to be considered. One or more parts of the vulnerable areas may be affected followed by one or more of the reflex action ailments.

Most Favorable Periods of the Year

June 22 to July 22
October 23 to November 21
February 19 to March 20

Herbs Necessary for You

Balm	Peppermint
Basil	Slippery Elm
Endive	Tamarind
Garlic	Camomile

Your Most Favorable Trees and Plants

Banana	Sugar cane
Breadfruit	All sap trees
Mango	Crabapple

Wines and Liquors

Tokay
Sparkling Champagnes
White wines

Famous Personalities Born With Their Sun in Cancer

Actors   James Cagney, Barbara Stanwyck, Gertrude Lawrence

Financiers   Nelson Rockefeller, John Wanamaker

Creative Artists   Stephen Foster, Gustav Mahler, Jacques Offenbach, Giacomo Puccini, Christoph Gluck, Richard Rodgers, Oscar Hammerstein II, La Fontaine, Petrarch, Kirston Flagstad, Camille Corot, Edgar Degas, Joshua Reynolds, Rembrandt Van Ryn, Peter Paul Rubens, Ernest Hemingway, James Whistler, William Thackery, Nathaniel Hawthorne, Nelson Eddy

Navigators   John Paul Jones, David Farragut, astronaut John Glenn

Theologians and Reformers   Mary Baker Eddy, John Calvin, Henry David
                             Thoreau, John Quincy Adams, Jean Jacques
                             Rousseau
Sportsmen   Jack Dempsey, Paul Charles Murphy
Personalities   Henry VIII, The Duke of Windsor, Dave Garroway

How to Deal With a Cancerian

Always be gentle, avoiding any coarseness. Remember that they don't like
jokes against themselves. Remember, too, that although the moon affects the
emotions and the Cancerian is very changeable to the point of being capricious, he's sensitive. The female Cancerian likes to bask in her motherly
attitudes, reacting through instinct, yet there's a tendency to inconstancy.

LEO ♌   The typical Leo is inclined to be tall, large
            boned and firm in figure—always moving with a jungle-cat
grace. Leos can be recognized by the magnificent size of the head set on
a strong neck. The forehead is broad, the cheekbones full and well
curved. The eyes are a striking feature—large, very flashing and com-
manding—usually blue, gray or green. The teeth are large—especially
at the front of the upper jaw and the lips are well shaped and sensuous.
The skin of the Leo is normally golden, but sensitive to the sun's rays
and easily freckled. Ears are round and well proportioned to the size of
the head. The hair is very profuse—generally ranging from sandy blond
to tawny brown in color.

Natural Element—Fire—Fixed

Ruling Planet—the sun

Gender—Masculine sign

General Characteristics

Virility
Vitality
Authority
Passion
Despotism, haughtiness, arrogance
Optimism
Opulence or ostentatious
Eloquent

Versatile
Extremes of conventional lawfulness and unlawfulness
Dignified
Paternal
Extremes of courageousness

Action and Reaction to Other Signs

Leo with Leo   A highly favorable business combination—not so good for romance

Leo with Virgo   Even powers result according to the needs of the time and to the intellectual qualities of both parties

Leo with Libra   Even powers in most cases, but, romantically, Leo will dominate

Leo with Scorpio   Scorpio dominates, especially in a romantic relationship Fairly good in business terms

Leo with Sagittarius   Leo dominates, and Sagittarius enjoys the domination. There can be difficulties in sexual relationships if other planets lead to masochistic qualities

Leo with Capricorn   Capricorn dominates in a business relationship, accepting responsibility and leaving Leo free to bask in the limelight

Leo with Aquarius   Leo dominates in a personal relationship; Aquarius prefers to indulge the caprices of Leo providing there's charm

Leo with Pisces   Even powers according to the sex. Leo male will dominate a Piscean male, but a Piscean female has no difficulty tactfully twisting Leo around her little finger. In business relationship, it's better for a Leo male to be with a Piscean female

Leo with Aries   Even powers in both personal and business relationships but not always of long duration

Leo with Taurus   Taurus dominates in business relationships, often able to supply the money which Leo enjoys spending. Taurus will rule the moneybags. In a personal relationship, the female Taurean inspires tenderness in the Leo male

Leo with Gemini   Leo dominates; relationships short but profitable

Leo with Cancer   Cancer dominates with charm, but must have tact, too

Most Favorable Climate

A warm or tropical climate suits the sun-loving Leo.

Being gregarious, Leo thrives in cities, but the deciding point is the climate.

Sports

Golf

Horseback riding

Tennis

Mountain climbing—but only certain types of Leo should attempt this strenuous sport as Leos are prone to heart trouble and suffer from strain at high altitudes.

Those born with the sun in Leo have the contrasting forces of being excellent at most sports and prone to major heart ailments. How the planetary patterns are placed in relationship to the sun sign becomes the deciding influence. Except when very young, most Leos rarely benefit from sports.

Flowers

Tall, dignified flowers such as long stemmed roses, gladioli and goldenrod

Perfumes and Incenses

Red sandalwood; frankincense; camphor; cassia; clove

Best Day of the Week

Sunday is the day of the sun.

Favorable Metal

Gold. There's a natural tendency for Leos to eschew silver and always wear something gold.

Favorite Precious Stones

Ruby; cat's eye; sardonix; diamond

Favorable Colors

All golden and orange shades through the full range of yellows as well as warm golden beige.

Your Musical Keynote

You vibrate to "D."

Your Best Number

The planetary number of the sun is 1.

Vocations

Public relations

Theater

Theology

Politics
The arts
Statesmanship
All positions where organization and authority is needed
Motion picture directors
Newspaper work
Psychology
Military leadership

Your Body

The most vulnerable areas are: the heart, back and spinal cord; the twelve vertebrae; the pericardium.

By reflex action, many other ailments can manifest themselves according to the pattern of other planets. The liver and kidneys, the nervous system, the eyes, nose and ears are all vulnerable at times. Reflex ailments are derived from the other two signs of the fire triplicity called Aries and Sagittarius.

Most Favorable Periods of the Year

July 23 to August 22
March 21 to April 18
November 22 to December 21

Herbs Necessary for You

Sage	Cinnamon
Thyme	Saffron
Rosemary	Cloves
Celery Seed	

Your Most Favorable Trees and Plants

Almond	Orange
Walnut	Palm
Olive	Ash
Grapefruit	Bay

Wines and Liquors

Cider or Champagne
Marsals
Kirsch
Chartreuse

Famous Personalities Born With Their Sun in Leo

Actors   Ethel Barrymore, Norma Shearer, Maureen O'Hara, Mae West, Monte Woolley, Billie Burke

Personalities   Jacqueline Kennedy Onassis, Princess Margaret, Dag Hammarskjöld, Henry Ford, Madame Du Barry

Creative Artists   George Bernard Shaw, Alexander Dumas, Edna Ferber, Aldous Huxley, Claude Debussey, Percy Shelley, Alfred Tennyson, Booth Tarkington, Izaac Walton, Rudy Vallee

Military Leaders and Statesmen   Napoleon Bonaparte, Sir Charles Napier, Herbert Hoover, Benito Mussolini

Motion Picture Directors   Alfred Hitchcock, Cecil B. DeMille, Samuel Goldwyn

How to Deal With a Leo

Always approach a Leo with dignity. Get to the point in conversation because Leo's a hasty person and hates repetition. Listen to his opinions and be ready for an exciting, adventurous companionship in which his strength can be noted and remarked upon. Praise that isn't redolent of flattery will earn the respect of the intelligent Leo.

VIRGO ♍   The typical Virgo is slender and graceful without being fragile, and there is a natural ability to keep slim, even after middle age. The facial structure is dominated by an oval-shaped head with a prominent forehead gracefully set on a long neck. The eyes are gray or green-flecked and deeply set—they can be beautiful, but there is a watchful expression. The nose of the Virgo is large in proportion to the face. Although Virgos have generous lips, the mouth itself is smaller than usual and often there are peculiarities of teeth because of too many teeth in a small jaw. The high cheekbones can be very exaggerated, and the chin is inclined to be bony and rather rounded. Complexion tends to ivory tints.

Natural Element—Earth

Ruling Planet—Mercury

Gender—Feminine sign

General Characteristics

Disinterested generosity
Aversion to demonstrative affection
Passive obedience
Tendency to intellectuality

Truthfulness
Analytical
Obstinacy
Persevering
Versatile
Interested in health
Compassionate but without sentimentality
Cautious

Action and Reaction to Other Signs

Virgo with Virgo   One of the most favorable combinations for business, and can result in millionaire status

Virgo with Libra   Libra dominates; generally a short-term relationship

Virgo with Scorpio   Scorpio dominates with romance more favored than a business relationship

Virgo with Sagittarius   Virgo dominates; this is a good business relationship

Virgo with Capricorn   Capricorn dominates in a business relationship which can be advantageous for both parties. Less likely to be a good relationship

Virgo with Aquarius   There are even powers. Generally the relationship starts very shakily with the parties leaving each other, but coming back when one needs the other and recognizes the need

Virgo with Pisces   Pisces dominates, especially in a romantic attachment, but can also be good for a combined business interest

Virgo with Aries   Aries dominates; often a short-term relationship

Virgo with Taurus   Taurus dominates; thrives best if Taurus is older than Virgo; fine for business

Virgo with Gemini   Virgo dominates and is tolerant with Gemini

Virgo with Cancer   Cancer dominates

Virgo with Leo   There are even powers if both are on a compatible level of intelligence

Although attraction and friendship is possible between two persons of any sign, it's rare that persons of adverse groups ever reach a true understanding. It's better to regard the incompatible persons as ships passing through the night where little constructive or mutual help will result. Environment, education and social status can provide a veneer which may pass for friendship.

Your Most Favorable Climate

Extremes of heat or cold rarely suit you, and you'll thrive best in a temperate climate. Live in small cities offering scope for cultural activities.

Sports

Cycling	Walking
Golf	Calisthenics
Horseback riding	

Flowers

Morning glory; cornflower; asters; petunias

Perfumes and Incenses

All woodland and fruit perfumes rather than sweet, flowery ones: bayberry; cinnamon; citron peel; red and yellow sander; mace; mystic resin.

Best Days of the Week

Wednesday and Friday

Favorable Metal

Silver or quicksilver. Many Virgos carry a thermometer which contains quicksilver.

Favorable Precious Stone

Diamond; agate; jade

Favorable Colors

Clear yellows; clear blue; certain types of muted checks

Your Musical Keynote

You vibrate best to "E."

Your Best Number

Your planetary number is 4, which relates to Mercury.

Vocations

With Mercury as your ruling planet, the versatile characteristics enable you to try many areas, success being dependent on the placement of other planets forming a satisfactory pattern.

Art criticism
Writing
Editorial work
Law
Dietetics
Medicine, especially of diagnostic type
Newspapers

Radio and television
Stenographer
Bookkeepers and accountants
Statesmen, politicians, patriots
Economists and financiers

Your Body

Your vulnerable areas are: the abdomen and small intestines; lower lobe of the liver; duodenum; lymphatic vessels of the intestines; all areas associated with assimilation; other areas such as the nervous system, skin and bronchial tubes, may be vulnerable by reflex action.

Reflex ailments are derived from the other earth signs as well, and are dependent upon the placement of the planetary patterns in Taurus and Capricorn. Because of the diversity of the ruling planet of Mercury which also rules Gemini, the nervous disabilities which affect Gemini may also be experienced by Virgo.

Most Favorable Periods of the Year

August 23 to September 22	April 20 to May 19
December 22 to January 19	May 20 to June 20

Herbs Necessary for You

Camomile	Hops
Fennel	Licorice
Mint	Mint
Guava	Parsley
Thyme	Red raspberry leaves
Sarsparilla	Sage
Chicory	Thyme
Dill	

Your Most Favorable Trees and Plants

Grapes	Apples
Quince	Blackberry
Fig	

Wines and Liquors

No particular one.

Famous Personalities With their Sun in Virgo

Creative Artists   Alexander Korda, Darryl F. Zanuck, Anton Dvořák, Arnold Schönberg, Luigi Cherubini, Frederick Ashton,

Creative Artists   Claudette Colbert, Greta Garbo, Maurice Chevalier, Sophia
                    Loren, Leonard Bernstein, Grandma Moses, Robert Crumb

Economists and Financiers   J. P. Morgan, Nathan Rothschild

Statesmen, Politicians and Patriots   La Fayette, Savanarola, Lyndon B.
                                       Johnson, William Howard Taft,
                                       George Wallace, King Louis XIV of
                                       France, Queen Elizabeth I of England,
                                       Cardinal Richelieu

Literature   Leo Tolstoy, H. G. Wells, Samuel Johnson, James Fenimore
              Cooper, John Gay, Christopher Isherwood, William Saroyan,
              John Gunther, Wolfgang Goethe, Maurice Maeterlinck

How To Get On With a Virgo

Virgos react through instinct, but reason and details must support all matters
when you approach them. This appeals to their practical nature. To end a
Virgo friendship rapidly, show no interest in his work, or forget to show an
interest in his well-being.

LIBRA ♎   Librans tend to be tall with long, not very
            well-shaped legs and sloping shoulders. The bone structure
is medium, with non-fleshy hands and legs. The natural Libran slimness
gives an ease of movement. Although one of the main characteristics of
the Libra is to have a long head, the face is small with a great delicacy
of structure—the profile his a chiseled, classical look. The eyes are dark
and expressive. The nose is long and straight with slender sensitive
nostrils. The cheekbones are high, slipping away to a well-moulded chin.
The mouth is usually one of the Libran's best features—well shaped
with long, finely sculptured lips. Most Libras have exquisite alabaster
complexions.

Natural Element—Air, Cardinal

Ruling Planet—Venus

Gender—Masculine sign

General Characteristics

Capacity for leadership
Intuition
Persistency

Absent-mindedness
Self-assertive
Mentally refined
Original
Physically lazy
Lover of harmony
Lover of the arts

Action and Reaction to Other Signs

Libra with Libra   Favorable combination if linked with mutual personal interests

Libra with Scorpio   Both have even powers, with Scorpio wanting to dominate and Libra accepting with mental reservations

Libra with Sagittarius   Libra dominates

Libra with Capricorn   Capricorn dominates, especially in business

Libra with Aquarius   Libra dominates in romantic relationships

Libra with Pisces   Libra dominates in either business or romantic relationships

Libra with Aries   Aries dominates, but the sensitivity of Libra suffers

Libra with Taurus   There are even powers according to each other's needs

Libra with Gemini   Libra dominates when both have respect for each other's minds

Libra with Cancer   Cancer dominates, but this can result in a battle of wills

Libra with Leo   Leo dominates emotionally

Libra with Virgo   Libra dominates

Your Most Favorable Climate

A climate ranging from cold to temperate and warm is most favorable to you. You thrive best in cities where there's a cultural element.

Sports.

Tennis   Walking
Fencing   Gymnastics
Skating   Swimming
Badminton

Flowers

Violets; roses; calendula

Perfumes and Incenses

Jasmine; musk; rose; violet; all mild perfumes, preferably from a flower base; satinwood; sandalwood

Best Day of the Week
Friday

Favorable Metal
For favorable vibrations, many Libras carry or wear an article made of copper, but there's a liking for all valuable metals such as silver, gold and platinum.

Favorable Precious Stones
Jade; moss agate; cornelian; diamond; beryl

Favorable Colors
Pastel shades and pale lavender

Your Musical Keynote
You vibrate to "A."

Your Best Number
The number of your planet is 6.

Vocations
The arts
Dealing in paintings, antiques and objects of beauty
Aviation
Military work
Architect
Engineering
Politics, statecraft and patriotic organizations

Your Body
The vulnerable areas are: the lumbar regions; kidneys; loins. Health warnings come through vulnerability to diabetes, uremia, renal caliculi and lumbago.

Reflex ailments occur from the other signs of the air triplicity, Gemini and Aquarius, and may result in the swelling of the legs, varicose veins, chest afflictions.

Most Favorable Periods of the Year
September 23 to October 23   May 21 to June 21
January 20 to February 18   April 20 to May 20

Herbs Necessary for You
Dandelion   Parsley
Juniper Berry   Peppermint

Kelp   Marjoram
Mint   All sweet-smelling spices

Your Most Beneficial Trees and Plants

Apples   Peaches
Apricots   Pomegranates
Grapes   Pears
Cherries   Quince
Figs

Wines and Liquors
No particular spirits.

Famous Personalities Born With Their Sun in Libra

Creative Artists   Brigitte Bardot, T. S. Eliot, William Faulkner, Thomas
                    Wolfe, Sarah Bernhardt, Eleanora Duse, Lillian Gish,
                    Helen Hayes, Deborah Kerr, Franz Liszt, Giuseppe Verdi,
                    Camille St. Saens, J. François Millet, Jean Antoine Wat-
                    teau, Virgil, Eugene O'Neill, Oscar Wilde, P. G. Wode-
                    house, Emily Post, Friedrich Nietzsche, C. P. Snow

Aviation   Edward V. Rickenbacker, Robert M. Webster, astronaut Michael
            Collins

Statesmen, Politicians and Patriots   Mahatma Gandhi, William Penn,
                                       J. H. Thomas, Sir Austen Chamber-
                                       lain, Georges Clemençeau, Admiral
                                       Lord Nelson, Eleanor Roosevelt

Military Leaders   Dwight Eisenhower, General Foch, Paul von Hindenburg
Architects   Sir Christopher Wren, H. H. Richardson, C. A. Platt

How To Deal With A Libran
Avoid all coarseness, be intelligent, tactful and, most of all, courteous. If you
use flattery, veil it with diplomacy. To end a Libran friendship rapidly, talk
vaguely without coming to the point, appear badly dressed, or speak coarsely.

SCORPIO ♏   The Scorpio's physical appearance
shows strength—the large-boned body structure varies from
medium to tall. The head is large and wide, but surprisingly shallow
and rather flat at the back. The eyes are vital and exciting, but they can
give the impression they are hiding an explosive secret. The nose has a
very slightly raised bridge and full, flaring nostrils. Round cheekbones
sweep down toward a strong jaw and round chin. There is a sensual

quality to the large, well-defined mouth. The teeth are squarish, with the two front teeth parted by a gap. The complexion has darker tones than usually associated with a water sign, but it is in keeping with the generally dynamic sultry quality of the face.

Natural Element—Water—Fixed sign

Ruling Planet—Mars, with Pluto as the co-planet

Gender—Feminine sign

General Characteristics
Self-determination
Obstinacy
Dramatic sense
Tenacity
Enterprising
Great mental agility
Fond of sensual pleasures
Passionate emotionally and to causes
Suspicion
Arrogance

Action and Reaction to Other Signs
Scorpio with Scorpio   Can be highly favorable combination
Scorpio with Sagittarius   Scorpio dominates
Scorpio with Capricorn   There are even powers in business relationships. Romantic associations are generally secretive
Scorpio with Aquarius   Scorpio dominates, often too dramatically for Aquarius
Scorpio with Pisces   Scorpio dominates in business; powers are much less evident in romantic associations
Scorpio with Aries   Although there are even powers, relationships fluctuate with each taking a turn as the catalyst to the other's emotions. Highly volatile, but the friction caused by one can produce some remarkable effects in the other
Scorpio with Taurus   Scorpio dominates, especially in a romantic relationship
Scorpio with Gemini   Scorpio dominates, but the relationship is good if both have good intellect
Scorpio with Cancer   Cancer dominates spasmodically
Scorpio with Leo   Scorpio dominates

Scorpio with Virgo   Scorpio dominates, but has to learn tact. Each can
hurt the other's feelings without too much lasting
ill-will

Scorpio with Libra   Even powers, as both recognize each other's need

Your Best Climate

Temperate to humid. Live in cities, if they're near a large river, lakes or the
ocean.

Sports

Swimming	Diving
Sailing	Wrestling
Boxing	Scuba diving

Flowers

Chrysanthemum or any exotic bloom

Perfumes and Incenses

All fragrances from odoriferous woods; pine; yucca; rosemary; cypress; briar
roses; dogwood

Your Musical Keynote

You vibrate best to "C," and this can be the high "C," beloved of opera
singers.

Your Best Number

Your planetary number, associated with Mars, is 3, but with the influence of
Pluto all characteristics associated with three are exaggerated. Pluto, having
many as yet unknown qualities, adds to the difficulties and complexities of
Scorpio.

Vocations

All areas of medicine including surgery
Scientific research
Detection
The arts
Adventurous exploration
Any work in transportation by sea or river
Theology
Dealing in liquids
Statesmanship
Military leadership
The law—ranging from judging to policing

Your Best Day of the Week
Tuesday, as in Mardi, the French for Tuesday, clearly showing the association with Mars, your ruling planet.

Favorable Metal
Steel or iron

Favorable Precious Stone
Opal; jaspar; malachite

Favorable Colors
Rich and dramatic colors; sometimes intense shades of scarlet, claret, magenta; strong blues and greens

Your Body
Your most vulnerable areas are: the generative organs; the rectum; the pubic arch; sacral vertebrae; red blood corpuscles.

The association with Pluto is causing many obstruse ailments which are difficult to diagnose. By reflex action, you can also feel the effects of the other signs of the water triplicity, Cancer and Pisces. Aries, which is also ruled by Mars, can also add reflex actions to your health problems; the feet, stomach and liver being the most likely areas.

Most Favorable Periods of the Year
October 24 to November 21   March 21 to April 19
February 19 to March 20   June 22 to July 22

Herbs Necessary for You
Capers	Mustard
Chickweed	Parsley
Cloves	Pepper
Coriander	Sage
Garlic	Seasalts
Ginger	Vinegar

Your Favorite Trees and Shrubs
Mango	Cacti
Melon	Hemlock
Papaya	Pine
Peach	Wormwood
Grape	Broom
Cherry	Box tree

Wines and Liquors
Port; champagne; Crème de Cacao.

Famous Personalities Born With Their Sun in Scorpio

Creative Artists   Georges Bizet, Aaron Copeland, Jean-Phillipe Rameau, Alessandro Scarlatti, Marie Dressler, Ignace Paderewsky, Franz Gall, Pablo Picasso, Jean Vermeer, Angelica Kaufmann, William Hogarth, Thomas Chatterton, Friedrich Schiller, Fyodor Dostoyevsky, George Eliot, Arthur Quiller-Couch, Voltaire, R. Stevenson, Vivien Leigh, Katherine Hepburn, Benito Cellini, Grace Kelly

Statesmen, Military Leaders   Sir John Moore, Rommel The "Desert Fox," Theodore Roosevelt, Jawaharlal Nehru

Theologians   St. Augustine, Billy Sunday, J. M. Eck, Billy Graham

How to Get On With a Scorpio

Avoid rousing his anger, be precise and straightforward. Remember that he'll react through instinct, especially when hurt, just like his symbol, the scorpion. To end a Scorpio friendship rapidly, you don't even have to try very hard. You have to learn to forget. But, remember, he rarely forgets.

SAGITTARIUS ♐   Sagittarians can be very tall with a well-boned, firm body; the appearance being stocky rather than fat. The head is long with a high forehead and a flattened formation of the sides rather than prominent cheeks that form a firm jaw and strong chin. The wide-set eyes are brown and warm, with a frank, open gaze. The nose is long with rounded nostrils and a broad tip. The mouth is fully arched, but not to be confused with a cupid's bow, and the teeth are strong and well arranged with a broad, flat look. The complexion is healthy with a well-scrubbed appearance. Hair can be wavy—shades range from brownish to dark red. The ears are large with large lobes. Hands and feet are large.

Natural Element—Fire, Common

Ruling Planet—Jupiter

Gender—Masculine sign

General Characteristics
Disinterested generosity
Compassion
Spendthriftness
Humanism
Prophetic
Passionately idealistic
Averse to demonstrative affection
Competent to strike at the target
Lover of freedom and liberty
Active mentally and physically
Genial
Good adviser
Stubborn

Action and Reaction to Other Signs

Sagittarius with Sagittarius   A favorable combination
Sagittarius with Capricorn   Capricorn dominates
Sagittarius with Aquarius   Aquarius dominates, but can be intellectually equal
Sagittarius with Pisces   Pisces dominates; a good business relationship possible when recognition of each other's needs is felt
Sagittarius with Aries   Aries dominates
Sagittarius with Taurus   Taurus dominates
Sagittarius with Gemini   Sagittarius dominates and is patient with Gemini
Sagittarius with Cancer   Cancer dominates, especially in romantic relationships
Sagittarius with Leo   Leo dominates but can lead to friction
Sagittarius with Virgo   Virgo dominates, and there can be mutual consideration based on intellectual understanding
Sagittarius with Libra   Libra dominates, but sometimes demands too much. Sagittarius is often sorely tried but remains faithful —often in the background
Sagittarius with Scorpio   Scorpio dominates

Your Most Favorable Climate

Most Sagittarians have stamina and can thrive in cold or extreme climates, but rarely in high humidity.

You can be quite happy in the country although financial conditions often make it necessary for you to live in cities. When this happens, it's best to try to be in a wooded or mountainous region. In no other sign do circumstances dictate so much where you live—and in the early days of your life, this isn't often where you'd like to be.

Sports

Track racing	Walking
Hurdling	Golf
Tennis	

Mountain climbing, although this shouldn't be overdone as fire element triplicity types are subject to heart trouble and discomfort from high altitudes. Almost all sports appeal to this sign.

Flowers

Most of the spring flowers; daffodils, narcissus, but also late summer's asters

Perfumes and Incenses

All odoriferous fruits; nutmeg; saffron; clove

Best Day of the Week

Thursday

Favorable Metal

Tin

Favorite Precious Stones

Carbuncle; amethyst; moonstone

Favorable Colors

Mixtures of red and indigo; the autumnal greens; the darker tones of yellow

Your Musical Keynote

You vibrate best to "G."

Your Best Number

The planetary number of Jupiter is 5.

Vocations

The law
The arts
Music, in particular
Public speaking
Theology
Salesmanship
Literary agencies
Statesmanship and politics

Your Body

Your most vulnerable areas are: in the region of the hips and thighs; also the ilium, the four coccygeal vertebra, sciatic nerves. Motor nervous system.

Hip weaknesses are common in later life. You may get kidney ailments, heart afflictions and eye infections, by reflex action influences from the other fire signs of Leo and Aries. The vulnerable physical parts do not necessarily have to be affected but preventitive care should be taken. Accidents through activities account for many of your afflictions.

Most Favorable Periods of the Year

March 21 to April 19
July 23 to August 22
November 22 to December 21

Herbs Necessary for You

Dandelion   Sassafras
Nutmeg   Thyme
Saffron   Sarsparilla
Sage   Aloe
Sesame seed   Aniseed

Your Most Favorable Trees and Plants

All berries and citrus fruits   Oak
Cherries   Olive
Berry-bearing trees and shrubs   Birch
All nuts, especially almond and chestnut   Cedar

Wines and Liquors

Burgundies
Champagne
Anisette
The heavier types of red wine

Famous Personalities Born With Their Sun in Saggitarius

Musicians   Maria Callas, Ludwig von Beethoven, Hector Berlioz, Manuel de Falla, Jean Sibelius, Virgil Thomson, Carl von Weber, Gaetano Donizetti, Morton Gould, Iturbi, Artur Rubinstein, Elizabeth Schwarzkoft

Other Creative Artists   Samuel Butler, Mark Twain, Noel Coward, William Cowper, John Milton, Heinrich Heine, Alicia Morkova, Walt Disney, Henri de Toulouse-Lautrec, Boris Karloff

Statesmen   Winston S. Churchill, Joseph Stalin

How To Deal With a Saggittarian

Approach him intelligently, taking care to discuss matters fully. Allow for the fact that he already has an opinion which isn't likely to be easily swayed. If you have to resort to flattery about some specific achievement, be sure your facts are right and that you're tactful at all times. To lose a Sagittarian friend show doubt that he has good intentions.

CAPRICORN ♑   The Capricon's body is tall with a long trunk and slender arms and legs. The long head is set on a long neck. The face is also long, but not symmetrically ovoid since the lower part is thinner. The eyes are small and rounded, usually a striking bright blue, deeply set under heavy brows. The nose is long; the mouth is long and thin lipped; the teeth are strong, small and slightly pointed in shape. The jaws are small, punctuated with a small chin. The skin generally tends to be dry, and the tones range in the darker shades. The hair is dark and usually fine.

Natural element—Earth, Cardinal

Ruling Planet—Saturn

Gender—Feminine sign

General Characteristics
Capacity for leadership
Executive instinct
Self-centeredness
Material ambition
Social climbing
Deliberate
Profound thinking
Great commercial promoter
Perseverance
Spiritual desolation

Action and Reaction to Other Signs
Capricorn with Capricorn   Generally favorable to both
Capricorn with Aquarius   Capricorn dominates, and is good for business relationships

Capricorn with Pisces   Capricorn dominates, but it can be an uneasy, see-saw kind of relationship

Capricorn with Aries   Even powers, each realizing his needs can be helped by the other

Capricorn with Taurus   Capricorn dominates; fine for business relationships

Capricorn with Gemini   Capricorn dominates; especially beneficial if male Capricorn is considerably older than Gemini female. Not so good vice-versa. Business relationship better than a romantic one

Capricorn with Cancer   Cancer dominates, especially in December-May romances

Capricorn with Leo   Capricorn dominates

Capricorn with Virgo   Capricorn dominates

Capricorn with Libra   Capricorn dominates, especially in romantic relationships

Capricorn with Scorpio   Capricorn dominates

Capricorn with Sagittarius   Capricorn dominates

Your Most Favorable Climate

Circumstances often force you to live in a cold climate early in life, migrating to a warm or even tropical one after middle age. You're one of the signs adaptable to living in two distinct extremes of climate. Live in country or city—again, you have the benefit of contrast. Where you spend your youthful days is rarely the same as where you spend your more mature life.

Sports

All ball games	Horseback riding
Golf	Yoga
Mountain climbing	Dancing
Track racing	Skating

Flowers
Carnations of the darker colors

Perfumes and Incenses
Fragrance from all odoriferous roots; frankincense; khus khus

Best Day of the Week
Saturday, the day associated with your ruling planet, Saturn

Favorable Metal
Lead

Favorable Precious Stones
Onyx; jet; moonstone; diamond

Favorable Colors
Gray; black; indigo; sage green; any of the darker, more somber tones

Your Musical Keynote
You vibrate to "F."

Your Best Number
The planetary number of Saturn is 7, the number associated with completion.

Vocations
All types of trading
Commercial promotion
Law
Politics
Mining
Undertaking
The arts
Tax collecting
Dancing
Banking, finance and economists
Statesmanship
Military leadership

Your Body
Your most vulnerable areas are: the bones, chiefly the knees and joint ligaments; afflictions of the skin. Many of you suffer from ill health from early years to puberty.

Reflex ailments are derived from the other earth signs of the triplicity, Taurus and Virgo, digestive disturbances being quite common. The tendency inflicted by Saturn produces melancholic periods which, in themselves, can upset the nervous system. Rheumatism and arthritis are constant hazards to health after middle age.

Most Favorable Periods of the Year
December 22 to January 21
April 20 to May 20
August 23 to September 22

Herbs Necessary for You

Caraway	Mint
Chickweed	Rosemary
Clove	Rye
Dill	Sarsparilla
Fennel	Sassafras
Garlic	Wintergreen
Hop	

Your Most Favorable Trees and Plants

Cypress	Bananas
Beech	Dates
Pine	Papaya
Yew	Quince
Hemlock	All citrus fruits
Apples	

Wines and Liquors
No particular spirits.

Famous Personalities Born With Sun In Capricorn

Creative Artists   Humphrey Bogart, Marlene Dietrich, Sir Edward Elgar, Alexandre Scriabine, Pablo Cassals, Josef Suk, Jean de Reske, Molière, Edgar Allan Poe, Cézanne, Carl Sandburg, Gary Cooper, Ethel Merman, Henri Matisse, Cecil Beaton, Danny Kaye, Ava Gardner

Dancers   Jean Coralli, Adelaine Genee, Kurt Joos, David Lichine, Vaslav Nijinsky, Moira Shearer, Paul Taglione

Politicians, Statesmen, Military Leaders   Hermann Goering, Alexander Hamilton, David Lloyd George, Thomas Woodrow Wilson, Joan of Arc, Marshall Joffre, Robert E. Lee, Benjamin Franklin, William Gladstone, Richard Nixon

How To Deal With a Capricorn
Be concise and practical and realize that he can't help being cautious. He's guided a great deal by outward show and can be flattered. The materialistic ambitions, with reaction through instinct, should always be taken into account. It's no use appealing to the emotions or humanitarian instincts as these are lessened by a leaning toward materialism. To lose a Capricorn friend, interrupt him when he's hard at work.

AQUARIUS ♒ Aquarians are handsome and distinguished-looking people—moderate in height with an exceptionally large head and high forehead. The facial features are well shaped—the Aquarian profile is one of the best of the Zodiac. The eyes are structurally beautiful, far apart, deep set in colors ranging from dark gray to bright blue. The nose is aquiline with finely chiseled nostrils; the cheekbones drift down toward the strong but neat chin. The lips are slim and sensitive, but rarely sensual. Aquarians have exceptional ivory complexions—perhaps due to the fact that many tend toward vegetarianism. The gait is quick, but there is a lack of coordination and the Aquarian is likely to trip easily.

Natural element—Air, fixed

Ruling Planet—Uranus

Gender—Masculine sign

General Characteristics
Determination
Sociological humanitarian
Blindness to adverse factors
Altruistic
Independent
Inventive
Intellectual
Hypersensitive to duty
Philosophical
Reserved
Honorable

Action and Reaction to Other Signs
Aquarius with Aquarius   Favorable when united by a business project
Aquarius with Pisces   Favorable when united by a business project
Aquarius with Aries   Aries dominates
Aquarius with Taurus   Taurus dominates, good for business relationship
Aquarius with Gemini   Aquarius dominates, but it's an uneasy relationship
Aquarius with Cancer   Cancer dominates in romantic relationship
Aquarius with Leo   Leo dominates, but can cause hypertension
Aquarius with Virgo   Even powers according to individual needs which override personal wishes and desires. A good combination for uniting in an humanitarian cause

Aquarius with Libra   Libra dominates, but this is a fine romantic relationship for an Aquarian male with Libra female. Not so good vice-versa
Aquarius with Scorpio   Scorpio dominates
Aquarius with Sagittarius   Even powers, each recognizing the other's needs
Aquarius with Capricorn   Capricorn dominates, especially in business

Your Most Favorable Climate

Cold, temperate to warm, not tropical. Circumstances often force you into city living where you thrive so long as you have access to a country retreat.

Sports

Fencing   Golf
Tennis   Walking

Flowers

Violets; spring flowers of the bulb, variety, such as daffodils

Perfumes and Incenses

All odoriferous roots; frankincense; pine; pepperwort

Your Best Day of the Week

Saturday

Favorable Metal

Stainless steel; aluminum; silver

Favorable Precious Stones

Garnet; amber

Favorable Colors

Silvery, electronic tones such as found in iridescent colors; electric blue

Your Musical Keynote

You vibrate best to "F."

Your Best Number

The planetary number of your ruling planet is 8, associated with inspiration.

Vocations

Medicine and surgery, also teaching in these areas
Philosophy
Scientific research

The arts
Aviation
Psychology and psychiatry
Electronics
Politics and statesmanship
Astrology and astronomy
Archaeology

Your Body

Your most vulnerable area is: the ankles.

By the reflex action of planets in the other two signs of the air triplicity, Gemini and Libra, nervous afflictions, poor circulation and hepatic disorders are not uncommon. Varicose veins can be a discomfort after middle age.

Most Favorable Periods of the Year

January 20 to February 19
May 21 to June 21
September 23 to October 21

Herbs Necessary for You

Balm	Sassafras
Chickweed	Camomile
Coriander	Sorrel
Dill	Basil
Gentian Root	Wintergreen
Hyssop	Garlic
Mint	Nettles
Parsley	Valerian
Rosemary	Sage
Rye	

Your Most Favorable Trees and Shrubs

Beech	Bananas
Cypress	Gooseberries
Pine	Grapes
Willow	Pears
Yew	Plums
Dates	Quince
Apples	

Wines and Liquors

No particular spirits

Famous People Born With Their Sun In Aquarius

Airmen and Astronauts   Charles Lindbergh, Walter F. Boone, Charles T. Myers, H. M. Trenchard, Astronaut Aldrin

Creative Artists   Jack Benny, Clark Gable, Jascha Heifitz, Fritz Kreisler, John Barrymore, Norman Rockwell, Claude Monet, Lord Byron, Robert Burns, Charles Dickens, Sinclair Lewis, Eartha Kitt, John Ruskin, Jules Verne, W. H. Ainsworth, Jerome Kern, Victor Herbert, Franz Schubert, James Dean

Statesmen and Politicians   Abraham Lincoln, Franklin D. Roosevelt, Kaiser Wilhelm II, Sir Robert Peel, C. J. Fox, Adlai Stevenson, Tallyrand

Astronomers and Astrologers   Galileo, Johann Mayer, W. H. Pickering

Philosophers and Humanists   Francis Bacon, F. H. Jacob, J. J. Rousseau, Swedenborg

How To Deal With an Aquarian

Don't beat about the bush. Approach all subjects from a practical point of view. He reacts through intelligence—not through emotion, intuition or instinct. To lose an Aquarian friend, bore him.

PISCES ♓   The Piscean's body structure varies as the birthdate approaches the Arian sign—the typical short, plump figure becomes a taller, firmer type. The head is large, the face round and broad, sometimes giving a top-heavy appearance. Pisceans are known for beautiful, expressive eyes—generally light in color—blue, green, gray. The nose can vary from retroussé to aquiline. The lips are sensitive, and the teeth are small and pearly with the front teeth having a distinct gap between them. The ears are small, slightly fleshy, but well shaped with rounded ear lobes. The arms and legs are short with small, nicely formed feet and expressive hands.

Natural Element—Water, Common

Ruling Planets—Jupiter and Neptune

Gender—Feminine sign

General Characteristics

Fond of tradition
Adaptability
Disinterested generosity

Compassion
Capriciousness
Spendthriftness
Passive obedience
Idealism
Philanthropy
Capable of sacrifice for other people's welfare
Spirituality
Impracticality
Supersensitivity

Action and Reaction to Other Signs

Pisces with Pisces   Quite favorable
Pisces with Aries   Aries dominates
Pisces with Taurus   Taurus dominates; good emotionally and in business relationships
Pisces with Gemini   Pisces dominates
Pisces with Cancer   Cancer dominates; generally long-lasting relationships
Pisces with Leo   Each recognizes the other's needs, and there are even powers
Pisces with Virgo   Pisces dominates. The relationship is never easy and takes time to show results to mutual advantage
Pisces with Libra   Libra dominates
Pisces with Scorpio   Scorpio dominates. This can be a good relationship both romantically and for business
Pisces with Sagittarius   Each recognizes the other's needs
Pisces with Capricorn   Capricorn dominates, with some resentfulness from Pisces. Better for a Capricorn male and a Pisces female than vice-versa
Pisces with Aquarius   If both parties are of a high intellectual capacity, this can have mutual benefits

Your Most Favorable Climate

Warm to humid. Live near an ocean, river or lake.

Sports

All water sports.

Your Favorite Flowers

Lilac; violet; lilies, including water lilies

Perfumes and Incenses

Clave; nutmeg; fragrance from all odoriferous fruits or exotic tropical flowers such as those found in Hawaii.

Best Day of the Week

Although Thursday is the best day, you're so adaptable to prevailing conditions that you can use Mondays and Tuesdays to advantage as well.

Favorable Metals

Platinum; silver; tin

Favorable Precious Stones

Moonstone; amethyst

Favorable Colors

Purple; orchid shades; silver; neptunian green; white

Your Musical Keynote

You vibrate best to "G."

Your Best Number

The planetary number of Jupiter is 5, while that of Neptune is 9.

Vocations

The arts
Astronomy and astrology
Social work
Design
Radio and television
Dancing
Law
Occultism
Military work
Literary work

Your Body

The vulnerable areas are: the feet, by reflex action due to having two ruling planets plus an affinity to the other two water signs, Cancer and Scorpio; you're liable to be subjected to numerous illnesses. This doesn't mean you'll have a lifetime of illness; simply that no sign can cram into it a greater variety of illness.

By reflex action, you can be afflicted with glandular, hepatic and pulmonary ailments. Circulation can be bad, the blood impoverished, and you can get illnesses like dropsy that have a watery content. All Pisceans should take care to prevent ill health and not be reckless in exposing themselves to sick persons. Carelessness accounts for much of the debilitation Pisceans suffer and can lead to having low resistance to diseases.

Most Favorable Periods of the Year

February 10 to March 20	October 24 to November 21
June 22 to July 22	November 22 to December 21

Herbs Necessary for You

All sweet-smelling spices	Dandelion
Aniseed	Mint
Agronomy	Nutmeg
Aloe	Peppermint
Balm	Plantain
Basil	Sage
Caraway	Kelp
Cedar	Sorrel
Coriander	Wintergreen

Your Most Favorable Trees and Shrubs

All berried trees and shrubs	Most types of berries and citrus
Almond	Cherry
Ash	Fig
Birch	Grapes
Chestnut	Mango
Maple	Melon
Mulberry	Peach
Oak	Pineapple
Olive	

Wines and Liquors

No particular spirits.

Famous Personalities Born With Their Sun In Pisces

Musicians   Niccolo Paganini, Andres Segovia, Marietta Alboni, Marion Anderson, Enrico Caruso, Catherine Cavaliero, Johann Sebastian Bach, Maurice Ravel, Nicolas Rimski-Korsakov, Gioacchino Rossini, Geraldine Farrar, Mary Garden, Lauritz Melchior, Adelina Patti, Frederic Chopin, Johann Strauss

Poets   Gabriele D'Annunzio, Henry Wadsworth Longfellow. W. H. Auden

Actors   Ellen Terry, Rex Harrison, Jackie Gleason, Margaret Leighton, Elizabeth Taylor, David Garrick, Jennifer Jones, Merle Oberon

Writers   Henrik Ibsen, John Steinbeck, Robert Lowell, George Moore, Victor Hugo, Jack Kerouac

Painters and Sculptors   Jules Dupre, Michelangelo, Augustus Saint-Gaudens, The Earl of Snowden, Pierre-Auguste Renoir, Salvador Dali, Henry Moore, Vincent Van Gogh

Military Leaders and Patriots and Statesmen	George Washington, Cardinal Newman, John of Austria, Carlos V, Andrew Jackson, Philip Sheridan, Sir Henry Wilson, Kemal Pasha

How to Deal with a Piscean

He'll respond best to kindness and courtesy and react through instinct. To lose a Piscean friend, call him a dreamer or betray a confidence. Lose his trust and you'll rarely stand the chance of regaining his friendship.